D1022379

The KAZDIN METHOD
for Parenting the Defiant Child

The KAZDIN METHOD
for Parenting
the Defiant Child

WITH NO PILLS, NO THERAPY,
NO CONTEST OF WILLS

Alan E. Kazdin, Ph.D.

WITH CARLO ROTELLA

HOUGHTON MIFFLIN COMPANY

BOSTON · NEW YORK

2008

Copyright © 2008 by Alan E. Kazdin and Carlo Rotella

All rights reserved

For information about permission to reproduce selections from
this book, write to Permissions, Houghton Mifflin Company,
215 Park Avenue South, New York, New York 10003.

www.houghtonmifflinbooks.com

Library of Congress Cataloging-in-Publication Data
Kazdin, Alan E.
  The Kazdin method for parenting the defiant child : with no pills,
no therapy, no contest of wills / Alan E. Kazdin ; with Carlo Rotella.
      p.   cm.
  Includes index.
  ISBN-13: 978-0-618-77367-1
  ISBN-10: 0-618-77367-3
  1. Problem children — Behavior modification. 2. Child rearing.
3. Parenting. I. Rotella, Carlo, date. II. Title.
  HQ773.K39 2008
  649'.64—dc22   2007018303

This book is intended to present the research and ideas of its
author. If a reader requires personal advice, he or she should
consult a competent professional. The author and publisher
disclaim liability for any adverse effects resulting directly or
indirectly from information contained in this book.

The DVD companion to *The Kazdin Method for Parenting the
Defiant Child* was produced by Vida Health Communications
(www.Vida-Health.com).

Book design by Victoria Hartman

Printed in the United States of America

MP 10 9 8 7 6 5 4 3 2 1

Contents

Acknowledgments

My name may be on the cover of this book, but what's inside is a distillation of many, many people's work and experience. Science is, almost by definition, a collective enterprise. We advance knowledge by rigorously testing and retesting other investigators' ideas and findings, as well as our own. The method I have developed for changing children's behavior comes out of a rich, complex web of collaborations. In the course of my career, I have worked, directly or by supervising others, with perhaps 6,000 children, 4,000 parents, 5,000 teachers, 3,000 therapists, and scores of fellow scientific investigators, scholars, and clinicians. The National Institute of Mental Health, Rivendell Foundation of America, Robert Wood Johnson Foundation, William T. Grant Foundation, and Leon Lowenstein Foundation, among others, have supported my work with generous grants. Yale University, the Pennsylvania State University, the University of Pittsburgh School of Medicine, and Northwestern University have provided me with good homes, inspired colleagues and students, and welcome support. Vida Health Communications gave my work a new life on video. All of these institutions and individuals have contributed to the development of my method, and thus to this book. I owe them all my heartfelt thanks, and I owe special thanks in particular to the superb clinical staff at the Yale Parenting Center and Child Conduct Clinic. To protect the privacy of parents and children, in this book I have changed and invented names and identifying characteristics.

The KAZDIN METHOD
for Parenting the Defiant Child

Introduction

Your four-year-old's tantrums have become more frequent and intense; they have started to dominate the life of your household. He's not just yelling and screaming anymore — now he throws things, hits, and kicks, too. The bedtime tantrum is the most predictable one, and the one that disrupts home life the most, but he has also taken his show on the road. You've been late to work recently because he melts down in the morning when you leave him at daycare. After other spectacular public performances at the supermarket, restaurants, and family gatherings, none of which you handled very well, you are sure that others see you as an incompetent parent — and you are starting to wonder if they might be right. And, deeper than that, it frightens you to feel the situation slipping beyond your control. You're losing your confidence that you can govern your child, your household, and when you lose your temper, yourself.

• • •

You want your nine-year-old to work with you, not against you. You're not asking for blind compliance, but more cooperation would be nice. Right now, she seems to fight you every step of the way, from getting up for school in the morning through homework and dinner and computer or TV time. Sometimes she insists on complete freedom and autonomy; sometimes she acts as if you have to do everything for her. She bickers incessantly with her sister, too. Is it asking too much for you to have a little peace around the house? You're tired of laying down the law, trying to understand her point of view, and using every other strategy that hasn't worked. Frankly, you are fed up with your own child. You find yourself wistfully wondering why you weren't one of the lucky ones who got a nice, easy kid to raise.

•   •   •

Your thirteen-year-old gives you nothing but attitude. On a couple of occasions, he has stolen something or committed an act of vandalism, the most worrisome pieces of a larger pattern of defying authority. You tell yourself that he's going through a phase, that he's just a normal preadolescent, but you fear that he may be heading toward serious trouble. You have tried to talk to him in every way you can think of — punishing, explaining, begging, crying — but nothing works. Your spouse says you are exaggerating, but you feel it's time to face the seriousness of what's happening to your family. Your child has a good heart, but that doesn't keep you from feeling always a little on edge, not knowing when the next crisis will develop.

•   •   •

Should you be addressing these problems *now*, before they lead to more serious ones? Or should you wait to see if a particular problem resolves itself? Perhaps you've gone online, Googled "tantrum" or "defiant child," and found that your child's behavior fits a dire-sounding label. Perhaps you're more concerned than your spouse is, or vice versa, and it's becoming a bone of contention between you — two devoted parents who find themselves disagreeing about what's wrong, how serious it is, how to put it right, or whether to try to fix it at all.

The tangle of confusion, frustration, fear, and anger inside you turns spending time with your child into a wearisome, long-running confrontation, even a chore that you secretly dread, and that feels very wrong to you. You've become a character you don't really recognize, or recognize all too well as the kind of parent you never wanted to be: a frequently irate, sometimes out-of-control shouter who spends altogether too much time ineffectively nagging, threatening, punishing, and even hitting the very child you love as much as you have ever loved or could ever love anyone. You feel off-balance, strange to yourself. You need a better way to be a parent, but you haven't gotten much useful help from the models you may have turned to: the way your parents, bless their hearts, did it; the many ways the child-rearing manuals suggest you do it; the way Supernanny does it on TV. With professional experts of all kinds promising that their way works, with friends and friends of friends telling you stories about how so-and-so's kid was turned around by a new parental strategy or miracle diet or whatever, it's hard to figure out what actually will work for you and your child.

The Method

There is a way to establish what actually does work. It's called science. To most people as they go about their daily lives, "science" means subjects such as the discovery of water on Mars, how birds spread influenza, and what trans fats do to our bodies. All of these are important and consistently newsworthy, without doubt, but science has also been quietly pressing forward in the effort to understand child development, child-rearing, parent-child interaction, and all sorts of other matters that affect your child's social, emotional, and behavioral adjustment.

Within the extensive research on human behavior in general, a great deal tells us specifically about the behavior of children. You may be surprised to hear that scientists have studied the most effective way to give a command to a child, or that they have rigorously compared the effectiveness of rewarding good behavior and punishing misbehavior. There are even studies that tell us very specific things like, for instance, the most effective way to speak to a child when asking her to do something she'd prefer not to do: brush her teeth, wear a jacket, get off the phone, or go to bed on time. Obviously, very few parents have the time or training to get up to speed on the latest research in psychology, not to mention child development and neurobiology and all the many related fields. But they can benefit profoundly from what researchers have discovered.

In this book, I present a method for changing your child's behavior that is based on good science — on what we currently *know* about children's behavior from the results of sound, well-conducted studies. I do not offer impressionistic beliefs or unsupported opinions about childhood. I'll be telling you something about the research and basic principles that underlie this approach, so you get a sense of *why* it works, but my emphasis will be on *what* to do and *how* to do it.

One great virtue of the method is that the same principles and techniques apply to the full range of situations for children and adolescents. I'm talking about everything from the milestones of normal child development — eating, toilet training, sleeping in one's own bed, not having tantrums — all the way to potentially more serious behavior problems like fighting or stealing. The method has been demonstrated to be effective even in those more difficult situations in which there are other problems in the home, such as when parents have physical or mental health problems, or engage in drug use or domestic violence. As long as you are committed to systematically taking this approach to changing the behavior of your child, even an imperfect and partial application of the method produces results.

First, you must shift your own focus of attention. As parents we tend to be experts on what we want our kids *not* to do. For example, *I want him to stop whining, talking back, and ignoring me.* I will teach you to focus more positively on what you *do* want your kids to do — *When it's bedtime, I want her to go directly, quickly, and quietly to bed* — and give you the tools to methodically reinforce that behavior until it replaces the behavior you don't want.

You'll learn how to build up the behaviors you want: how often your child must practice the good behavior in order for it to "take," how to set up situations so that the behaviors you'd like to see are much more likely to occur, how to create more chances to practice, how to praise most effectively, how to set up and give rewards that work, how to get from the desired behavior never happening to seeing it happen a lot, how to troubleshoot and improve a program that's not working well enough. I will have much to tell you about the details, because they can make all the difference between success and failure.

When you commit to positively reinforcing the behavior you want, you can be kinder to your child while being more systematic. We tend to fall into a trap of believing that getting serious about behavior problems means getting negative: more punishment, tougher standards, "zero tolerance." But positive reinforcement requires a very different kind of effectiveness from a parent: better praise, more purposeful rewards, greater attentiveness to a child. It draws you and your child closer together as it makes you a more effective parent.

Parents who use my method often find great relief in discovering that getting down to business doesn't have to mean bearing down even harder on their children. Being more effectively gentle and positive with your child doesn't mean being spineless. The reverse, in fact, may be true. Flying off the handle, perpetual anger, shouting, hitting — those are the truer signs of a defeated, ineffective parent. Positive reinforcement tends to calm a household because it offers clear, attainable objectives for parents and children alike to aim for in shaping behavior.

My method does not require a lifelong commitment. The program you'll set up for changing your child's behavior works like a frame you place around a growing plant to train it up straight and healthy. The plant is better behavior, and once it can stand on its own, you'll take down the frame. You will not be awarding points or keeping track of rewards forever. In fact, most parents find that such concentrated interventions take effect very quickly and can be largely discontinued after a relatively short time, like a month or two. The intention here is that you build the frame of this method around your child's changing behavior, but once the desired behavior takes deeper root and gains in vigor, you quickly scale down the frame and then take it down entirely.

Where the Method Comes From

I did not set out to specialize in helping parents improve their children's behavior. I started down the road that led to this method when somebody gave me a problem to solve and I turned to the research for help.

That occurred back in the early 1970s, when I was a graduate student at Northwestern University. The director of a local clinic that treated children who had emotional problems asked whether I could help his clients. The one I remember best was Sharon, a fifteen-year-old girl who had terrible, destructive tantrums whenever anyone said no to her or there was even the slightest unexpected change in her routine. When told we would be breaking for lunch, for instance, Sharon would blow up. She threw things, swore with amazing virtuosity, and shouted at the top of her voice. The predictable pre-lunch tantrum could be controlled by announcing to her sixty and then thirty minutes before lunch that lunch was coming, but if the clinic's staff forgot to do this, the tantrum was inevitable.

After consulting with researchers around the country, I created a program for Sharon and other clients at the clinic by adapting techniques on learning and behavior that had proved effective in treating adults. The program did not produce overnight miracles, but it did bring about gradual transformations with clear, lasting effects. We could see and measure the changes and, more important, others working with our clients and their families saw the changes. In the case of Sharon, we entirely eliminated her tantrums in about three weeks, step by step, by instituting a system of rewards for small positive changes in her behavior. She reached the point where she would smile mischievously instead of blowing up when we interrupted her. And once we ended the programs, the improved behaviors continued. The programs were temporary; the changes endured.

The treatment did not make any attempt to get at a root cause of behavior — to determine, say, the ultimate cause of Sharon's rages. We proceeded upon the idea that if you can help the child in the short term to change her behavior, over time you will change the child. The research tells us that building up a better response to replace tantrums, if the new behavior is repeated often enough, will in effect rewire that child's brain so she doesn't jump to rage as the default coping strategy for difficult situations.

Sharon's was an extreme clinical case, but I also wanted to bring the research to bear on the more everyday behavior problems that all parents have to deal with. I was appalled by the unending stream of bad "expert" advice to often desperate parents, who understandably snatched at anything that looked like a tool and rarely had the training to tell what was based on good science and what was not. So I began conducting parenting classes in which we discussed and practiced techniques for changing behavior that parents could use at home. Often the behaviors we addressed were utterly normal ones, like getting a child to eat certain foods, using the toilet, getting ready for school, doing homework, practicing a musical instrument, playing nicely with a sibling, respecting property, and not teasing or hurting a pet. The programs did not always succeed, especially at first, but we constantly evaluated whether change was happening and whether it was happening fast enough. We would adjust the program, measure our progress, and adjust again.

I also began working with schools, and when I moved from Chicago to take a job at Pennsylvania State University, I applied what I had learned to help children in local schools there. There were many challenges — such as a memorable five-year-old girl who would self-induce vomiting whenever she was mad, thoroughly disrupting the class every time she did it. (She actually turned out to be an easy case.) But as the research on behavior made the leap from the laboratory to meaningful application to the lives of real people, and as the body of that research built up, we had more equipment with which to face those challenges. The accumulating studies began to show conclusively that what many of us do as parents — from harsh punishment to endlessly explaining to a child why his behavior is wrong — may not work at all and can even make our children's behavior problems worse by giving attention to them.

We began teaching parents to "catch their children being good," instead of unwittingly reinforcing unwanted behaviors by shouting, hitting, explaining, or otherwise attending to them. And the developing body of scientific research began to show conclusively that small, temporary changes in what parents do at home have large, lasting effects in changing children's behavior at home and at school.

After a decade at Penn State, I moved to the University of Pittsburgh School of Medicine, where, in addition to continuing my research and directing an inpatient service, I continued training parents to change their children's behavior at home over the long term. My colleagues and I also used federal grants to study the techniques we taught, refining them and making them more effective.

In 1989, I took a position at Yale University and moved my clinic there. It continues as the Yale Parenting Center and Child Conduct Clinic, which I direct. I am also the John M. Musser Professor of Psychology and Child Psychiatry, and for four years I directed a large research and clinical operation at the Child Study Center at the Yale Medical School. At the Yale Parenting Center and Child Conduct Clinic, the most hands-on of these responsibilities, my staff and I see families of children from ages two to sixteen and apply programs to change child behavior in the home and community. Five days a week, every week, we work with parents who need help with their children. Some families bring us children who are referred by the schools, other mental health services, or law enforcement agencies. These are children with severe problems. But at least half of the parents who come to us face less severe difficulties. They just want our help in stopping their children from arguing or teasing so much, or in getting their children to do homework, to take more responsibility, or to not melt down so often. And we know how to help them. We can help families break the cycle that pits defiant child against exhausted parent until one or both gives way.

Getting the Word Out

Discovery has been my job, and I love it. I've spent more than three decades refining my method — thirty-plus years of research, grants, scholarly conferences, clinical applications, follow-up studies, all the routines of scientific scholarship. I've written or coauthored forty-four books and almost six hundred articles, chapters, and papers. But they were addressed almost exclusively to other professionals in my field. Now it's time to get the word out as widely as possible to the people who need it most.

The scientific evidence that demonstrates what works best in changing children's behavior is overwhelming. That wasn't true when I first began working with children, but it is now. There's always more vital research to be done, but scientists have to think beyond research, too. How do we get this technology — because that's what a scientifically supported method that produces reliable results amounts to, a technology — into the hands of people so that they can put it to use? I'm both sobered and motivated by recalling that children are still being crippled and killed by polio half a century after researchers discovered a vaccine for it. Research *must* go hand in hand with dissemination if it's going to help people. Misbehavior isn't as scary as polio, but it's far more pervasive than polio ever was. (And sometimes it's pretty scary in its own right. Children's misbehavior at its worst — conduct disorder, a psychiatric diagnosis for extreme aggressive and antisocial behaviors — is a fantastically expensive, widespread, persistent problem affecting millions of families.) Scientists, including me, have not worked hard enough to ensure that their relevant findings reach beleaguered parents. I wrote this book to distill that scientific expertise in the form of practical help you can use to address behavior problems in your own home.

My job is made more complicated by the sheer volume of advice and therapeutic approaches, much of it misguided, that's already out there. Parents who come to my clinic often have a mishmash of good and bad and irrelevant parenting lore already floating in their heads. Sometimes they have tried other treatments, including some that superficially resemble methods that actually work, and those treatments have not helped much.

I feel for these parents. They're looking for workable solutions in a field with insufficient quality control. There are over 550 therapies for children and adolescents. Over 90 percent of them haven't been tested with any scientific rigor. We simply don't know if they work or don't work. But there's no public outcry of *What's the basis for this?* There are no hoops through which a therapy must pass to get on the market, no equivalent of the Food and Drug Administration's approval process for a new drug. What's out there *might* work, but it's often being used in place of things that are *known* to work. And a few widely accepted treatments have actually been proven to make behavior *worse*.

This is the fault of the mental health professions, not of parents, who make what sense they can of the tsunami of seemingly authoritative information constantly coming at them. I'm doing what I can to effect change in my profession from within. As president of the American Psychological Association, which has over 150,000 members, one of my main goals is to encourage the recent turn in clinical work toward greater accountability to scientific standards.

But there's still a lot of poor advice out there. For instance, one parenting book that's been in circulation for years says that if a brief time-out doesn't work, keep upping the ante and make it longer, even going to a so-called monster time-out lasting four hours or more. But the research shows us that more intense punishment does not lead to greater change in behavior. If you are giving more and longer time-uts, it means your strategy is failing. The answer is not to escalate — just the opposite, in fact. If you're giving more and longer time-outs, this should tell you that you need to do more to positively reinforce good behaviors to replace the unwanted behaviors.

Speaking of time-outs, plenty of experts explain that you give a child a time-out so that he can think about how he got into trouble. This is a complete misunderstanding of time-out, which is not about thinking at all. We know this because animal research proves that time-out works with all sorts of mammals that do not have our cognitive power. In a time-out, we simply withdraw attention for a brief period. Getting a child to think about things is really good for lots of reasons but not as a way to change the child's behavior. Getting the child to *do* things differently, on the other hand, will change behavior *and* the child's thoughts about it.

One widely read author assures readers that if children can tell us they are angry, they will not kick us or otherwise express their aggression in unacceptable ways. This is an outdated view not supported by evidence. A large body of scientific work tells us that talking about aggression will not reduce aggressive behavior. In fact, talking about aggression sometimes actually increases aggression. In any case, it will certainly not help a child develop nonaggressive solutions to behavior problems. The whole approach is based on misguided psychology derived from an old hydraulic model, which treated the human psyche like a steam engine that must release pressure in order to function smoothly.

But ideas discredited by science can continue to circulate for years, even decades. Some of the advice — about punishment, for instance

— is actively harmful. Some of it is basically benign; it may not hurt, except to the extent that it gets in the way of finding and applying more effective solutions. Often, the advice offers fine general tools for living but not direct paths to addressing your concerns about your child's behavior. In addition to teaching practical skills, this book will equip you to read the parenting advice with an informed critical eye.

Perhaps the greatest danger posed by bad advice is that it discourages parents from pursuing solutions that really do work. Some of the bad advice out there looks superficially like the good, evidence-based advice. All kinds of experts tell you to praise your child, or set up a point chart, or use time-outs instead of harsher punishments. But most of them don't pay any attention to the good research on how to make these strategies effective. Nor do they systematically connect the strategies to the real reason why they work, which is that they encourage *reinforced practice* (of which I'll have more to say in chapters 1 and 2) to occur. Success and failure are determined in the details, and scientists have studied those details with an exactitude that I want you to be able to take advantage of. If you happen across mediocre, impressionistic advice that's not based on good science, and you try it, and it fails to change your child's behavior, you may decide that praise or point charts or time-outs don't work at all. And that would be a tragedy, because when done right, they work very well indeed.

This book is all about doing it right. My main goal is to put the science at your disposal in a practical, efficient way that you can *use* to improve your child's behavior.

So, Relax

Before we get started, I think it's important to establish some perspective. Your child is most likely perfectly normal, which is to say that she is wonderful in many ways but occasionally misbehaves (and the research shows that even the very best-behaved kid listens only about 80 percent of the time).

Kids are people, and people respond to the method of positive reinforcement this book teaches; it works. Our research shows that about 80 percent of even the most serious cases of child conduct disorder respond well to my method, and chances are good that even the very worst moments you confront with your child fall far short of the threshold that all of these serious cases exceed.

And take heart, too, in the knowledge that kids aren't as fragile as we sometimes make them out to be. Stop worrying that you have somehow inflicted permanent "psychological scars" on your child with less-than-perfect parenting — which is, of course, the only kind there is. Think, instead, of your child's behavior as a complicated bundle of habits and routines. It's never too late to change those habits and routines by reinforcing different ones, and when you improve your child's behavior, you give both your child and yourself a chance to feel better about everyone involved. Change the behaviors; the feelings will follow.

I intend this book as a resource you can use to build a better family life. It explores how both parents and children see the world and themselves, and how both children and parents often come to express that self-conception in troublesome behavior. Such behavior can drift into a self-perpetuating destructive pattern, but the cycle *can* be interrupted and the troublesome behavior changed, bringing greater harmony to the family. I have distilled the science into practical guidance — sample dialogues between parents and child, for instance, and explanations for why one dialogue has been shown to be effective while another has not. I keep foremost in mind the necessity of answering practical questions like, *If I want to start applying these methods today, what exactly do I do?* or *What exactly should I say?*

The scientific research has clear and often surprising things to say about even the most common and typically unquestioned practices we all employ, from explaining to nagging to punishing. So keep an open mind. Help is here, and it's the best help science can offer.

1

Seven Myths of Effective Parenting

My first daughter was supposed to be going to sleep in her crib. But I was standing there at cribside, enthralled, marveling joyfully at this little creature. She was squirming, making sounds, and looking at me, in no way moving toward sleep. My wife entered the room and fired off two questions: "What are you *doing?*" and "Is this the way to get her to *sleep?*" She was pointing out, in nonscientific marital shorthand, that by standing there I was attending to our daughter's behaviors — squirming, making sounds, looking around, being awake — and thus reinforcing them. As a clinical child psychologist, a scientist who studies human behavior, I supposedly knew not to do this. After all, I devote my days to teaching parents how to shape the behaviors they want in their children and how to stop reinforcing the behaviors they don't want. But what came most naturally to me was to stand there gawking at my wonderful baby daughter, even though this was rewarding her for not going to sleep.

Sometimes what comes most naturally is what works best in child-rearing. Parents feel a natural urge to be affectionate toward their children, and it's a good thing they do. Every hug or kiss, every warm word, does important work in helping to build a child's confidence, sense of security, and self-esteem. Parental affection strengthens both the child-parent bond and the child's ability to bond with others. In fact, holding and cuddling can enrich development of the brain, one of the concrete biological benefits of warm physical contact between parent and child. There's much more to raising a child than managing behavior. Heed the natural urge to hug your kid, and heed it often: it's one of the best things you can do as a parent.

But when it comes to shaping and changing a child's behavior, what comes most easily and naturally to parents is often the opposite of what works best. In the normal course of family life, parents are frustrated not just by their children's misbehavior but also by a sense that their own ineffectiveness has much to do with shaping that misbehavior. It's not that we're bad parents; rather, when it comes to behavior, most of us share some basic instincts and assumptions as parents that don't do us or our children much good. We turn instinctively to punishment as option one for changing behavior. We nag. We clutter the airwaves with ineffective talk. We endlessly explain to our children *why* they should behave better. We concentrate so intensely on the behavior we want to eliminate that we forget to praise and reinforce the behavior we do want. We say, *I know you know how to use the toilet/dress yourself/clean your room/do your homework! You've done it before!* We say, or think, *Your brother/sister/cousin/friend, who's younger than you are, has no problem using the toilet/dressing herself/cleaning his room/doing her homework. What's wrong with you?* We believe that our misbehaving child is "just being manipulative."

The assumptions behind each of these common habits are wrong.

I'm going to teach you a new set of basic assumptions, a new and more effective set of parental instincts distilled from what thirty-plus years of scientific research and working with families have taught me about how to improve a child's behavior. These revised basics are simple, there aren't many of them, and they're not hard to grasp, but they may feel counterintuitive at first. As you learn new habits, you can break unhelpful old ones. So, in this chapter, I want to start by addressing some common myths of parenting, assumptions that come easily to us and can steer us down the wrong path in raising our children. Let's think a little about the beliefs behind what you do now —

what any parent does — and why the parental strategies they lead to might not be working as well as you'd like.

Myth 1. Punishment will change bad behavior. Parents typically assume that punishing a child will teach a lesson by "sending a message." So punishment is often a parent's first and last option when it comes to changing a child's behavior. Depending on your style of parenting and your mood at any given moment, you decree time-outs, take away a privilege, shout *Stop that!,* or use nonverbal displays of exasperation like eye-rolling and sighing. Maybe you hit a little, or even a lot. If you're like most parents, you start out with milder punishments and escalate to more severe ones. Whether you do it mildly or severely, calmly or angrily, systematically or randomly, you probably find yourself punishing your child a great deal, and when you're not punishing, you're threatening to punish. The whole process can be difficult and distasteful, but, you tell yourself, it's what you have to do to stop kids from doing the wrong things and teach them to do the right things.

That's not really true. Punishment can have its uses, as we'll discuss in later chapters, but study after study has proven that punishment all by itself, as it is usually practiced in the home, is relatively ineffective in changing behavior. Why? Because it does not teach a child what to *do,* nor does it reward the desired behavior — which is the only effective way to get the child to do it. Punishment also has bad side effects that can make it harder for you to work with your child to improve his behavior: it increases his aggressiveness, drives him to avoid and escape you, and prompts him to adapt quickly to punishments in ways that make them useless.

Beginning when their children are very young, parents tend to fall into the punishment trap. It goes like this. Your child does something genuinely annoying or bad: hits his sister, breaks a lamp, or just screams and whines. You punish him for it, and he stops instantly. The experience of the punishment making the behavior go away has a profound effect on you. Next time this misbehavior occurs, you're more likely to respond with punishment. And there will be a next time. A great deal of scientific evidence shows that the unwanted behavior temporarily stopped by punishment usually returns at the same rate in the hours or days to come. All the punishment did was stop the behavior for a moment — which isn't bad, but you probably felt you had accomplished something more than that. As a child adapts to the punishment, the unwanted behavior tends to return faster. If the instantaneous stopping effect lasted for two hours, soon it's ninety minutes, then an hour, and so on.

So you step up the scale of punishment. After all, if a little punishment worked pretty well, more punishment will work better, right? If you were giving time-outs, you make them longer. If you were taking away a toy or a privilege, you take it away for a longer period. If you shouted, you shout louder, longer, and with a meaner expression on your face. Maybe you escalate to a smack on the behind. Or you grab the child by the shoulders and shake. Maybe you roughly shove her away so that she falls, or you smack her face. You wouldn't be alone. More than 90 percent of American parents report spanking their young children.

Each time, punishing your child stops the behavior for a moment. Maybe your child cries, too, and shows remorse. In our studies, parents often mistakenly interpret such crying and wails of *I'm sorry!* as signs that punishment has worked. It hasn't. Your child's resistance to punishment escalates as fast as the severity of the punishment does, or even faster. So you penalize more and more to get the same result: a brief stop, then the unwanted behavior returns, often worse than before.

Punishment doesn't work very well to eliminate a particular unwanted behavior, but it does produce all kinds of changes in behavior — only they're usually not the kind you want. The apparent positive effect of punishment is instantaneous but fleeting, while the negative effects take a little longer to reveal themselves, but in the long run prove far more significant.

For one thing, punishing a child can dramatically change the behavior of *parents*. Falling into the punishment trap tends to escalate the frequency and severity of punishments. Bear in mind that about 35 percent of parents who start out with relatively mild punishments end up crossing the line drawn by the state to define child abuse: hitting with an object, harsh and cruel hitting, and so on. The surprisingly high percentage of line-crossers, and their general failure to improve their children's behavior, points to a larger truth: punishing changes parents' behavior for the worse more effectively than it changes children's behavior for the better. And, as anyone knows who has physically punished a child more harshly than they meant to — and that would include most of us — it feels just terrible.

Parents who use relatively harsh punishments should also bear in mind that they're modeling unwanted behavior for the child they punish. Hitting teaches hitting as the way to respond to the problems raised by life; yelling teaches yelling; becoming visibly angry teaches anger, and so on. Modeling is a very strong way to teach behavior, stronger than punishment, which helps explain why the harm you do with harsh punishments can multiply and last a long time. You hit your daughter, your daughter hits her little brother, and then you spank her for it and yell, *We don't hit people in this house!* In fact, you've effectively modeled hitting for your daughter, who's not dumb, and she's learned her lesson well. This is why children whose parents hit them a lot will hit their peers when they are mad or trying to resolve problems, and why children whose parents shout at them will shout at their peers when they are trying to change their peers' behavior. The research finds consistently that children "discipline" other children in the way their parents discipline them.

Bear in mind, too, that punishing a behavior is still a form of paying attention to it, and *any* kind of attention can encourage your child to do it again. You're actually perpetuating the behavior when you descend on your child and punish her for it, especially if you accompany that punishment with lengthy explanations of why what she did was wrong and how the punishment is good for her. The lesson is *When you hit your brother, I pay a lot of attention to you; so next time you want attention, try hitting your brother. I may shout, I may rage, I may lecture you and take away privileges, and I may even hit you, but I won't ignore you.*

Finally, punishment tends to increase your child's aggression and desire to get away from the parent who punishes her — which makes for more unwanted behavior, which gives you more opportunities to punish, which tends to encourage more punishment, and so on, as you sink ever deeper into the punishment trap.

I'm not saying that there's no place for punishment. As I'll show you in later chapters, punishment can be a small but effective part of a program that also features lots of positive reinforcement of the behaviors you desire. The kind of punishment that helps eliminate the behaviors you don't want is mild, brief, sparingly used, and, if possible, occurs early on in the behavior, so that it short-circuits an unwanted sequence of actions before that sequence can get fully under way. Sometimes, a well-timed look or word can stop misbehavior. Technically, that look or word is punishment, or the threat of punishment, and it can be very effective. But parents typically wait until the misbehavior has run its course, then punish severely, frequently, and often angrily, and that usually doesn't work. I'm going to show you how you can punish less *and* be more effective as a parent; in fact, one leads directly to the other.

Myth 2. More reminders lead to better behavior. Because sometimes our kids actually do what we want when we ask or tell them to do something, we cling to the faith that if we just keep reminding them to do it, they'll do it eventually. When they don't, we're baffled and angry. We shout, *I've told you fifty times!* as if having said it fifty times increases the chances of our child doing what we want. In fact, studies show clearly that saying it fifty times is usually *less* effective than saying it once or twice. Nagging makes the desired behavior less likely to occur. Like punishment, excessive reminders become aversive, encouraging a child to escape physically or mentally from the person who gives them.

The technical term for asking or telling your child to do something is an "antecedent." An antecedent is an action that comes before a behavior and sets the stage for it. "Will you please clean up your room?" is an antecedent, and it sets the stage for the child cleaning up the room, the "behavior." The third piece of the sequence is called the "consequence." You ask the child to clean up the room; the child cleans up the room; you give the child praise or some other reward. (Punishment is a consequence, too, a negative one, but it doesn't work nearly as well as a positive consequence.) The sequence is clear: antecedent (please clean your room) leads to behavior (cleaning the room) leads to consequence (reward for cleaning the room). It's easy to remember: ABC.

- A for antecedent
- B for behavior
- C for consequence

But what happens if your request (the antecedent) doesn't cause room cleaning (the behavior) to happen? What happens if your child isn't listening or just doesn't do it? Well, repeating, *Will you please clean up your room?* fifty times does not make it fifty times more likely that the child will do what you're asking him to do. In fact, the likelihood goes down. Why?

First, it's because every time the antecedent doesn't lead to the intended behavior and consequences, the effectiveness of that antecedent to produce that behavior diminishes. Requests or instructions lose their effect if they don't lead directly to the rest of the sequence. In fact, nagging also reduces the chances that your child will do what you ask *next* time as well.

Second, repeating the request usually affects the *parent*'s behavior for the worse, which in turn makes it more likely that your child will not behave as desired. As stress goes up in your voice and manner — *I've told you* fifty *times to clean up your room and you're* still *not* doing *it!* — you almost guarantee failure. Strong statements made with lots of intensity (and anybody who's been after a kid to do something knows what I'm talking about) can become aversive, like punishment. Your child just wants to get away from this crazy-angry person who's hounding him. You're guaranteeing failure, because nagging your child will lead to his wanting to escape before it will be effective in producing the behavior you want. Nagging is like a medicine that just gives you side effects without curing the disease, and the side effects of a bad antecedent (nagging, or any other form of ineffective request on your part) can be similar to those of punishment.

I'm going to teach you to give fewer but more effective commands. The insights gleaned from research on child conduct can help you improve the *quality* of your communication with your kids by reducing

the *quantity* of extraneous reminders — instructions, threats, reprimands, updates, warnings, much of which a child hears as mere white
noise — that add up to nagging. I'll show you how you can get better
results by being more specific, clearer, calmer, and more gentle in asking or telling your kids what to do.

*Myth 3. Explaining to your child why a behavior is wrong will
lead him or her to stop that behavior.* Exasperated parents often find
themselves repeating things like, *You know better* or *I have told you
time and again why you should not do this.* While there are many
sound reasons to rationally explain good behavior to a child, doing so
is very unlikely to *change* your child's behavior. This statement applies not only to children. Sexually active adults who know about
sexually transmitted diseases still do not use protection. Most adult
smokers, overeaters, and kleptomaniacs know that they are doing
wrong and hurting themselves or others but continue the destructive
behavior. Kids are no different. In children and adults, recognition
that one is doing wrong does not automatically trigger a process that
will alter the improper behavior. You can say, *Don't be a racist! It's
morally wrong!* or *Save your money! You'll regret it if you don't!* to
people all day long, and they may know that you're right, yet it won't
change their behavior in any significant way.

Let me be clear that explanation has an important place in raising kids. Explanation is wonderful for building IQ, for developing a
child's powers of rational reasoning, and for teaching the difference
between right and wrong. But while explanation improves understanding, it's rarely an effective tool for changing behavior. The most
effective way to teach a general principle like "It's not right to take
from others" is not just to preach it in the abstract but also to reinforce your child's good behavior in specific situations in which he
chooses not to take from others.

Adults typically grasp the weakness of the link between understanding and behavior when it comes to themselves (*I know I shouldn't
eat these chips and that trans fats are bad for me, but I'm going to eat
them anyway*), but not when it comes to their kids. They insist on explaining and explaining why a behavior is wrong, even though verbal
instructions have proven to be one of the weakest interventions in

changing behavior. Explaining, when used all by itself, is an anteced-ent with no consequences. (Remember, an antecedent is anything you do to set the stage for a behavior, to prompt it to occur, and conse-quences are what happens after the behavior — reward, praise, pun-ishment — that teaches a child to do it again or not to do it.) An ante-cedent without consequences doesn't do much to change behavior.

Explaining what was right or wrong about a behavior once the be-havior is over is a relatively weak tool, too. It can work to change the behavior of unusually motivated, competent people — if you tell a competitive ice skater that she's not performing a jump properly be-cause her arms are in the wrong position, she's likely to adjust her be-havior at once — but that's a small and exceptional subset of human beings. For most people, the understanding that comes from feedback after the fact does not work wonders.

That said, the research does tell us how to explain more effectively if you're trying to change behavior. I'll teach you not only how to be specific and helpful when you talk with your child about good behav-ior, but also how to give him opportunities to *practice* that good be-havior so that you can reward and reinforce it. That's the key — pair-ing explanation with actually practicing the behavior — and we'll work on it.

Myth 4. Lots of praise just spoils your child. Praise is one of the strongest ways to influence your child's actions. It can be the essential ingredient in improving behavior, or it can make behavior worse. The result depends on the quality of the praise and upon how and when it's delivered. Parents often offer plenty of positive comments to their kids but deliver those comments in ways that undermine or even re-verse their potential good effect on a child's behavior. So while there may sometimes be a sufficient *quantity* of parental praise out there — to the point where it feels like a trip to the park is just an opportunity to hear *Good job!* repeated hundreds of times in a dozen different voices until the words have no meaning — the *quality* of its delivery is very uneven, causing much of it to miss its target.

You don't necessarily have to speak to encourage your child to-ward particular behaviors. Giving her a hug, a kiss, or simply your undivided attention can all serve to reinforce a behavior. They can all be very effective — think about how you used them all to encourage your child when she was just starting to walk — but they can be misused, too. For example, your being on the phone is often a cue for your child to make all sorts of requests: *Can I have a snack? Can I go outside? Can I have a pony when I'm twelve?* Finally, you cover the phone with one hand and hiss, *Yes! Yes! Whatever! Can't you see I'm on the phone?* Attending to the requests and giving in to them just serves to reinforce the habit of interrupting you on the phone. Your child, noting that asking for things while you're on the phone tends to get attention and positive answers, will probably do it again next time. The solution? Tell her, *When I'm on the phone, please don't ask me for things. It can wait until I'm off the phone. If you ask when I'm on the phone, the answer will always be no. If you wait until I'm off, the answer may be yes or may be no, depending on what you're asking for.* Then, of course, you have to follow through and really ignore your child while you're on the phone.

Misguided or poorly delivered praise can make it effective in exactly the wrong way, or make it ineffective. One good example is the practice of praising the child's general qualities — *You're so smart, What a good girl you are, You're the greatest* — and not the specific behavior you want the child to do more of: *I'm so impressed that you sat right down and practiced the piano for twenty minutes, like a big girl.* Another example of ineffective praise is "caboosing," in which the parent adds a negative comment to positive praise, thereby diluting its useful effect. Parents will often say something like, *It's good you cleaned up your room,* and then caboose it with a zinger, like, *Why can't you do this every day?* The implicit reprimand for past bad behavior tacked on to praise for good behavior actually weakens the reinforcement of the lesson that cleaning up is desirable.

Most parents do not, in fact, praise their children's behavior too much, even if they think they do. There seems to be a hardwired Eeyore in us all that accentuates the negative. The human brain is set up to be super-responsive to negative stimuli, far more responsive than to positive stimuli. Parents, therefore, respond much more to misbehavior than to good behavior, and when they're under stress, that's even more the case. We tell our clients at the clinic to "catch your child being good" — to look for chances to notice good behavior and praise it.

A lot of very good research tells us that praise, properly used, is one of your most reliable tools in changing your child's behavior. I will teach you the nuts and bolts of how to praise most effectively. It's not complicated, but praising your child the right way is more precise and purposeful than simply filling the air with cries of *Good job!*

Myth 5. Doing it once or twice means your child can do it regularly. We mistakenly assume that because a child has performed a behavior correctly, he now knows how to do it every time. Studies show that performing a behavior once, or a few times, does not mean that it can or will be performed consistently. Consistency of performance — doing the behavior regularly — often has to be trained. Just as, say, training a runner for long distances is not the same as training her to sprint, training your child for consistency is somewhat different from teaching him to do it right on one occasion. This is nothing strange or unique to children. Do you exercise regularly? Do you eat healthy meals every day? You might mean to, but it doesn't always work out that way, does it? It's no big deal to go to the gym once or to pass up fries in favor of salad once, but doing it consistently is another matter entirely.

As a parent, you'll find yourself thinking, or saying, *I know you can clean up your room; you've done it before,* or *I know you can do your homework on your own; you've done it before.* And because the child *has* done it before, parents tend to assume that not doing it now must be intentional and malicious, an act of defiance aimed at them. In that sense, parents have unrealistically high expectations of their children. *If you dressed yourself once, you can do it again right now.* And that expectation leads directly to conflict when parents assume *If you're not doing it now, it's because you're defying me, or you're lazy, or you just don't listen.*

It might help to think about the consistency of your child's behavior as a matter of establishing actions in her repertoire, a set of moves your child can make without special effort on your part or hers. You don't help to establish a behavior in your child's repertoire by berating or punishing her when she doesn't do it; you establish the behavior by praising and otherwise rewarding her when she does it. So it's not very helpful to say, *Can't you be with your brother for two minutes without fighting? You sat and watched this show yesterday with no problem! Why can't you do it now?* Better to prompt the children with something like, *Remember how well you watched TV together yesterday?* and then, when they're watching the show without bickering, look in and praise them for it.

The term for this kind of purposeful repetition of behavior and reward is "positive reinforcement." Nothing is more crucial to helping a child master a behavior and perform it reliably over time. The best way to make a behavior come naturally to your child is an intensive (but, thankfully, relatively brief) period of reinforcement, a stretch of days or weeks in which you create repeated opportunities for your child to do the behavior and be rewarded for it. Repetition is crucial.

If you're a regular reader of parenting advice, I know what you're thinking at this point: *I know* that. *He's talking about sticker charts, point charts.* And maybe you're thinking, too, *I've tried charts and things like that, and they didn't work so well.* Maybe you did try a point chart, and maybe it didn't work. But that's almost certainly because you got bad or incomplete advice on how to use one. I say this with confidence, because I have spent altogether too much time in my career repairing badly flawed reward programs in homes, schools, and institutions. Like many of the strategies I'm going to teach you, positive reinforcement sounds familiar and simple, but that doesn't mean that everybody automatically knows how to do it right. And you can't just proceed intuitively, winging it as you go along, because some aspects of successful positive reinforcement go against the instincts that most parents bring to child-rearing. Reliable research and a great deal of clinical experience shows us the right and wrong ways to use positive reinforcement, and success lies in getting the details right.

So I will teach you how to set up a system of rewards, how to pick rewards, how to reward properly, how to add small but telling wrinkles to a reward program to improve results, and even more important, how to practice a behavior with your child, how to combine praise and more tangible rewards, and how to fade your participation most effectively so that your child takes on more and more responsibility for a behavior until she can do it on her own.

Myth 6. My other child did not need special training or a program, so this child shouldn't need them, either. If my other child learned to use the toilet or eat with utensils or do homework without any special training, why does this child need special training? No one knows the answer to this very frustrating question. Nor does anyone know why some of us are better than others at painting, math, showing empathy, or sumo wrestling. That there are great individual differences in all human abilities, aptitudes, and behaviors is a scientifically demonstrable fact. Your different children may well require different kinds of training, as do we all.

Studies of parents' attitudes toward their children show that they typically do not appreciate just how great the differences can be between siblings or between children of the same age — even between identical twins. For instance, the rate and level of learning varies wildly from individual to individual. All kinds of genetic and environmental factors go into this variation. Even pairs of identical twins can have very different brains, and thus learn at different rates, just as they have different fingerprints. People tend to be misled by the physical similarity of twins, a principle that applies more generally. People are fooled by similarity in age, for instance. *My other child was toilet trained when she was three,* we tend to think, *so therefore all kids should be capable of toilet training at the age of three.*

Let's think for a moment about the developmental average, the age at which a child "should" be able to do something. First, boys will often be slower than girls, developmentally speaking. Second, if the developmental average is, say, four, that means some kids might be able to do it when they're two, and others not until they're six. However, if the behavior under discussion is toilet training, you (and the kindergarten teachers) are unlikely to be patient with a six-year-old who's still not toilet trained.

But calendar age is not a very good measure of what a person can do. The process of developing is really a sequence of processes, and they proceed at different rates in different people. In some children, the eyes develop faster; in others, bowel control comes sooner. Two children conceived on the same day and born on the same day nine months later can have very different bone ages — bone age being a measure of how the bones have formed, how the processes of calcification and ossification have proceeded in the body, at any given moment. Such differences become very clear, of course, in old age. Stand two sixty-five-year-olds next to each other. One looks like she's fifty; the other looks like he's eighty. We think nothing of seeing such differences in sixty-five-year-olds; we expect them. We don't expect them to occur across the range of four-year-olds, or across the range of babies, but those differences do exist.

The development of behavior is much the same. Instead of thinking of it as a series of benchmarks that have to be met by such and such a calendar date, think of it as the process of your child achieving a level of mastery of behaviors you want. That process will require different amounts of effort on your part at each stage for each kid — not different principles or techniques, but different applications of technique and effort. Don't burden your child or yourself with the requirement that he be statistically average; think instead about how to help him master behaviors according to his own particular strengths, weaknesses, and sequence of development.

Myth 7. My child is just being manipulative. When a child goes against our wishes, we often explain away the misconduct by saying that she's just being manipulative. But research shows that children are no more manipulative than the rest of us — and actually probably much less so, since coming up with a strategy for getting one's way by anticipating and managing the behavior of others is beyond most children's abilities. What parents interpret as manipulative behavior by a child is often just a tendency toward irritable actions, which the parents themselves may have unwittingly reinforced and turned into a pattern. Your child screams; to stop the screaming, you give him your undivided attention and perhaps submit to his demands; this trains him to turn to this behavior to get more attention from you. Calling a child manipulative often substitutes for recognizing that we may have reinforced the wrong behaviors in that child.

Parents are right, in a sense, to see their child's behavior as designed to get their attention. But the "manipulation" is rarely conscious on the child's part. He's not thinking, *I think I'll get some attention from my mom by driving her crazy,* although he might be thinking, *I get attention when I do this, and I like attention.* If you ask a difficult five-year-old how he gets his mother's attention, he usually won't say, *I misbehave.* His response to his parents' cues occurs well below that conscious level. Mostly, the child is just responding to the consequences of his previous behavior. If screaming has proven before to be a reliable way to get attention, he'll go to screaming as a first option in his repertoire. We've done studies in which we had parents change their responses to behavior, and it's amazing how fast the child adjusts to the change. If we have parents ignore screaming and pay a lot of attention to asking nicely, the child will switch to asking nicely as the better, more reliable way to get attention. Now, who's "manipulating" whom?

Another study tried to isolate the effect of praising good behavior by setting up a mini–training program in a schoolroom. We had a child engage in free play, and we had teachers come in one by one to interact with the child. We instructed one group of teachers to notice and praise good behavior 100 percent of the time (when a child played nicely and put the toys away properly, the teacher was to always notice and praise that behavior), one group to notice and praise 50 percent of the time, and one group zero percent of the time (no matter how often the child played nicely and put toys away, the teacher was instructed to never notice or praise that behavior). Thus, during the training period of the study, a child would be in the room participating in free play, and different teachers would come in and praise good behavior all, some, or none of the time, depending on which group each teacher was in. After a while we would stop this training, return the child to a normal classroom situation with other kids, and send in the different teachers who had interacted with her during the training period. When the teacher who praised good behavior 100 percent of the time came in, the child behaved well in class. When the teacher who praised good behavior 50 percent of the time came in, the child's behavior was uneven but acceptable. When the teacher who praised good behavior zero percent of the time came in, the child, to use a nontechnical term, bugged out. What is this telling us? Adults shape the behavior of children in their responses to it. Our kids are not manipulating us; in part, they're expressing what we train them to do.

• • •

The training of children is never over. It's never too late. Parents are right to be amazed at how their children appear to be born with temperaments and personality types already seemingly built in, but they don't always appreciate just how malleable a child's behavior really is. And the decisive factor in shaping a child's behavior is what parents and other adult caregivers do.

I realize that being a parent is challenging even on a good day. There are normal stressors on a child: a four-year-old's fears, a twelve-year-old's sensitivity to peer pressure — there's always something. Parents are under stress, too. Time and money are usually in short supply, and new demands and problems seem to spring from out of nowhere. *Braces? Kung fu lessons? You broke* what? Beyond merely coping with what comes up, though, you're also trying to teach your child how to be a good person, how to make his way in the world. It can seem hard or impossible to do everything at once, and sometimes it seems as if you can't do even the simplest thing — sit down to a family dinner, for instance — without a crisis.

And now, on top of all that, I come along and tell you that some or much of what you assumed about parenting is wrong. But that's just step one; in the chapters that follow, I'll show you what you can do right to be a more effective parent.

I regard the debunking of myths as a necessary preamble to my nuts-and-bolts work, which is to help in the practical day-to-day business of child-rearing. I will show you how to develop behaviors in your child that ease daily life but also build the long-term habits and values that you want for your child. When you manage the day-to-day issues better, you will be much more effective in helping your child for the long term as well. My method focuses on behavior, but behavior affects how the child copes, interacts with others, and develops as a thinking and feeling person. Changing behavior has broad ef-

fects on how well a child, a parent, and a family function — and fortunately, we know a great deal about how to change behavior.

Parenting is a craft. It can be done better or worse. It's time to
move on to the next chapter, in which we establish the principles for
doing it better.

2

Everything You Need to Know
(Except *How*)

I've already touched upon some of the basic principles behind my method for changing children's behavior. I'm going to summarize those principles here, so they're all ready to hand in one place. Then I'll answer some questions you might naturally have about them and about the method built upon them.

The Positive Opposite

Let's change one parental habit right now, and for good. Instead of thinking of your child's behavior in terms of what you *don't* want — *He has too many tantrums* or *It drives me crazy when she doesn't listen* — start thinking in terms of the behavior you *do* want.

The key is the idea of a "positive opposite": the behavior you want, which will replace the behavior you don't want. The positive opposite approach to *He has too many tantrums* might be *When he gets frustrated, I want him to tell me so with nice words and a calm body*. The positive opposite approach to *It drives me crazy when she doesn't listen* might be *I want her to listen to me the first time I say something.* It's much easier to build up a behavior you want by positively rewarding it than it is to wipe out a behavior you don't want via punishment or other negative means. When you get rid of a behavior by rewarding its opposite, the effects are stronger, last longer, and do not have the undesirable side effects of punishment. So concentrate on the positive opposite and the principle of replacing what you don't want with what you do want. I have offered some examples of positive opposites in the table below. Take a look at it, but try making your own, too, by listing five things you don't want your child to do and then thinking of a positive opposite for each.

You want to get rid of . . .	Positive opposite
Siblings fighting over a TV show (or use of a computer game)	Sitting and watching TV together nicely (or taking turns with game), without shouting or hitting
Child throwing his clothes all over the floor in his bedroom	Placing clothes in his dresser or closet
Child not doing her homework	Sitting quietly at her desk and doing schoolwork for twenty minutes
Child getting out of bed again and again for a drink of water to stretch out bedtime	Going to bed, getting up no more than once for a drink or bathroom, and remaining in her room
Child arguing and shouting at me whenever I say no to something	Expressing anger calmly
Child refusing to eat vegetables at dinner no matter how I prepare them	Trying a few bites of vegetables with dinner
Child's annoying habit of rubbing the back of his head when he is talking	Let it go — this behavior will probably drop out by itself before long

Positive Reinforcement

When you consistently connect a behavior to rewards, that's "positive reinforcement," one of your most basic and powerful tools. Positive reinforcement should be as consistent and as immediate as possible, directly following the desired behavior and clearly connected to it. Ideally, when you're working on a particular behavior, every time your child does it you should be right there with a good consequence. Let's say you're working with your child on minding the first time you ask him to do something. Every time he minds you the first time, you positively reinforce it with attention, praise, a privilege, or a token.

We'll talk much more about these rewards in the chapters that follow, but rest assured from the start that they don't have to be extravagant, and in fact they should not be. Often, the simple fact of your attention and some enthusiastic praise will be plenty. And you won't have to do this forever. The period of intense positive reinforcement required to make a permanent change in your child's behavior can be relatively brief, but during that time you will have to reliably connect reward to behavior often enough so that your child learns to connect them as well.

But rewards are not enough to change behavior permanently. Too often, positive reinforcement is misinterpreted as simply throwing rewards at behavior. There's more to it, especially the two crucial concepts that follow: reinforced practice and shaping.

Reinforced Practice

This is the best way to build up a behavior you want. If there's one concept in this book to keep foremost in mind, make it this one. "Reinforced" means that when the child performs the behavior, you notice and reward it with positive reinforcement. "Practice" means that the child has many repeated opportunities to do the behavior right and to be rewarded for it. During the time when you're working on the behavior, you need your child to have a lot of repetitions — perform the behavior, get the reward, perform the behavior, get the reward — in order to establish it in his repertoire by associating it with clear consequences. In the chapters that follow, I'll teach you ways to do that, including simulations: setting up practice situations in which your child can successfully do the behavior so that you can reinforce it.

Shaping

You shape a complex behavior by breaking it up into doable steps and then reinforcing each step until you build up to the bigger accomplishment. Parents who come to my clinic will frequently say something like, *I'd like to reward my child for doing the right things, but he can't ever take no for an answer* [or *go to bed on time*, or *leave a friend's house*, or *get through a family dinner*] *without having a tantrum. That's why I'm coming to you.* In one sense, they're right. If you wait for your child to do some challenging behavior perfectly so that you can reinforce it, you may wait forever and never see it happen. One of the greatest parental mistakes is expecting too much good behavior — asking that performance be perfect or near-perfect before you notice and reward it. Yes, your child may well be physically capable of doing exactly what you want, but you may have to adjust your expectations so that you can reward him for doing partial, incomplete, and flawed versions of what you want. These much-less-than-perfect versions can, if properly rewarded and sequenced, lead to his doing exactly what you want, and to doing it every time.

You can work up to meeting even the most challenging goals if you think about shaping behavior in discrete steps. This, of course, holds true for everybody, not just children. If you've never played the piano before and want to learn to play a piece by Beethoven, you don't just start trying to play the piece. Instead, you build up to it in gradual steps: you learn to read sheet music, learn scales and exercises, move to more difficult exercises, play easy pieces and then more challenging ones, then you try limited chunks of the Beethoven piece, and so on until you're good enough to master the whole thing.

If you want your child to do two hours of homework on her own every night, you don't withhold praise and rewards until she does two hours of homework without being asked to. You start by setting goals for smaller units of work and for doing it without being asked over and over to do it, and you gradually build up to her doing two hours of homework on her own. You reinforce success as you go, always looking out for and praising any aspect of her behavior that comes even a little closer to your desired goal. When your child performs a behavior that's not quite right, ask yourself, *Was there anything about it that's a component of what I'd like her to do?* If the answer's yes, and it almost always is, then jump on that component: *It was great that you did X* (whatever she did right). Then you can push her a little further toward the goal: *It would be really, really great if you did X and Y* (the part she didn't do, or didn't do correctly). Be careful not to caboose; one way to guard against caboosing is to avoid using "but" when you praise.

Fortunately, you've already had good practice in shaping your child's behavior. You did it when your child began to walk, for instance. You praised him wildly when he pulled himself up from a crawling to a standing posture. You held his hands and helped him to take a few steps, encouraging him by exclaiming, *Look at you! You're walking! What a big boy!* He was not walking, of course. He wasn't ready to perform such a complex behavior, but you were shaping that behavior by reinforcing the stages on the way to it: pulling up, walking with your assistance, walking with less assistance from you, cruising on his own from one piece of furniture to the next, then the first halting true steps. That's an excellent example of shaping, and the principle applies to much more complex behaviors.

Extinction

You might expect that the most effective flipside of positive reinforcement would be punishment — *I'm taking away your stuffed bear until you stop whining* — but it's not. "Extinction" often proves to be the better tool. You extinguish a behavior when you don't give your attention to it, like removing oxygen and fuel from a fire. In the chapters that follow, I'll talk about when it's best to ignore a behavior, even one you might ordinarily notice and react to. And I'll talk about the importance of coupling extinction with reinforcement of the behaviors you do want to encourage. That is, you ignore whining, for example, which you don't want to encourage, but you couple that with rewarding something you very much want to encourage — such as when your child makes a request just once, in a normal, nonwhiny voice, and says please. Extinction, by itself, is not the strongest way to change behavior, but when combined with reinforcement of the positive opposite, it can play an important role.

Putting It All Together: ABC

In the last chapter, I talked about how to put all this together using the ABC formula. Here's a slightly expanded definition of the formula:

- A for antecedent — everything that comes before a behavior, including the way you model behavior for your child, the instructions you give, the prompts you offer to guide your child, and the context that sets up the behavior.
- B for behavior — when you identify positive opposites, when you shape a behavior by breaking it down into doable steps, when you give your child repeated opportunities to do something right, you're working on the behavior itself.
- C for consequences — what comes after the behavior, such as praise, attention, and other forms of reinforcement.

When you put them all together — ABC — you set the stage for the behavior with the right antecedents, you give your child repeated opportunities to perform the behavior, and then you deliver reliable consequences. When you see its effect on your child's behavior, there appears to be magic in this sequence, but in fact it's the result of good research done by many dedicated scientists. I have seen this research be a great help to parents, but in many cases it has not yet been translated into practical advice that most parents can find and use. I'm writing this book to present the science to you in a way you can use.

I should add that ABC holds the answer to a concern sometimes raised by parents who come to my clinic: *I have praised and praised until I'm blue in the face, and I've done point charts before,* they say, *and they don't work with my child.* Praise and points are part of the C portion of ABC — they're consequences. But A and B are critical, too. Often, it's the case that the parents have been very generous with rewards but less careful about the way they set the stage for the behavior (A) or about consistently noticing and responding to the behavior itself (B). When praise and points don't work, it's usually because they are used improperly, and that's often because the earlier stages that come before consequences have been neglected.

Q & A

Okay, with these basic ideas in place, let's move on to some questions you might have about the program we're about to undertake and the principles underlying it.

Why do I have this problem in the first place? Is it my fault? Did I mess up my kid?

Mothers, in particular, tend to blame themselves for their children's misbehavior, but there's really no point in blaming yourself. Taking the blame does not help you to change your child's behavior. More important, that kind of self-accusation is based on a false premise. Yes, there is much you can do to change your child now, but explaining how he got the way he is in the first place involves many factors, and we truly don't know how these many factors come together in any individual. Let me put it this way: science offers no conclusive evidence in support of blaming yourself as the sole or dominant cause of your child's misbehavior.

Only in very rare and unique cases can we attribute a child's misconduct to a solitary cause. Usually, the causes are multiple and interrelated, so that attributing a child's misbehavior to any one factor is inaccurate. Children, like adults, differ in temperament, personality, and social characteristics. Some are simply more sensitive, anxious, argumentative, or annoying than others. They're complicated, and the ultimate sources of their behavior may well remain mysterious to us. Indeed, we may describe our own behavior in rational terms that tell a sensible story, but we really do not know much about why we do many things: why we have kept some habit or interest from childhood but not another, for instance, or why we engage in some parenting practices we learned from our parents but are adamant about avoiding others. Why do we have this foible or that? Why does your spouse continue to engage in a certain habit — refusing to replace the toilet paper when it runs out, offering helpful advice to you when you're driving — even after years of careful instruction to the contrary by you? We do not know the *why* behind most behaviors, even when we talk as if we do.

For instance, we know that some people who are beaten as children become criminals when they grow up, but most do not. If being beaten is a cause, shouldn't everyone who is beaten as a child become a criminal? But if a child is beaten *and* has a minor genetic abnormality that affects the functioning of a brain transmitter, the chances are really high he will grow up and engage in criminal behavior when compared to another child who is beaten but does not have that genetic characteristic. Which "caused" the criminality, the beatings or the genetic abnormality? The answer, of course, is both, and neither (by itself).

For our purposes, it may help to distinguish between original causes (how a behavior came to be a part of the child's repertoire) and current causes (what triggers and guides the behavior right now). While we may not be able to figure out original causes, we can identify and work on the current causes. That's what a parent can do best: pay close attention to current causes and try to change behavior by changing them.

In other words, we can treat a problem without necessarily knowing everything about its cause. You have a headache, you take aspirin, and the headache goes away. Why, exactly, did you have a headache? Sometimes you think you know why, and sometimes you don't, but what matters is that the aspirin worked. Similarly, when you take steps to improve your children's behavior, you take on yourself the primary responsibility for solving a problem, but it doesn't necessarily follow that you are solely responsible for the problem's existence in the first place.

What are the most important concepts underlying the method?
Start by changing behavior, not by trying to get to the root causes of your child's misbehavior. Kids have rich psychological and emo-

tional lives, and we don't want to ignore that. But, for the moment, we want to concentrate not on what's going on within the child but on what's purely outward, as observed in the child's behavior and the child's relationship with others. All the principles I've introduced in this chapter so far — positive opposites, positive reinforcement, reinforced practice, shaping, extinction, ABC — give us names for ways to work on behavior, and behavior is one key to relationships with others.

On occasion, parents with a defiant, oppositional child have told me that they no longer love their child as they once did. Years of pain and conflict have produced a kind of emotional divorce between parent and child. More commonly, parents feel frustrated and inept, and are angry at the child for making them feel that way. They still love their child, but their love has gotten tangled up with all sorts of negative feelings. Now, to my knowledge, science does not know how to cause one person to love a particular other person or to love another person in a more heartfelt way. But we can change interactions between people, as expressed in behavior, and cause both child and parent to be less irritable, less angry, less hurt, and less hurtful in their interactions with each other. When we smooth interactions at the level of behavior, more often than not we also see immediate results in feelings such as appreciation and love. When relieved parents tell me things like, *She's a completely different person — she used to be spoiled and selfish but now she's so decent and thoughtful,* they're really putting a label on a collection of behaviors. They're saying, in effect, *My child used to consistently do behaviors X, Y, and Z, which I call "spoiled," but now she consistently does behaviors A, B, and C, which I call "thoughtful."*

That's why it makes sense to work on behavior. We know how to change it (without resorting to pills), and it affects everything else, including the deep feelings that we tend to think of as the root causes of behavior. Studies show that reinforced practice, over time, actually changes the brain. Chemical and structural changes occur in the brains of violinists, for instance, who practice regularly for years. These studies suggest a dynamic, two-way relationship between behavior and the brain, between action and mind. So when we alter our

children's outward behavior in a purposeful way, we're also addressing those internal aspects of their being that are harder to define and
address — the inner life that we tend to think of as who we truly are.

*Why does it work? Why does changing behavior in essence change
the child? And, given that it does work, more questions arise. What
are the implications of changing something so closely associated with
my child's self-image as her behavior? Will I be getting my child to behave at the expense of his fragile ego? Will I be beating back my child,
setting her up to be beaten back by others when she's an adult? Am I
changing my child's personality?*

Let's take them in order. First, why it works: repeated practice
helps lock particular behaviors into your child's repertoire of behaviors, a process that involves changes in the brain. Going back to the
example of the accomplished violinist, we know that he doesn't read
an A-flat on his sheet music and say to himself, *Let's see now, that requires me to depress the E string exactly this far up the fingerboard.*
His brain has learned to bypass the rational process and go directly to
the previously learned response. Recent technological advances in the
study of the chemistry and structure of the brain have given science
the capacity to see how this process plays out on the molecular level,
but that research is still in its early stages. For now, suffice to say we
know that repeated practice changes the brain, and we're still trying
to figure out exactly what those changes look like. It would be beside
the point to worry that following the program outlined in this book
might cause changes in your child's brain; *every* behavior your child
learns and practices, whether it comes from you or from another
source, causes changes in the brain.

As for a fragile ego — there's no such thing. I work with a child's
capacity for seeing himself and negotiating reality, a child's equipment
for handling life. As a child's behavior improves, he also builds competence, develops socially acceptable habits, and enables interactions
with other people. Our internal strength comes from our connections
to others and how well we function every day. Science does not know
how to change egos, let alone break them, especially since "ego" is
just an idea with no real counterpart in the brain. But behavior is real,

and we know how to change it, and by changing it how to inspire individuals (both children and parents) to see themselves better.

You're not "beating back" your child by positively reinforcing good behavior. If anything, the typical overwhelmed parent at wits' end, who screams and hits, does a lot more beating back. The child of that typical harried parent receives many more psychological nicks and gashes from inept parenting than he ever will from calm, systematic, effective parenting. And let me reiterate here that of course we care about a child's — and a parent's — thoughts, feelings, self-confidence, and other important attributes that don't fall under the category of behavior. But developing good behaviors and concrete competences can affect all of these, an effect that goes far beyond a simple change in the ability to perform a particular behavior. In homes where we change a child's behavior, for instance, we find decreases in parental stress and in parental symptoms of depression and other disorders, and we find improvements in family relationships. Our studies have repeatedly established this connection between changing behavior and changing the inner lives of individuals and the shared lives of families. Changing behavior isn't about forcing or beating back a child; it's about helping that child engage with the world and with others, and therefore it's also about enriching that child's inner life.

Finally, the question of personality. One significant part of what we call personality consists of temperamental differences that are already evident when a child comes into the world. (This is what people mean when they say of a new baby, *You never know who's going to get off the train.*) Your child's inborn temperamental qualities are not likely to change much as a result of any improvements you might reinforce in her behavior. The same goes for personality characteristics, such as being outgoing or being conscientious, which tend to remain fairly stable throughout a life. That said, we must first note that there's great variation in how these traits may be expressed. And, second, changing a child's behavior will affect how the child expresses those traits that seem innate. It is clear that parents, through their daily interaction with their children, have a dominant role here. As a parent, you are bringing about behavioral changes, even when you don't consciously intend to. The important question is this: will the changes you bring about help or hinder your child's development into a contributing and achieving adult?

I've tried some of these things already. I reward good behavior, I've kept point charts and all the other stuff you're talking about, but it hasn't worked. Why is it going to work this time?

It's going to work this time because we're going to do it right, and we're going to rely on a deep body of reliable scientific research to show us how to do it right.

When working with parents at my clinic, I'm often reminded that one of the virtues of this program is also one of its curses: it takes very familiar concepts and presents them in unfamiliar ways. The things I ask you to do to change your children's behavior are not like quantum mechanics; they're not mysterious or ultrascientific-sounding. Most of what I ask you to do looks like common knowledge or common sense, and parents often make the mistake of assuming they know all about it just because they've done something like it before. But, in fact, success usually lies in the details, and the details can be fresh and surprising.

Sometimes it's obvious when a parent is misapplying a technique we use in our program. I've had a mother tell me, *I've tried time-outs, and they don't work,* and then go on to admit that her idea of a time-out is for the child to spend all day in his room — all of Saturday, and all of Saturday night — with meals slipped in the door. That kind of drastic measure will not produce anything resembling the behavior a parent wants.

Another parent, a father, made his child earn dinner by cleaning up his own room. If the room was not perfect, the child did not get to eat dinner, and he would not get breakfast or lunch the next day, either, unless he did the job right. The father called it "tough love," although "desperate parenting" would be a more accurate description. The father felt that he had dramatically taken charge of the situation, and he did indeed eventually get his son to clean up his room. But that's doing it the hard way, and the side effects of such drastic measures — the child's greater inclination to avoid and distrust parents, the increase in the child's aggression — will more than cancel out any benefits in teaching an appropriate behavior.

You probably scoff at those examples of misapplied techniques and say, *I'd never do anything like that.* Well, consider these examples of improper use of consequences:

Your child does something very wrong, and you take away the privilege of using his bicycle for two weeks. The punishment fits the crime, you think, and that will teach him not to do whatever it was he did wrong. But our studies show that you only need to take away the bicycle for a day or so in order for taking away the bicycle to influence the child's behavior. That is, thirteen of the fourteen days of the two-week ban are excessive and don't add to its effectiveness. And the two-week ban will have other, undesirable effects. It will reduce the child's socialization with the other children with whom he usually rides his bike, and we very much want to encourage that socialization; it does not let the child earn back the privilege with a desired behavior; and it places an unnecessary wedge in the parent-child relationship and will foster ongoing resentment, because no matter how good the child may be during the two weeks that follow, he will still not get his bike back.

Or how about this one? You decide that your child can go to a concert or some other special event only if she does all her homework for the next two weeks or does not get a bad grade when report cards come in next month. This approach is almost certainly bound to be ineffective. It does not reinforce specific behaviors along the way (no shaping) and does not provide regular, repeated opportunities to do a desired behavior (reinforced practice). Also, the reward is much too delayed to influence behavior effectively; the links between antecedent and behavior and consequence are very weak. It sounds great — a big prize for a big accomplishment — but it very rarely works. And on top of that, parents will often relent, even though the child didn't do what was expected of her, and let her go to the concert anyway, since she was looking forward to it so excitedly and they don't want to break her heart (or put up with her whining). That's even worse, of course. Even though this kind of delayed mega-reward isn't a very effective reinforcer, if you give in and let her go to the concert anyway, you are ultimately rewarding *not* doing the behavior.

The point here is that the difference between success and failure often lies in getting the details right. Think about learning to land an airplane. You've seen lots of airplanes land, and you've probably seen pilots do it on TV. That doesn't mean you know everything there is to know about how to do it. When there are lives at stake, you don't say, *Hey, I can do this because I've seen airplanes land before, and I put my car in the garage every night, which is sort of the same thing. You just point the plane downward, and it lands.* No, you say, *What exactly do I need to do, and in what order?* It's the difference between tootling around on an instrument and making systematic progress by learning scales and working on specific skills and techniques. When you've got a planeload of passengers — or a family you're responsible for — the stakes go up.

Let's move on to the details.

3

Putting the Method in Place
Transitions, Tantrums, and a Very Young Child

Let's start with the kind of problem that parents of young children face all the time: a four-year-old whose temper tantrums threaten to completely take over his family's lives. But this chapter is essential reading for parents of children of any age, because this is where I'll lay out most fully the basics of the point chart method: how to begin by identifying the positive opposite behavior you want to build up, how to set up a point chart, how to select and award rewards, how to explain the program to your child, how to practice the program with your child to drastically improve your odds of success, and how to adjust household routines to give the program the best chance to work. With this chapter under your belt, you'll be ready to adapt this basic approach to other problems common to very young children — toilet training, say — and also to a much broader range of problems presented by older, even much older, kids. We'll see more of those problems in the chapters that follow. For now, let's concentrate on the basics, and on a child who has turned bedtime into the family tragedy.

I'm going to concentrate on a single case, that of a four-year-old boy named Davey, to illustrate the method in this chapter. As you read along, bear in mind that there's nothing about any of this that's specific to boys — other than trivial things, such as differences in what boys and girls might consider a good reward (although there's also a significant degree of overlap there). In this book, whether my example in any given passage is a girl or a boy, I'm talking about kids in general.

Define the Problem and Its Positive Opposite

Jen and Mel, Davey's parents, are sitting in my office, looking not very happy. Jen, who spends more time with Davey, describes the problem.

She tells me that Davey typically throws his fits at times of transition, like when he's being dropped off at daycare, when one parent goes off duty and the other takes over, or when leaving a place where he's been having fun. But, Jen says, the main problem is going to bed at night.

"Usually it starts like this," she says. "He is playing his video toy or watching TV and then about 7:15 we say, 'Okay, Davey, it's time for bed. Go into your room.'" I can hear in the way she imitates herself, her voice sweet and gentle and trying not to provoke, that the whole family walks around on eggshells, hoping Davey won't blow. But he does.

"His tantrum begins then," Jen continues, "and the next hour or so is one hundred percent predictable. He screams, flops around, maybe hits or kicks. If there's something nearby that he can pick up and throw, he might do that. He's tipped over a lamp before, grabbing at things to stop us from carrying him out of the living room and into his room. Any neighbor who heard his carryings on would think we were beating him or something worse. Sometimes we can walk him to his room during the tantrum and even get him into bed. We tell him to stay in his room, and close the door, but he comes right back out, crying, and we have to take him back. This can go on for an hour or more, and finally he gets so exhausted that he stays in his room and goes to sleep. By this time we are all spent, and everyone has lost it at some point."

I ask her to say more about the physical aspects of the tantrums.

"We try not to let Davey make us mad with his hitting or kicking or throwing things, but sometimes, especially if he hits somebody in the face, one of us gets fed up and spanks him, or kind of shoves him into his room. I don't think of us as people who shout or hit, and my husband and I certainly don't blow up at each other, but when I think about what happens in the evening, I have to admit that I don't like how rough it gets."

This kind of detail is very helpful. She and Mel have paid close attention to Davey's tantrums, and they have a clear sense of the behavior they want to get rid of. We also can clearly identify the behavior they want to replace it with: an easy, peaceful transition, a bedtime routine in which Davey gets ready for bed, goes to bed, and stays there, without shouting, screaming, or other drama. We now have plenty of information and can start addressing the problem. We're not merely trying to figure out how to cope with it, I remind them. We're going to fix it.

Get Started Right Away

First, because we want to get started right away, we are going to focus solely on the bedtime tantrums, the worst part of the problem. There may be other areas of Davey's behavior you want to work on, I explain, but for now it's important to begin somewhere and get one set of behaviors — bedtime tantrums — under control. We won't wait until you are experts on this method or until we have a comprehensive list of every one of Davey's behaviors that needs attention. We want to get started right away. We can make a little progress now, and this will make the home more peaceful for everyone.

To begin with, I tell Jen and Mel, you have to abandon your current approach.

You will no longer be focusing on stopping your child's temper tantrums. Instead, beginning one calm afternoon when both Davey and you are relaxed, you'll tell him about something that will catch his attention immediately — a way for him to win some new rewards. With Davey's help, you will put up a point chart on the refrigerator that you've created earlier. The chart shows how many points Davey can earn for going to bed without a fuss and what those points can buy him — what types of rewards he can earn.

Before you can do that, you'll need to design a point chart — the kind that will really work.

Step 1: Starting a Point Chart

What's a point chart (also known as a sticker chart)? It's a day-by-day way of keeping track of and displaying the positive behaviors your child has accomplished and the rewards he or she can earn for them. Research shows several special advantages to a point chart (for children of all ages — and adults, too). It keeps everybody honest about what has been earned. It provides a special incentive to your child to see the points piling up. It reminds you, the parents, to do the program — which is important, given how busy your life can get — and it's a trigger for you to praise your child. Its very presence also serves as a setting-up event, a condition that makes the desired behavior more likely to occur.

Some parents make elaborate or cute charts, reasoning that if the child likes the chart itself, she will be more enthusiastic about the program. I've seen special stickers of cartoon characters, taped-on Cheerios and Cocoa Puffs used as point markers, a picture of a garden on which butterfly stickers were added to mark points, and so on. Fun is fine, and by all means let your creativity flow, but the research shows no significant connection between how much a child enjoys the chart itself and how well the program goes. A plain chart will work just as well. The chart is just a way to track and prompt the process of doing the behavior and earning praise and other rewards. That process — reinforced practice in action — is what makes the program work.

Success will lie not in the presence of the chart itself but in how it is employed. Decades of behavioral research tell us how to set up the most effective point chart plan and use it in the most effective way. I don't need Jen and Mel to be perfect in how they apply this technique, but I need to underscore that the *how* really matters.

For Davey, we'll use a fairly simple chart. Down the left-hand side are the days of the week. He can earn points at bedtime and by practicing bedtime earlier in the day, so moving across the chart are two boxes, spaces to be filled in with check marks, stars, stickers, or any other positive marker to keep track of the points Davey can earn —

up to four per day, two for a good bedtime and two for a good practice, or even six (on rare occasions), if he practices twice. I urge Jen
and Mel to ask what he likes, or at least give him a choice about what
to use to mark his points. He's partial to dinosaurs, so dinosaur stickers would be a great choice.

POINT CHART FOR DAVEY

Days of the Week	Two Ways to Earn Stickers		Total
	Practice	Big-Boy Bedtime	Total Stickers Today
Monday			
Tuesday			
Wednesday			
Thursday			
Friday			

Total for the week: _____

Saturday and Sunday could be added, but it is fine to begin with
five days.

In each box, place stickers or check marks if Davey earned points
for doing the behavior.

If he did not do the behavior that day, merely put in a dash (do not
leave blank).

Decide early on whether you want to apply the program during the
weekend as well as the weekdays. If you have any doubt, stay with
five or even fewer days a week. Better to do the program well for five
days a week and take the weekend off, than to do it less well for all
seven days, or to do it haphazardly on the weekends. (There are times,
at my clinic, when we encourage a family to use the program only one
or two days a week, if their home situation only allows them to do it
consistently and well on those one or two days.) It's much more important to do the program well than to do it all the time.

The *where* matters, too. Where you place the chart can make a difference. Put it somewhere conspicuous, where everyone can see it,
and see it often. The refrigerator would be a perfect spot. The more
often you see it, the more likely you will be to keep track and praise
your child. It's important for your child to see it often as well. It will

motivate him or her to earn more rewards. Conspicuousness, in general, can help. For instance, delivering rewards where others can see or hear you do it will make those rewards more effective in changing behavior.

Step 2: Buying Rewards

Once you've set up the chart, you need to select some fun, appropriate rewards and set the terms for "buying" them with the points your child earns on the chart. I go over the ground rules with Jen and Mel.

First, do not take away. We absolutely do not want to take away anything Davey is "getting" now. So if he has a computer game or TV time, they're off-limits to you as rewards on his point chart. Taking away an existing privilege would cause Davey to resent the program. This can lead to more tantrums and maybe a little aggression, even from children who don't usually have tantrums. We want to *add* new rewards, although it's also fine to add more of a reward the child already receives.

Begin with the small rewards. To get started, we need some special privileges that can be earned for very few points and will be made available right now if Davey has a good day. Davey is young enough that a grab bag would work as one of the small rewards. You can put small, inexpensive items into a bag (or into separate little bags) — things like a little plastic car, an animal, a soldier, a puzzle, a ball. You decide what Davey would like and maybe even ask him to help select the small rewards at the store. Have at least six choices. Six is not a magic number. A few more would be better, but the important thing is that one or two is too few for now. Candy and snacks can be used, but I recommend staying away from these. Using food as a reward raises problems we don't really want to deal with — like, for instance, what if Davey wants to claim his ice cream cone reward twenty minutes before dinnertime?

In addition to small toys and other such goodies, think of privileges and other treats as rewards. Privileges might include, for example, selecting the menu for dinner, getting a break from doing a chore or task, playing a special game, going on a small outing, and having one of you sit with him when he watches TV. You don't have to spend a lot of money on rewards; in fact, I would urge you not to. Since Davey loves stories, an extra story will seem like a great prize to him, especially if he earned it with his own behavior. So will ten extra minutes before bedtime.

Price the rewards so that they are readily attainable. Davey can earn a maximum of four points on a typical day, at least to begin with. We do not expect perfection, so he may not earn this many points, especially in the beginning. But even if he earns fewer, we want to price the rewards so that he can buy something each day. Or, another option for Davey, he can save them up for a more expensive reward. We want both options to be in play. So, if you have six rewards, make a couple of items worth two points, a couple (that he prizes more highly) worth four, and a couple (that he regards as even more desirable) worth six or more. A chance to reach into the grab bag for a little toy would be, for example, a two-point reward, something he could earn by doing some but not all of what you're aiming for on any given day.

Timing matters. There must be little or no time delay between behavior and awarding points. If Davey earns two points on Tuesday night for going to bed without a tantrum, show him the points on his chart as soon as he wakes up on Wednesday morning. The link between behavior and consequence has to be as short and as direct as possible. If it's not, the program will probably fail, no matter how carefully you address every other aspect of it. Also, have prizes selected and ready to go, so he can cash in his points right away if he wishes to. The exchange of points for prizes doesn't have to be immediate, though. Just make sure he has regular changes to cash in during the week.

Adding in more "expensive" rewards. When we do add them in, special rewards (for ten points, say, or more) can include privileges like going out for a meal, or going on a more significant outing — maybe ice skating, or to a special playground with a friend. Don't be extravagant (nothing like, *And for 500 points, you get a real suit of armor!*), but do pick rewards that he'll be excited about and will regard as worth the extra effort it will take to accumulate points and not spend them on smaller, more easily attained prizes.

The table below shows what Jen and Mel picked for Davey, with his help, and in the appendix there's a more extensive list of suggested rewards for different age groups.

REWARD MENU FOR DAVEY

Item	Number of Stickers Needed
Pick from the grab bag	2
Going through a magazine with mom or dad for 10 minutes	2
Extra bedtime story	4
Staying up 15 minutes later on Saturday night	4
Choosing dinner for the family	6
Playing cards with parent for 15 minutes	8
Watching a rented movie (at home) on the weekend	8
Ice skating	10
Using the cell phone to call grandma	12
Disposable camera	15

(leave spaces to add if you or Davey think of new items)

A common problem with larger rewards requiring many points is that their delivery isn't immediate. When developing behavior, especially early in the program, the emphasis should be on small rewards that can be earned daily. Having your child save up all his points for one big, much-desired reward will lead to an ineffective program. It's true that things or events your child values usually make for good rewards, but it is *how* they are delivered that dictates whether they change behavior. We want points and praise that are immediate, and we want rewards to be readily available.

Here is how to get the best of both worlds. In addition to the usual little rewards that your child can buy with two, four, or six points, and in addition to the more expensive rewards costing ten or twelve points, you can also choose a more delayed, larger back-up reward that requires a lot more points to achieve. If your child wants a football helmet or a princess costume more than anything else in the world, that's a good one, or the reward could be a trip to the circus, or some other exciting event. For this, we need a second chart that keeps track of *all* the points your child has earned, whether he spent them or not—like an end-of-the-year wage earnings statement. It might look like this: a picture of the moon at the top of the chart and a rocket ship that can move up each week based on how many points were earned that week. Just transfer the Total Points for the Week number from his chart to the special rocket-ship chart, even if he spent those points on smaller prizes, and have him witness and even participate in that little ritual. When the rocket ship gets to the moon, the large back-up reward is earned. Let's say that your child has to earn thirty-five points to get that football helmet (in which case you might want to make the chart represent a rocket heading for a football-helmet-shaped moon) or that princess costume (in which case maybe it's a rocket to the Moon Princess's castle). At a maximum of four points a day, twenty points a week (if you don't do the program on weekends), even if your child is very good it will take more than two weeks to accrue enough points. More likely, it will take three or more.

DAVEY'S ROCKET SHIP TO THE MOON

You made it!! SUPER GREAT!!!!

35 points _____

30 points _____

25 points _____

20 points _____

15 points _____

10 points _____

5 points _____

Add a cutout rocket and move the rocket up each week when you transfer the total points for the week from Davey's point chart to this one.

The larger back-up reward is a bonus, an add-on to spice up the game. The emphasis of the program should still be on praise and more frequent and immediate rewards. Successful programs do not require this bonus, but it can add useful excitement and interest by adding more incentives and novelty for your child.

Step 3: Explaining the Program

Jen and Mel are ready to present the program to Davey. Put smiles on your faces, I tell them, as you describe to Davey how this fun program will work. Play along with his excitement as he chooses his personal point markers and tells you about the first five things he'd like to earn as rewards. Don't be afraid to suggest things he wouldn't think of himself, such as daddy taking him to work one day or to the library to pick out a new book. Davey wants to please you. Your job is to tell him how to do it.

In this case, just make sure you clearly identify the behavior that will earn him a point on the chart: a good bedtime, or what Jen and Mel call a "big-boy bedtime." Be very specific about what this means: he needs to go into his room, get into his pajamas, and get into bed. Explain to him that when he does all of those things, he earns two points.

Jen asks, as parents sometimes do at this stage, "Is a four-year-old capable of understanding the reward system?"

Yes, most of them get it right away. And when you immediately follow up the explanation by practicing the behavior, praising Davey for getting it right, and awarding him points that he can turn in for a real reward, you'll know he gets it. It's not critical that Davey be able to explain the whole program back to you. Experiencing the consistent connection between behavior and positive consequences, and experiencing it often, will establish the relationship in his actions, and that's what counts.

Mel, looking doubtful, says, "But Davey's smart. Once he gets it, he'll realize that it's like a game, and he'll figure out ways to get the rewards without being really sincere about behaving better."

I tell him and Jen that their job is to *help* Davey game the system. Don't worry that he's going to "manipulate" the rewards system. You *want* him to manipulate it, to the best of his limited ability. Remember, this arrangement of rewards and reinforcement is temporary; it's going to go away as the behavior takes root. It's perfectly fine if he starts out doing the right thing for the wrong reasons, just as long as he practices doing the right thing.

Parents "game" their children to teach them many other things. For example, with a small child, you lead him over to his grandmother and say, *Now say "Thank you" to grandma for the nice gift.* He's saying thank you mostly because you told him to, and because everybody will exclaim, *What a good boy!* — praising him, which is a key to reinforcing behavior — when he does. Then, when he's a little older and more practiced at saying thank you, you prompt with, *What do you say?* Then, when saying thank you comes to him without prompting, you stop prompting entirely. By then, if you've raised him right, he says thank you because he has good manners, or because he feels grateful and that's the best way he knows to express the feeling. (If you're still hauling your twenty-six-year-old over to grandma and saying, *Now say "Thank you" to grandma,* you and I have more work to do together, but it's work for another time.)

The interplay of sincerity and gaming the system works in much the same way for parents and children. Even if at first you don't feel entirely sincere in praising your child effusively just for doing something she should be doing without praise in the first place, do it anyway. It doesn't matter if you feel as if you're acting. You'll grow more comfortable over time — especially as you see the praise and other rewards leading to better behavior in your child. You and your child are both building habits, and this comes from practice. That's how the actions become established and ingrained, natural and automatic. The first stage — getting the behavior to occur regularly, and providing the proper consequences — is often the hard part, because it feels unnatural at first. But it will soon feel natural, and soon *not* doing the behavior will feel unnatural. People who begin an exercise program often have to force themselves to keep to it at first, but regular exercise changes their outlook to the point where they look forward to their daily exercise and are disappointed if they can't do it. The behavior becomes a habit; departing from it comes to feel awkward or foreign.

Step 4: Practice

Once you are finished explaining the program, you can immediately begin the first practice session. I suggest to Jen and Mel that they start with something like, *Okay, Davey, let's practice this to see what you can earn and how it works. I'm going to ask you to go to bed now — this is just pretend — it isn't bedtime, but just pretend it is — and if you go to bed during pretend time without a fuss, you can earn points and rewards right now.*

Then, when he's ready, tell him you are about to begin the pretend bedtime, and, playing yourself, say, *Davey, please go to bed now.* Then you can slip out of your pretend role — lean over close to his face, smile, and whisper, *Now we go to your room. Remember, this is just pretend.* The moment he starts to walk to the room, say something like, *Davey, you're so good at pretending!* Walk with him — with your arm around him, if possible, touching and guiding without pushing — and praise him as he is walking and going to his room, help him get into his bed, and then say goodnight and give him a pat or a kiss goodnight. Let him know that you will be returning in just a minute, because this is not bedtime but pretend bedtime, but if he is still in bed when you do return, you will then help him put the two points he earns on his chart. Make sure there is something he can buy with them right away. Give him his reward. Be sure to praise, too. The points do not take the place of the praise. Both should be used; the combination maximizes the effects. We will not need such heavy practice, praise, and reward points as the program goes on, or as we move to other behaviors. The systematic use of practice and rewards will be new for Davey — and for you — and this early part is more labor intensive than later parts.

If your schedule allows, practice bedtime with Davey once more on the first day — for instance, right before dinner. Again, tell him, *Davey, here is a chance to earn some points . . .* Don't worry that he's racking up too many points on the first day. You want him to experience the connection between his behavior and its consequences and to experience it on several occasions. You will scale back soon.

Each day of the program, try to practice at one time other than bedtime. If you can't practice every day, just try to practice a few times a week. It's fine to do it twice on one day if you missed on the previous day (which is why I say he can earn a maximum of four points on a *typical* day; on those rare two-practice-session days he can earn six). It can be useful to connect practicing to some other routine. One father I am working with drives his daughter to school each morning, and they practice their behavior in the car. The problem they're working on is that the daughter frequently lies when asked what she did with her friends or whether she took something she wasn't supposed to. So they set up pretend situations in the car each day as part of the trip to school, and she works on telling the truth. They don't need special reminders to practice because it's built into the routine of going to school. Remember, your practice routine won't last forever — just a week or two, at most.

Practice is important, but if you or your child are tired or irritable, or it seems like not a good time because things are not calm in the house, just skip the pretend-practice opportunity. Your child will not want to pretend if these sessions are a chore, or if you are tense during them. In the beginning of developing the behavior, we want to be extra careful to do the program properly under the best possible conditions.

Step 5: The Routine

What comes before a behavior, what sets the stage for that behavior, is just as important as what comes after. Jen and Mel need to establish a bedtime ritual that helps Davey settle down. Asking a child to go to bed at 7:15 may not be ideal if he is typically in the middle of a TV show that ends at 7:30. The interruption will predictably lead to a minor tantrum. We need to be sure he will not be in the middle of anything too exciting or active in the thirty minutes before bed.

It might help to think of it this way. Remember the ABC (antecedents, behavior, consequences) sequence from chapter 2? We're talking about antecedents here, which come before a behavior and make it more or less likely to occur. There are two kinds of antecedents that matter. One kind is called "prompts" — specific statements or actions aimed at getting a particular behavior to happen. Typical statements would be *Please go pick up your toys, Let's pretend now,* or *Please use a fork when you eat that.* The category of prompts also includes direct demonstrations, like doing a behavior along with your child or modeling it for him: showing him exactly how to do the behavior you want by picking up and putting away a toy, for instance.

But there's another category of antecedents which is not specifically focused on the behavior but also comes before and helps set the stage for it, arranging the situation so it is conducive to the behavior and therefore makes it more likely to happen. These are called "setting-up events," and they include things like establishing quiet time before getting to bed, or the routine of washing hands and setting the table before sitting down to a meal. A bath, a story, and a calm half hour before bed — a ritual that comprises a great setting-up event — significantly increases the likelihood of going to bed on time and without fuss. In contrast, computer games, action TV shows, phone calls, or roughhousing with siblings or a parent would not be good setting-up events for getting to bed. For some kids, it doesn't matter that much what you do before bedtime, but if bedtime is a problem in your household then the wrong setting-up events can make all the difference.

In Davey's case, bedtime is a point of contention, so we really need a pre-bedtime ritual that starts a transition from being a normal active boy to being a quiet person ready to go to sleep. Here is one scenario, just to make the point about transitioning in easy steps to bedtime, although there's nothing magical about this particular sequence.

I tell Jen and Mel to guide Davey to a quiet activity after dinner and a bath: reading with you or peaceful play — doing a puzzle together might be fine if he doesn't get frustrated — rather than a TV show with loud action and ads.

Ask Davey to get ready for bed and then into bed — praising and mentioning that these are chances to earn points, of course.

Read or tell a story with only one lamp or dim light on. You can set a timer or simply say that you can read or tell only one story, and stick to that rule, so this step doesn't make itself available to him as a natural opportunity for tantrums and begging.

Leave the room quietly after tucking him in. Praise him for being such a big boy and going to bed so nicely. For four-year-olds the "big boy" comment, given with surprise and enthusiasm, often helps a great deal.

What to Expect the First Week

The goal this first week is to start the program, not to perfect it. Much is new here, for the parents even more than for the child. We do not want perfection from Davey, I tell his parents, nor from you. We expect that he will not comply perfectly; we expect that you will not be perfectly consistent. Normal children, adolescents, and adults rarely comply with anything perfectly.

He's probably not going to change the first night, or he may perform miraculously well on the first night but then backslide on the second. You have to be ready for no-point nights at the beginning. Give the *Please go to your room, put on your pajamas, and get in bed* instruction in the usual way and start to go into his room with him. If he complies, great: help him get ready for bed, tuck him in, tell him he'll get two points on his chart in the morning, and be sure to show him the points — or let him mark them himself — first thing next morning. If he says no and starts a tantrum, say, *Davey, this is a chance to go to bed and earn points,* and repeat the *Please go to bed* statement *once,* gently. Don't escalate or show your power; don't take the tone of your voice up a notch, which will make things worse. Don't give him chance after chance, warning after warning. If your second and final request goes unheeded, make the judgment that he will not go right away, and then say, *Okay, maybe tomorrow you will be able to earn points for going to bed.* Now leave the room. Try to make the environment sterile, with nothing to stimulate him further — turn off the TV, turn down lighting, and so on. Get him to his room, but he cannot earn points once he has missed out. Don't weaken on this front. If he did not go right away the first or second time, he cannot undo that. Just say, without sarcasm or edge in your tone, *Maybe tomorrow you will be able to get points.*

If he goes to bed properly and earns his two points but then comes out of his room again, take him back into his room and warn him that the next time it happens he'll lose a point. If it happens again, take away a point. No arguments, threats, or explanations; be matter-of-fact. If he comes out again, take away the second point. After that, treat him just as you would in the situation I just described, when he didn't go to bed and didn't earn any points.

Be sure not to fall into parental quicksand by explaining everything to Davey when he's resisting. Your attention and explanation will actually reinforce the tantrum. Attention from you is weaker than effective praise, but it is strong enough to keep a bad behavior going.

If there is one obstacle likely to emerge this first week, it will be that Davey's behavior only approached what you wanted him to do and maybe wasn't even good enough to earn any points. Be sure to praise all that you saw that was good and was an improvement over past behavior. So you may have wanted Davey to go to his room and get in bed and stay there, but he only got as far as going to his room. This is great progress for the beginning of our program, so don't hold back praise until he can do all the behaviors in sequence. Praise what you saw that was good, praise the little steps along the way to the desired behavior, and praise whenever you give points. Remember that praise for the behaviors, all by itself, is pivotal, even if points are not earned.

Let's turn to some crucial things for you to keep in mind as you apply the example of Jen, Mel, and Davey to working with your own child.

Keys to Success

Success will require changes not only in your child's behavior but, in all likelihood, also in your interactions with him or her. I've gathered together in this section some guidelines for you to follow once you begin the program. There are six of them, but really there's one absolutely essential one — how to use praise as effectively as possible — and then everything else. Praise matters most, and I'll give it close attention before turning to the other keys to success.

1. Praise is all-important. Studies show that the quality and quantity of the praise you give to your child correlates with the success of the program: poor or mediocre praise produces less improvement in behavior; good praise produces more improvement in behavior. Praise is more important than points or anything else. Effective praise should include three components:

- Enthusiastic verbal praise (with feeling, joy, and excitement: *Great! Fantastic!*)
- A very specific statement of exactly what your child did that you liked
- A gentle touch, like a pat on the shoulder or head, a hug, a high five, a smile, a thumbs-up or okay sign, to add a tangible non-verbal reward to the verbal praise

In addition to these three things, there are three guiding conditions to keep in mind. Effective praise should be

- Contingent: you praise when the desired behavior happens, so that the link between the two is strong
- Immediate: your praise comes right after the behavior that earns the praise
- Frequent: especially at the beginning, you should look for (and create) as many chances as possible to praise the behavior

That may seem like a lot to keep in mind, but I think an example will show that it's not too hard to do. Let's return for a moment to Jen and Mel, who want a little more nuts-and-bolts guidance on how to praise Davey's good behavior at bedtime.

It's still early on in the program, one of the first nights, so you're making sure to notice and praise every good move he makes. The moment he starts to walk toward the room, say something — with a nice smile and enthusiasm — like, *Davey, that's great! I asked you to go to your room and you started right away.* Kiss his forehead or pat him gently; try a high five, or a hug; you decide what fits. There, you've already hit most of the high spots: the praise was enthusiastic, specific, and nonverbal; it was contingent and immediate, and, because you're looking for every chance to praise, probably also frequent.

When the two of you get to the room, you say, *Davey, you're doing so well! You are here in your room.* Praise him again once he gets into bed. You're enthusiastic; you specifically identify the good behavior (*What a big boy! I asked you to get into bed and you got right in!*); and you offer nonverbal reinforcement to show how pleased you are. You do not always need to make sure you include every single element of effective praise every time; you might be across the room and cannot get over to touch him for some reason. But if you can combine these three elements most of the time and give them contingently, immediately, and frequently, you will be surprised, even shocked, at the effect.

Whether you're practicing or it's actually bedtime, whenever Davey goes to his room or gets into bed without a tantrum or with only a little resistance, praise him. Give "clear and clean" praise. "Clear" means that you say exactly what he did that was good and you liked; be very specific. "Clean" means that you don't caboose — you don't add anything negative or judgmental to your praise at the end. You don't say, *This was better than last time.* You don't ask, *Why can't you do that every time?* Don't even add the usual parental explanations. This is not a moment to educate; it is a moment to build and shape the behaviors you want, step by step, through reinforced practice. Concentrate solely on that. Remember that adding other information to the praise dilutes the reinforcing effect of the praise.

After you praise his success in doing the parts he did do right, let there be a clear pause, and then you can add, *You can earn even more points tomorrow if you also do* [whatever he didn't get right]. Most parents fall into the "close but no cigar" trap — that is, they withhold praise because the behavior they see in the child is close or closer to what they want to see but isn't quite there yet. Don't fall into that trap. Always praise steps along the way to the good behavior.

And bear in mind, especially when dealing with a child as young as four, that when I say "enthusiastic," I mean ENTHUSIASTIC! Most parents who come to the Yale Parenting Center and Child Conduct Clinic hold back too much. They don't become effusive enough until we model it for them. Think cheerleader-level enthusiasm — that's what works best. I'll tell you a story that illustrates what I mean. When we first opened the parenting center and clinic, it was in a building that wasn't soundproofed, and there were other offices in the building that provided talk therapy for adult patients with adult problems: depression, anxiety, the woes of life. When our therapists worked with families and demonstrated the right level of effusiveness, their voices would go right through the walls, ceilings, and floors into these other offices. We tried everything we could think of — we brought in architects to design soundproofing, we tried white-noise boxes for the other offices — but our therapists' voices still came through loud and clear. Adult patients would be talking about their difficult relationship with mom, or plumbing the depths of sexual pathology, and offstage cries of *Great! Way to go! You did it just right!* would inappropriately punctuate their therapy sessions. Eventually we had to move; we needed more room, anyway. But I'm talking about that kind of effusiveness. Ham it up: big smile, eyes lit up, gushing tone. This is not an occasion for understatement and subtlety. Think of yourself as standing on a mountaintop and trying to communicate "I'm thrilled and impressed!" to a person standing on a neighboring mountaintop.

When you praise, concentrate on the behavior, not the person. The advice books and online parenting guides are full of ineffective sample praise on the order of *I love you, You're so great, I'm proud of you, I respect you,* and so on. These are all perfectly nice things to say to your child, but they're not specific praise for behavior. Instead, try phrases like, *It was great when you . . . , I like it when you . . . , Terrific! You did . . . , You were really a big girl when you did . . .* — and then, of course, finish the sentence by specifying exactly what it is you are praising.

And don't forget to add nonverbal reinforcement to the verbal praise. You show in your facial expression that you are thrilled, and you add some kind of positive physical touch.

I know that many of you are thinking, *But my praise wouldn't always be sincere, and don't I have to be sincere for this to work?* No. You have to praise effusively, and that's more important than anything else. But you will find that you *become* more sincere as you do this and see progress. Remember your child's initial thank yous and I love yous? They were lamentably rote and insincere, but as they grew more sincere you grew more sincere in your response to them. After five or six days of praising the behavior you want in the ways I have described, you will find that you genuinely feel differently about your praise and its sincerity. And remember that enthusiastic praise, however sincere you may feel it to be, is always much more effective than sincere punishment, which is the usual alternative.

A related concern: *Will I teach insincerity to the child?* No. Lessons in sincerity or insincerity will come from how you behave in everyday life around the house. When you ask a question, do you care about the answer? When you hear someone was hurt or is ill, does your reaction reflect genuine concern? Do you model truth-telling or lying for your children? Sincerity comes from other places than our behavior-change program, but soon it will come from your praise, too.

2. Make noncompliance a nonevent. Try to ignore your child if he does not comply with your request. Say, matter-of-factly and without rancor, *You won't get a point for staying in your bed. Maybe next time.* Then if possible leave the room or ignore him. The risk is too high that attention or a little nagging will make his behavior worse. I am not saying that you should never punish your child. But, I tell Jen and Mel, just for this week, when we're first starting the program, let's get the chart and praise going and concentrate entirely on rewarding him for what he does right. Once you've made some progress and the behavior is going well, you may introduce some mild punishment to help speed up that progress. I'll have more to say about punishment in later chapters, especially chapter 6, which is entirely devoted to the subject. For now, let's stay away from punishment and concentrate on positive reinforcement.

3. Begin with "please." When you ask your child to engage in the behaviors you want, begin with the word "please." This isn't just courtesy or good manners. *How* you ask is very important in almost all human interactions. Please is a setting-up event that makes it more likely your child will comply, because it's noncoercive and implies that she has a choice. Also, the changes that using please makes in your own tone reduce the chances of inspiring a defiant response in your child. The research is clear that choice, or the appearance of choice, increases compliance. Snapping orders at her or threatening punishment, in effect removing even the appearance that your child has a choice, increases the likelihood of an oppositional response. So begin with please.

Some parents tell me that they don't feel they should have to say please. They say that they're in charge, and saying please treats the child as if she were an equal, which she isn't. I understand that, and I sympathize. But the science is very clear here: Please produces much better results than *Do it now, or else!* So, I tell them, concentrate on your own greater effectiveness, rather than being touchy about your imagined dignity. Better to say please once and have the child do what you ask, than to say, *Do it now, or else!* ten times and get nothing but defiance in return. In the long run, I think there's more parental dignity in getting compliance with self-assured gentleness than in acting like an ineffectual tyrant who can't put down the perpetual rebellion that you yourself feed with your own harsh measures. If you're truly in charge, or want to be, you can afford to say please.

4. The tone ought to be warm and gentle. Don't bark it out or put extra force in your voice. This is not a command; it is an instruction. In fact, if you say it like a command, I can almost guarantee you will not get compliance from a child presently inclined toward defiance. The research shows that your child is more likely to comply if you use a warm and gentle tone, a setting-up event for compliance; similarly, a harsh, tense, or commanding tone is a setting-up event for oppositional behavior. A good rule of thumb is to anticipate compliance. Then you won't feel anxious, and your voice will communicate that you do not expect to be in conflict.

5. Don't ask a question when you are instructing your child to do something. Do not say, *Why don't you get ready for bed?* Adults understand that putting a directive in the form of a question is less confrontational, but a child hears the question as a question, not as something he needs to do. Also, don't just say, *It's time for bed.* That's not as definite a directive as parents think it is. Be absolutely clear, explicit, and direct: *Please go to your room and put your pajamas on and get in your bed.* Clarity is not only good for your child, it's also good for you and your family. An important part of the program is knowing and specifying exactly what you *do* want your child to do (the positive opposite of the behavior you don't want). We often refer to this as the "stranger test": can you specify the behavior so clearly that a stranger would understand exactly what you want your child to do? In general, if we can specify the behaviors clearly, we can probably develop them in our children.

6. *Physical closeness counts.* When you ask your child to do something, get close; it helps. When you ask him to prepare for bed, walk with him into his room. If you can guide him gently with your arm around him to take him there, that's good, too. But do not guide or direct physically if you are prone to use a little force to get your child to move in one direction or another. Also, at this early point, if your child is prone to hitting you, for now we can avoid the gentle physical guidance.

• • •

We're ready to move on to other problems and other solutions. You have under your belt a thorough, basic account of how to set up a program for changing a problem behavior. We'll be dealing in subsequent chapters with other problems, older kids, situations extending beyond the home into school and public settings, and so on, but you've got the fundamentals in place now, a good base to build on.

4

Your Six- to Twelve-Year-Old

Supermarket Scenes, Late for School, Sibling
Squabbles, Homework Avoidance, and More

She's a terror when she's in one of her moods." I hear a lot of that kind of thing from the parents of children between the ages of six and twelve — no longer little kids, but not yet adolescents, or even preadolescents. "It's like we're a hostage to him" is how one parent put it. "We can't go anywhere or do anything outside of the house because we're too worried that he's going to make a scene. Even when we're in the house, it's as if he's in control. Sometimes it seems we have to cater to him and listen to him more than he has to mind us."

In some ways, children in this age range are inclined to be more independent than parents would like. They want to be free and unsupervised, especially when they're with friends, and can be headstrong to the point of meanness. Even as their capacity for embarrassment grows, building toward the preadolescent state of being permanently embarrassed by their parents' existence, they are still capable of staging a nasty dispute in public with you if they don't get what they want.

But, on the other hand, I often hear from frustrated parents that their child relies on them too much, stalling and refusing to perform tasks that children "at his age" usually do. Getting ready for school in the mornings and sitting down to do homework, for instance, commonly generate daily struggles that leave everyone in a family angry and exhausted.

Children of this age still need you to closely guide their lives but often actively defy or passively resist your authority. And as they get older they get better at fighting back as a near-equal, which makes the struggles more serious. It's the kind of situation that can lead you to feel stumped.

Let's approach this problem by recognizing that a six- to twelve-year-old offers some special challenges.

First, don't underestimate her ability to put stress on you, to make you react and lose your cool. When she was younger, she might have had tantrums or screamed *No!*, but now she can question and challenge your authority in ways that push your buttons far more effectively: *You're ugly, and I don't want to grow up to look like you,* or *Who cares about your stupid rules,* or simply *I don't love you.* Parents tend to react to such provocations by coming down harder, with harsher reprimands, threats, and aggressive gestures: *You do what I tell you when I tell you, young lady, or you can kiss your bike goodbye for a month!* Who is this parent, so angry her voice is shaking, melodramatically pointing a finger at her eight-year-old daughter? It doesn't even sound like you.

A defiant child between six and twelve, old enough to have mastered getting your goat, is probably very good at pushing you to jump to the conclusion that you're in a battle for control of the household. Too often you respond by exerting control for its own sake, just to remind everybody who's boss. But when you do that, you just end up making your child more aggressive and driving her away, encouraging her literally or figuratively to escape and avoid you. Meeting defiance with redoubled force might (if you're lucky) momentarily suppress the behavior you don't want, but the effect is very temporary. Research consistently shows that the bad behavior comes back just as frequently and just as badly as before — and it will probably get worse, since cracking down tends to amplify defiance.

Second, the older the child, the more likely the parents are to have unrealistic expectations for that child's behavior. *He's ten years old,* you say to each other, exasperated. *He should know how to*

. . . You can finish that sentence with whatever behavior you want him to do that he's not doing: *get ready for school by himself, get through the supermarket without embarrassing us, play with a friend without melting down,* or *sit down and do his homework.* Most parents find *He's ten years old* more persuasive than *He's seven years old* . . . or *He's five years old* . . . The older the child, the more likely you are to assume that he can perform the behavior and is simply choosing not to do it because he's manipulative, spoiled, or just plain rotten. And when you see his conduct that way, you're more likely to punish failure to do the behavior and less likely to reinforce the steps toward doing it consistently. The result, of course, is that you're less likely to do what needs to be done in order to help him behave properly.

So we begin by adjusting parental expectations. Put aside the notion of a struggle for control. Forget about what you think your child can do or chooses to do. Instead, we'll start by recognizing what she does right now and by stating clearly what you want her to do. Then we can work on shaping the behavior we want to replace the behavior we don't want.

But, before we do get down to cases, we have to recognize a third distinct challenge posed by a child who has already begun to live in the wider world in her own right. A seven-year-old, or an eleven-year-old, goes to school all day and may also have afterschool and weekend activities. That means an expanding circle of relationships to friends, classmates, teammates, neighbors, teachers, coaches, friends' parents, and so on. Even when she's home with her parents, she might be online, instant messaging with her friends, or on the phone. In short, she's not under your direct authority that often, actually — mostly just in the early mornings and in the evenings, and on weekends, and not always at these times, if you take into account gymnastics, soccer, music lessons, dance class, visits to friends' houses, sleepovers, expeditions to the mall supervised by friends' parents, and other such activities.

Being out in the world gives a child chances to form opinions and tastes and to take on responsibilities. Your child has a far better developed set of likes and dislikes than he did when he was younger, he takes greater responsibility for taking care of himself (washing, dressing, and so on), and he has more duties as a member of the household and even as a member of society: chores and homework, for instance. This greater autonomy is a necessary part of growing up, of course, but also creates more opportunities for problems to come up.

Also, your confrontations with your child tend to occur more often in the public eye and tend to be more difficult than they were in the past because they're more two-sided. You might have felt self-conscious when your three-year-old screamed in the grocery store, but you could always just pick her up and haul her out. The self-consciousness you felt back then pales in comparison to the outright humiliation you might feel if your six-year-old talks back sarcastically or calls you names when you don't give in to her demand for candy at the supermarket checkout.

Bear in mind, finally, that a child in this age range has had plenty of time to absorb your example and has a much more highly developed capacity to mimic you. Some parents who come to my clinic complaining about their child's swearing, teasing, lying, and so forth are shocked to discover that they have been effectively modeling such behaviors for their impressionable child. If you're serious about changing your child's behavior, you may well have to attend to your own habits as a source of it. This doesn't mean that your child's behaviors all come from you or that you are solely to blame for his misconduct, but too often I find that parents who ask me to treat their children are invoking a double standard: *Do what I say, not what I do.* That doesn't work, because the *do,* the behavior they model, is ultimately a much stronger influence than the *say,* the behavior they preach.

So, yes, in many ways a six- to twelve-year-old offers a greater challenge than a four-year-old who won't go to bed without a fight. But take heart. You do have the power to shape an older child's behavior, and you can call upon the basic principles and skills we have already discussed in previous chapters. However, you must adapt them to the special challenges presented by a child who has begun to strike out on his own into the world, yet still needs your close supervision. The nature of rewards has to change to reflect the priorities of the age range, of course, but at times you must also adjust your general assumptions about your own authority. To continue to shape your child's life effectively as his autonomy grows, you must be prepared to give up some control, to negotiate with him more and dictate to him less, and to be subtler in how you reinforce the behaviors you want — even as he displays greater aggression toward you and a more sophisticated ability to provoke you, both of which can undermine your good parental judgment by making you angry.

Supermarket Scenes

And what's more angry-making than bad conduct in public places? Annoying as struggles within the household can be, embarrassing behavior in front of onlookers is much more traumatic for parents. Even if nobody's around to witness your shame, the feeling of powerlessness, of not being in control of your own kids, can really burn.

So meet Will, a six-year-old boy with all kinds of energy and a heroic sweet tooth. School personnel have referred to him as "hyperactive," but he's not really. He's just active and very quick — so quick, in fact, and so coordinated that he's already quite good at baseball. His athleticism and energy serve him well on weekend afternoons at the park, but his parents have just about had it with his conduct at the supermarket. His habit of putting items in the shopping cart is annoying but bearable. His mother usually just puts them back. No, the problem at the supermarket focuses on the predictable struggle at the candy display at the checkout counter. It has become the low point of their week.

Let's pause here for a moment to appreciate the evil genius of those who decided to put candy within reach of even the smallest shopper at the supermarket checkout counter. Those evil geniuses are responsible for a lot of whining, demanding, and out-and-out grabbing-and-running by children, and also, because they stack the deck against parents, for a lot of less-than-ideal parenting. After forty minutes or so of shopping — keeping the kids from wrecking the store, dealing with crises, trying to get everything on the list, alternating between conciliatory negotiating and laying down the law with ever more dire threats of punishment — they get to the checkout counter, with the light at the end of the tunnel clearly in view, and that's when the kids, driven half-mad by all that candy near at hand, launch a last-ditch assault.

Parents come to know and dread that impending assault, and the tension increases even before they're ready to head for the checkout counter. That's why so many parents make the mistake of improvising new rules on the spot in the supermarket, shooting from the hip in a panic as they lay down new conditions as fast as they can think of them: *Okay, okay, if you stop screaming right now I won't take away TV for six months like I said I would when you punched your sister in aisle five. And look, if you stop hurting your sister right now and don't touch anything on the shelves and don't spit on the floor anymore, I'll think about maybe letting you buy some candy at the checkout counter.* The public stage of the supermarket makes every conflict seem like a major control issue. When every little behavior problem seems to raise the question of who's in charge in public, parents find themselves in a rapidly escalating situation in which they feel they have to punish or reward in an extreme way. Often, they end up creating consequences that reinforce exactly the wrong behavior.

That's what happens when Tania, Will's mother, takes him to the store. He starts begging for candy early on during the shopping expedition. *No,* Tania says. *Candy's not good for you. It rots your teeth and makes you hyper and ruins your appetite for real food.* Filling her shopping cart with healthy, nourishing food, she feels virtuous, even righteous. *Please,* says Will. *Please, please, please!* Tania sticks to her guns: *No.* Will's whining escalates, and he promises everything under the sun: perpetual goodness, second helpings of liver and spinach, no more requests for treats until he turns twenty-one. Irritated, Tania escalates in return. She takes her voice up a notch and adds a hissed threat: *Now stop asking. You're embarrassing me in front of all these people. If you ask again, there will be no candy for a week!* Will, sensing that it's time to play hardball, counterescalates, pulling out all the stops. He tries hyperventilating, dignified sobbing, insults — whatever it takes.

A humiliating public scene rapidly takes shape, one that Tania fears might even inspire the intervention of the supermarket's security forces. She's tempted to just haul Will out of there and go home, but she has an almost-full shopping cart that she doesn't want to abandon now, when the week's shopping is almost done. *Okay, fine,* she says, giving in all at once as other shoppers look on like rubberneckers at a car crash. *I don't care! Go ahead and spoil your appetite and rot your teeth! Just take the candy and shut up!* Or words to that effect. She's not proud of it, but that's often what happens. Candy in hand, Will becomes a tear-stained angel, at least for the moment.

Will has, in effect, pressured his mother with bad behavior and then rewarded her for giving in by removing the pressure, ceasing the bad behavior. He is shaping Tania's behavior (to get him to stop behaving badly, buy him candy) and Tania is shaping his (to get candy, behave badly) in ways that will make the next expedition to the supermarket only more difficult.

Now, with Will's parents in my office, wearing that desperate look I've come to know well, it's time to get down to work. I start by suggesting that, rather than escalating the threats and then giving in, it would have been better, actually, just to buy Will the candy the first time he asked, especially if Tania made asking nicely a condition for getting it. Or she could build buying the candy into the conditions of going shopping in the first place, clearly stating in advance the limited amount that Will can have and making it depend on a certain level of behavior, and then — here's the hard part — sticking to those conditions. Or let's say Tania's a no-candy parent; she could still reward Will for asking nicely: *You can't have candy because it's not good for you, but since you asked so nicely and were so good in the store, we can rent a movie instead.* Or if he has other favorite snacks that Tania approves of — animal crackers, a muffin, a fancy fruit — then Will could earn one with good behavior in the store.

I tell Tania she shouldn't try to preempt Will's meltdowns by giving him a snack as soon as they enter the store, though. In that case, he would get the reward before having done anything to earn it, making the consequence no longer contingent on the behavior by reversing their proper order. He could have his snack and then switch to misbehaving for the rest of the shopping expedition. Anyway, giving the snack early would not necessarily preempt the misbehavior and resulting public scene, since Will's meltdowns may happen more because he gets tired and irritable from shopping and Tania has a prior history of responding poorly under pressure at the checkout.

If Tania is worried that once in the store Will won't be able to control himself and will start nagging, then they should practice in the car before going into the store or right at the beginning of shopping when they get the cart. I tell Tania to try something like, *Okay, Will, let's practice asking nicely for a treat.* Help him with the words and tone, even if he has to repeat your words exactly. When he does it right, praise him, have him practice again, praise him again, and don't forget to tell him, when you praise, exactly why it was great. Now, as you begin shopping, say, *If you ask nicely like that when we get to the checkout line and you behaved well in the store, you'll get* [whatever the prize is that you've agreed on]. While you are shopping — after you've gone through the first aisle or two — you can say something like, *Will, you're doing so well, you're being such a big boy. You're behaving so nicely and not asking for treats.* The challenge of our program is to catch your child doing the behavior you want and to reward that behavior — with praise, above all. And if you can't catch it often enough because the behavior doesn't occur often enough on its own, then you practice it. Once the behavior is developed, the praise and other rewards will become unnecessary — right now, though, they're crucial.

But let's take a step back from the conflict over the candy and think about conduct in public as a more general issue. That's what Will's parents really want to address when they talk about embarrassing trips to the supermarket. Lurking behind the supermarket are all the other public places where your child can make a scene, demonstrating for all to see your inability to control him: gatherings of family and friends, restaurants, doctors' waiting rooms, airports (there's no parental nightmare quite like a long airline delay). So we want to address the supermarket problem with an eye toward other such situations.

To begin with, I tell Will's parents, now that we have a clear description of what actually happens in the store, let's see if we can state the positive opposite you want to achieve here. In framing a positive opposite, let's try to use positive terms: what to do, rather than what not to do. Instead of *No whining,* for instance, you can say, *Ask questions with a big-boy voice.* (If you need to define whining for your child, which can be hard to do in the abstract, an imitation of a whining child might be your best bet, but be sure to do it with a little humor.) Instead of *Don't touch the stuff on the shelves,* you can say, *Keep your hands to yourself unless I ask you to get something off the shelf.* Instead of *No running around,* you can say, *Please walk when we're in the store, and stay where you can always see me.*

So let's say we have our positive opposite for the supermarket clearly defined. *We're going into the store now, and if you can use a big-boy voice and keep your hands to yourself and walk when we're in the store, then you can get a prize when we leave the store.* If Will consistently makes it through the whole store on pretty good behavior in order to earn a reward, then you might just keep mental track of his progress: does he get the prize or doesn't he? But if asking him to behave well throughout the whole shopping expedition in order to get the reward is asking too much, then you can break it down. Chances are you'll have to do that, at least at first, since his behavior in the supermarket has been a problem.

It's time to set up a point chart, not unlike the one used by the parents of Davey, the boy in the previous chapter. You might use a three-by-five-inch index card to keep track of points, because you want to have it with you in the store. At first, if Will has a really hard time in the supermarket, you may have to award a point for good behavior in each aisle. This is the extreme scenario. Let's say there are ten aisles. He can get a point at the end of each aisle. If a total of ten points is possible, one way to arrange it would be that for six points he can buy a reward at home, but for eight points he can pick anything he wants at the checkout counter, as long as it costs a dollar or less. (I'll have more to say about points and rewards in the next section of this chapter.)

If Will develops some consistency in handling the extreme aisle-by-aisle scenario, then perhaps you can go to two points for every two aisles (but no points if he misbehaves in either one of the two aisles), then three for three, then five points for half of the store, and so on, until you've worked up to the scale of behaving throughout the entire trip to the store. Whatever the scale, he can cash in the earned points for some immediate reward: a treat at the checkout, an activity immediately after it (renting a movie, for instance), or something he can buy with the points when you get home.

When you enter the supermarket with Will, lean close to him and say, *All right, Will, here we go. Let's see if we can earn enough points for a prize today.* If he's really having trouble behaving in the store and you're assigning points for each aisle, then prompt him frequently as you go through the store: *Here's a new aisle coming up. This is a chance for a point.* Remember to praise his progress all the way through the store, and remember to be specific: *You're doing really well, Will. You're using your inside voice, and you haven't touched anything on the shelf in this aisle.*

Unpraised behavior is likely to drop out, so it's critical to praise little steps, good tries, and almost-behaviors, even if they're not enough to earn a point. Don't be stingy about this. If you're going to be giving points only at the end of the shopping expedition, be sure to praise five or ten times along the way: *This is amazing. We've gone down two aisles and you had no trouble at all, didn't touch anything, you're listening so well. Way to go.* And supplement the verbal praise with a touch, a smile, or both.

Late for School

In many households with children, the morning routine has all the stress and suspense of a space shuttle launch in iffy weather. The countdown clock starts ticking when the alarm clock goes off, and a hundred or more finely graded details have to go just right — everyone has to get up, wash up, get dressed, eat breakfast, gather together school or work materials, put on shoes and jackets, and get out the door to the car, the bus stop, the train, a walking route, however everyone gets to where he or she needs to be in the morning. Especially in households with multiple kids and working parents, the difference between stepping out the door at 7:27 or at 7:36 can become the difference between a functional morning and a day that has already begun to crash and burn. The slightest delay can seem like a catastrophe.

That's why the parents of Sarah, who's nine years old, get so furious when she lingers in bed after being told three times that it's time to get up, or takes twenty minutes to choose a shirt, or stares off into space twirling her hair with her finger when she's supposed to be finding her math homework and putting it in her backpack. And, as they've found out the hard way, shouting, *Let's go! Hurry up! We're going to be late!* dozens of times every morning doesn't really speed things along very much. We need to come up with a better way to address the problem, by returning to the principles we've already employed.

Defining the Problem and Its Positive Opposite

The first step is simply to observe and describe. What does your child really *do* in the mornings? Break it down. Sarah's parents start out by telling me general things like, *She just drags her feet through everything,* but eventually they're able to make it a little more specific — *She stays in her room too long before breakfast* — and finally we get it down to something precise and useful: *She gets up when we tell her to, but then she gets back in bed until we yell at her. That all takes maybe an extra fifteen minutes. Then she takes up to twenty minutes to choose her clothes; then she wants to play with her younger brother or watch TV or play a video game instead of coming to the table for breakfast; then she takes too long to gather up her homework and other things to take to school.* For the moment, I tell them, forget about what you think she should be able to do, or what you know she has done once or occasionally (yes, of course she gets dressed by herself in one minute flat on Saturdays before gymnastics, but let's not worry about that right now), and just figure out what she does consistently on school-day mornings. Once we develop a clear picture in our heads of her morning as a series of behaviors, some of which we want to change, we can then concentrate on shaping her behavior so that she moves faster, offers less resistance, and requires less prompting.

Next, we consider positive opposites of those behaviors we want to change. The ultimate positive opposite of a rushed, conflictual, chaotic morning routine might be something like this: *We want her to get up on time in the morning, get dressed quickly and calmly, come straight to breakfast, get her school things together, and be ready to walk out the door at 7:30, and we want her to do it all without having to be constantly reminded to do it.* But we can't accomplish all that at once. We pick our spots and change one or two behaviors at a time until we've shaped a morning routine that everybody can live with.

So begin by selecting one or two behaviors that you find most bothersome, that you want most to change, and in each case think of a behavior that would be a step in the right direction — a move toward the positive opposite. For instance, Sarah's parents tell me that she lingers in bed for about fifteen minutes and then takes about twenty minutes to get dressed. Getting out of bed is the key behavior, because that begins the whole sequence of getting ready for school. Our new guideline, then, is this: if Sarah gets up within ten minutes of being awakened (either by an alarm clock or by a parent), she gets a point. If she comes downstairs to the breakfast table, dressed, within twenty minutes of being awakened, she gets another point. You can set a kitchen timer or snooze alarm to mark out the time periods. Also, think about ways to set the stage for the morning routine to go more smoothly — such as, for instance, having her pick out her clothes the night before.

Points and Rewards for an Older Child

We're going to reinforce and track Sarah's progress with a point chart. It's the same approach we used with Will and Davey, using praise, points, and the further rewards that the points can buy to reinforce steps in the right direction — that is, toward doing the desired behavior most or all of the time. But we have to tailor the point chart system to a nine-year-old's level.

We're going to go over the details in a moment, but first let's recall the general guidelines for setting up a point chart from chapter 3. You'll need to make the chart itself, choose the "currency" (points, stickers, and such), attach value to specific behaviors (one point for this, two points for that), and choose the rewards that Sarah can buy with her points. Also, remember the keys to effective use of the point chart: it needs to be posted prominently where she regularly sees it, so it can act as a setting-up event for the behavior you want; you need to award points as soon after the successful performance of the behavior as you can; you should always accompany awarding the points with effective praise; and you need to be consistent about awarding points and rewards. She should get the points every time she does the desired behavior, and she shouldn't get the rewards or other benefits without earning the points by doing the desired behavior. The point chart has to be predictable and reliable for her, strengthening the link in her mind between behavior and consequences.

Now, some details. We'll begin with rewards. Most of them should be relatively minor, the kind that cost just a few points, so that Sarah can earn one nearly every day, especially at the beginning. The nature of these rewards must fit Sarah's age and tastes. In the case of the smaller, daily rewards, there may be inexpensive little items that will work well — a piece of fake jewelry, for instance, or the right to rent a movie, a cheap gift certificate to a store she likes, IOU's for music downloads or cell phone minutes — but you should also think in terms of privileges and control, rewards that don't cost anything extra. Giving her the right to make decisions about free-time activities, or what the family eats for dinner, letting her stay up a bit later than her usual bedtime, giving her breakfast in bed, doing one of her chores for her, cooking or baking with her, preparing a favorite food, letting her win the right to keep the DVD player in her room for the weekend, letting her leave her room messy for an extra day or two — these can all work just as well or better, depending on your child's preferences.

Now we price the rewards. If we're going to work on getting out of bed, getting dressed, and getting to the breakfast table more quickly and without being nagged, we might set up the prices like this: Sarah gets one point for getting up within the new time limit of ten minutes after wake-up time, she gets one point for being dressed and downstairs within the new time limit of twenty minutes after wake-up time, and she can earn one bonus point if she gets both of the other two possible points on any given morning. So, at the outset she can earn up to three points per morning, for a total of fifteen during the week (since we're working on weekday mornings, we'll relax and let her sleep in on weekends). As was the case with Davey's program in the last chapter, choose six rewards, a big enough number to start with, and price two of these six rewards at two points, two at four points, and two at ten to twelve points. (For suggestions, consult the table of age-appropriate rewards in the appendix.) Obviously, you want to place the most desirable (the "biggest") rewards in the ten- to twelve-point category, the midrange in the four-point category, and the least significant ("smallest") rewards in the two-point category. This way, if Sarah does a good job on any given day, she can earn a reward, and if she has, say, an okay day followed by a perfect day (one point for Monday, three points for Tuesday) then she can buy a slightly bigger, midrange reward on the second day, even though she can't buy any reward on the first day.

We're also going to create a second category of rewards: special bonus prizes like the football helmet that Davey could earn by completing his rocket-to-the-moon chart. These are big-ticket items Sarah can work up to over a longer stretch of time, such as a sleepover with a friend with pizza and a movie, or an expedition she's been looking forward to. If she loves going to the water park, then a trip to a water park might do nicely. You know your child best, so you're the best judge of what she will regard as a major reward. With these special bonus prizes, the price is high — say, thirty-five points, which means she might take a month to get there — but she earns them with the *total* accumulated points that she spends on smaller rewards. As with Davey's rocket-to-the-moon chart, start another chart for this special bonus prize that's marked off in increments of five or so points. Every week, transfer her total earned points for the week—including points she cashed in for prizes—to the special bonus prize chart. When she reaches the total on the special bonus prize chart — when the rocket gets to the moon, or whatever's thematically appropriate for her chart — she gets the big prize. This kind of added incentive works very well for nine-year-olds, who usually get the logic of the special bonus prize right away and take pleasure in tracking their progress.

As for the point chart itself, we'll need to make it age-appropriate. While a younger child might want to keep track of her points with stickers of animated characters, a nine-year-old may well go for a little more dignity: check marks or stars might be preferred. The chart should still be posted somewhere prominent, where Sarah will see it regularly. The visibility of the point chart is itself an antecedent, because seeing the chart sets the stage for good behavior by reminding Sarah that such behavior will produce rewards. Sports teams do something similar when they prominently post announcements awarding points or other recognition to athletes who attend practices regularly. Seeing the announcement, which rewards hard work with praise, encourages team members to come to practice and work harder. Some college football teams go one step further and award little decals for merit that players wear on their helmets during games, a conspicuous reward system that functions as both consequence (a helmet full of stickers says, *This player did a good job* in a very public way) and antecedent (because it reminds all the players on the team of the praise they can earn by behaving properly). Even big tough college football players are not too old for stickers, it seems, but your nine-year-old may well want something a little more understated.

Remember as always that praise is absolutely critical to the success of the program. Think of awarding points as a cue for you to give effective praise. Also, praise the steps along the way to awarding points. For instance, it would be worthwhile to go back to Sarah's room in the morning shortly after wake-up and say, *Great, you are getting ready so nicely and so independently. Sometimes I think you're all grown up already.*

Speaking of praise, you will also need to adjust the tone of praise for a nine-year-old. You should still be enthusiastic, but you don't have to lay it on quite as thick as you would with a younger child. Sarah's not quite of eye-rolling age yet (we'll get to that in the next chapter), but it's just around the corner. So praise her, and when you do, remember to be enthusiastic and specific, and to combine verbal praise and touch as often as possible, as before, but you can try a slightly quieter enthusiasm than you would employ with a four-year-old. Some nine-year-olds will already regard everything a parent does as uncool. In this context, the definition of "uncool" includes anything that strikes the nine-year-old as childish or simply too pleasing to the parent. So if your child doesn't want a high five in addition to verbal praise, do a high five in the air with her (a "ghost" high five). Your praise for a younger child should border on the gushiness of a cheerleader, but for a nine-year-old try: *That's great, Sarah, here you are at the breakfast table right on time,* a pat on the shoulder, and that's enough.

One more important note on rewards: fight the natural urge to be stingy with points. Parents often want to hold out for perfection in their child's behavior before they'll consider awarding points on the point chart, and that's a mistake. Remember, we're *shaping* behavior here, and you should be looking for excuses to reward positive steps toward the desired outcome. Go into this program with the mindset that you and your child are looking for a way to put points on the chart and to win rewards. That doesn't mean you reward her for behavior she really doesn't perform, but it means that you should resist the urge to act as if the points are precious and can't be lightly awarded to a mere child whose behavior is less than perfect. Just give her the points when she does what she's supposed to do, and give them happily.

Once you've got the program under way, make an effort not to nag. If Sarah isn't doing what you ask, remind her once, then let her know that she won't get the point this time, and we'll try again next time. If she's showing signs of progress in doing what she's asked without being reminded, you can also add a wrinkle as you go: if she can get out of bed and come down to breakfast on time without being asked or reminded to, she gets an extra point. What we're trying to do here is fade your participation, so that Sarah gets in the habit of being responsible for herself in the morning. Such fading is crucial to the success of the program. Remember that the program is intended to be temporary, a dynamic process that you taper off until the behavior is a habit and you don't need the structure of prompts and rewards around it.

Keeping the Program Fresh

After three days or a week of this program, you should see signs of progress. If you do, keep the program going, and you might add another reward: points for consistency. This will be especially important if Sarah performs well on some days but not on others. In that case, you can declare a new wrinkle: she gets one additional point for each two days in a row in which she earns three points. When Sarah qualifies for a consistency point, you award her the regular points for that day, as usual, then you award her the extra point. Be specific in identifying the extra point and in praising her for earning it: *Hey, not only did you get up and get down to the table on time today, but you did it two days in a row. That's fabulous, and you get the extra point.* If she begins to consistently earn this two-day dividend, then you can drop the two-day bonus and move to an extended four- or five-day dividend: if she can get three points per day for four days in a row, she earns two extra points, or if she can go a whole week getting three points per day, she gets three extra points.

If you like the progress you see, you can start picking other aspects of the morning to shape. Sarah can, for instance, earn points by setting the table for breakfast and clearing her plate. I also tell her parents that it may help to arrange to let Sarah overhear them discussing her success: *Did you see how she came right down on her own and got her own breakfast? Yeah, that's great. She's really growing up.* That's a form of praise that can work well to reinforce Sarah's progress.

Not Enough Progress?

If you're not seeing enough progress, look right away to the ABC's. Start with B, for behavior. Did Sarah do any of the desired behavior at all? Did she get up or get dressed a little quicker at least some of the time? If the answer is yes, then immediately look to make small but telling changes in A (antecedents) and C (consequences). Let's start with the antecedents. What can be done to better prompt the behavior? Try reminding her right before it's time for her to do the behavior, because arranging the shortest possible gap in time between prompt and behavior is most effective. Or you can do the first part of the behavior with her, to get her started. Combining antecedents with consequences, you might offer the usual point if she does the behavior with a gentle reminder but double points if she does it without the reminder.

If the answer to the question about behavior is no, if after a few days of the program she didn't do any of the behavior you want, then it's time to tweak the program more drastically. Start with A — more prompts, lots of help. Think of yourself as helping her game the system of the program: *Let me help you get some points, Sarah.* This may require staying in the room with her and handing her articles of clothing — a temporary measure, so don't worry that you're going to have to do this every morning until she leaves home for college. Your being there (as opposed to just verbally reminding) is a powerful antecedent, as is actually helping her get dressed.

Now we look to B, the behavior itself. Maybe you've set too tight a time limit. If you're trying to reduce her getting-dressed time from twenty minutes to five and it's not working, try reducing from twenty to fifteen, then, if that works, fifteen to ten, and so on. Remember, we want to set up the change in the morning routine so that it's a step in the right direction *that she can make.* We want her to succeed. Don't set the bar needlessly high.

Let's also look at C, the consequences. The main thing is to look for and praise any progress toward the behavior you want; look for any kind of success, and reward any steps along the way. As for the rewards that she buys with her earned points, it may be necessary to double-check that the rewards you've chosen are appealing to Sarah and that she values them. Ask her. She'll tell you. Also, consider adding more challenge and fun to the process of completing the behaviors and earning points. You can declare some days double-point days — once or twice a week, say, or on any day that it's raining (since that tends to make people more sleepy), or any day she chooses (but, again, no more than once or twice a week). You tinker with the consequences by adjusting how they are presented, the number of points that can be earned, and how Sarah gets to control how and what rewards are delivered. On a double-point day you can playfully remind Sarah of the opportunity to get extra points by teasing her a bit before she gets ready: *Oh no, you could break the bank and get too many points today.* (Being playful is a setting-up event that will make her want to earn more points. The comment and the nonpanicked, nonanxious, nonnagging style in which you deliver it are actually antecedents increasing the likelihood that Sarah will do the behaviors you want her to do.)

I want to reiterate one crucial point about parental expectations. Too often, parents begin with standards for behavior that are too stringent and unrealistic: *Do this every day, every time, and then we'll see about giving you a reward.* When we shape behavior, we can start small. We aim for one good day, or one good step toward a good day, and we reward that, and we build from there toward the point where the child does the behavior most or all of the time. The morning routine, composed as it is of so many intermediate steps, is a perfect candidate for shaping. You can always find some piece of it that lends itself to defining a positive opposite and rewarding progress toward that positive opposite.

For more suggestions about what to do if you don't see enough progress, see chapter 8.

Sibling Squabbles

Here's a news flash: siblings squabble a lot. But the normal friction between siblings, especially when they're close in age, can rev up to the point where a household can no longer function. Lisa and Christine's parents come to see me because their daughters, ages nine and eleven, have fallen into a pattern of behavior that makes it impossible to leave them unsupervised. Despite the age difference, the girls look almost like twins; Christine's only a bit taller than Lisa. They also look impossibly sweet-tempered, even angelic, with matching heads of long curly hair. When they first arrive at my office, I have trouble imagining them doing anything worse than blowing the down off aging dandelions.

But, it turns out, they can't seem to get along. They get bored, they bicker, they get into screaming matches or physical fights, then they sulk. They can't even watch TV together in peace or share a video game; they always argue over whose turn it is to hold the remote or to pick the game. "You can't leave them alone for more than five minutes," says their father, who works at home and is usually in charge of them. "They don't want a parent hanging around, watching them, but they can't get along by themselves. So I'm running in and out, separating them, trying to jolly them out of their moods, suggesting new activities. I've got work to do. I can't afford to have my workday end when they get home from school. I wish I could just leave them to be together on their own in the next room, but I can't."

The positive opposite is fairly easy to define here. We want the girls to spend time nicely together, to share activities, toys, and decision-making, to use calm voices and keep their hands to themselves. There's a wrinkle, though, in the way we shape their behavior to arrive at this desired state: we're going to treat them as a unit, not as individuals. If they're both good, they both get rewarded. If one screams or hits, they both lose out on the rewards.

First, I tell their father, you need to make very clear to the girls what you expect. Don't just say, *You need to behave;* lay out the positive opposite in specific terms. You can simulate it with them, too. Pick a time when they're getting along for the girls to practice "spending time together nicely" and be sure to praise them when they do. Be specific about what you're praising: *That's great, girls. You took turns with the video game, you used calm voices. This is going really well.* This will help them to know exactly what you expect of them.

The point chart can look the same as it would for just one child, but the points are awarded to both of them as a unit, not to either one girl or the other. Post it somewhere near where they spend time together, somewhere where they'll see it. Break it up into twenty- or thirty-minute blocks, say; whatever they can handle without parental intervention. For each time period in which they play nicely and without incident, they get a check mark or a point. If they're having trouble taking turns and sharing, it's probably best if you put the point on there yourself, rather than letting them do it, because you want only one check mark or star — to reinforce that it's a single point for the both of them — and you don't want to create an opportunity for them to squabble over who gets to put it on the chart. You're going to be looking in occasionally to check on them, rather than hovering in the room with them all the time; give them as much responsibility as they can handle. Be sure to praise them when they do earn a point: *This is working out really well, girls. You're spending time together so nicely.* If you can add some reinforcing physical contact to the praise, a pat on the shoulder or something like that, do so, but don't force it.

You might use a kitchen timer to mark the twenty- or thirty-minute periods (or longer, if they can handle it). When the timer dings, you come in and tell them whether they got the point or not. Our studies show, by the way, that once kids get used to the timer, their behavior tends to get better and better as the ding of the timer approaches, behavior is best right when the timer dings, and it's worst right after the timer is reset for the next period. One way to mitigate this effect is to add in bonus chances for points. In addition to coming in to check on them when the timer dings, you can occasionally drop in on them when it doesn't ding. If they're behaving well when you look in, they get a bonus point for that. If you look in fairly early on in the timer period, you create an incentive for them to behave better when they're inclined to behave worst.

Set up the structure of rewards so that they can earn privileges together with their points: a special outing together, or whatever else appeals to them. If you are worried that they will not want the same reward, or that they won't want to spend even more time together doing a joint reward, then offer a menu of rewards, and when they've earned a reward, let each one choose one item from the menu. The reward can consist of two separate items, but the important thing is that either they both get a reward or neither sister gets one. You're rewarding a "group behavior," so they both have to perform in order to qualify for a reward, even if it's an individualized reward.

One way to work this program is to make the continuation of an activity dependent on good behavior. If there's misbehavior, they get one warning — just one — and if it happens again then the activity they are doing comes to an end and they don't get a point: *Sorry, girls, there's no point this time. But we'll try again later.* You can also use a snack or some other natural break to "reset" them halfway through. Let's say that the girls usually tend to get testy after about an hour. They have the first half-hour session and it goes fine, so you give them a point and let them continue that activity. The second session also goes fine, so they get another point, and be sure to praise them every time you award a point. If they naturally start to erode after about an hour, this is a good time to break for a snack, after which they can either return to that activity or start a new one. But here's the catch: you shouldn't break for a snack or start an exciting new activity after a half-hour period in which they failed to get the point, because that would make the snack or the exciting new activity seem like a reward for misbehaving.

Squabbling Friends

You can apply this sibling approach to a child's constant strife with friends, too, and in fact that situation gives you at least one other good tool to work with. Let's change the scenario so that the squabbling pair consists of an only child and her best friend. It's not uncommon for so-called best friends to bicker too much when they're together. You can set up the same program for a pair of friends that Lisa and Christine's parents set up for them. You'll probably want to check your use of the program with the friend's parents, and depending on your relationship with them, even get them to do something similar when the girls are at their house. But if the friend's parents can't or won't participate, you can still improve the girls' behavior together at your house, which is a big step in the right direction.

You will definitely need the friend's parents' cooperation for an advanced variation of this program, in which you make the length of the visit depend on behavior. Sometimes, it's not possible to send a child home early. If her parents are counting on you to have her until 6:00, you can't very well deposit her on their doorstep at 5:00. If it is possible to end the visit early, though, that gives you a powerful tool for shaping behavior. As long as the two play together without incident, they get to keep going. If voices are raised or there's some other problem, they get a warning. One warning is sufficient for the whole visit. If after the warning they still misbehave, then the friend goes home. You don't need points in this case. The reward is extending their time together, and they get it right away.

No matter how you set up the program, be sure to look in and catch the girls being good. Don't wait to come into the room until they're bickering or in trouble, because then it's too late. Instead, stick your head in when it's quiet and they're getting along fine, and say, *This is so great; you're playing so well together.* And you can even back it up with a bonus reward. Come into the room at a random moment and announce, *Bonus point time! You two are doing soooo well* [and be specific about what they're doing right], *and you can still earn your regular reward, but this is a bonus for super-grown-up behavior.*

Your intention, over time, is to fade your participation and the rewards you're offering. You want to come in less and less often, and gradually eliminate all rewards except praise, and eventually the praise, too.

Homework Avoidance

Schools are piling on the homework these days, and parents are expected to be involved. It's often a big time commitment for parents on school nights, and when on top of that a child won't do homework without a fight, or won't do it at all no matter how hard the parents push, homework can turn into a major family problem. Kevin, an eleven-year-old, is a quick and competent student. His teacher has said he has "remarkable potential," and his hand will sometimes be the only one raised in class when the other students are sitting there looking confused. He's particularly good at math and science and has begun to show some facility for the saxophone. We know that schoolwork is not intellectually beyond him. Rather, the problem is that he won't sit down and *do* it. He has always resisted homework and has gotten by so far on quick wits, spotty effort, and altogether too much parental assistance, but now he's in the fifth grade and the problem's worse than ever. His parents have decided it can't go on any longer.

As they describe the typical weekday afternoon and evening, Kevin stalls and avoids homework by playing video games, watching TV, snacking, wandering around, volunteering to walk the dog — anything not to sit down and apply himself to his work. And when, after much yelling and pleading and drama, his parents do get him to sit down to do it, he pops back up again as soon as they relax their vigilance. "He's not hyperactive," says his mother. "He can sit still just fine in other situations. He just doesn't want to do his homework." They're angry and concerned, and they have pretty much concluded that they're not going to solve the problem by promising him an electric guitar if he gets A's, forbidding him from playing basketball ever again if he doesn't, or shouting things like, *At this rate you'll never go to college! You're killing me!*

So, let's get down to business. We have a good picture of what he does now. He tries to avoid sitting down to work, and when he does work he tends to go no more than ten minutes before getting up again. We also have a good picture of what we want him to do: sit down and work steadily for, say, thirty minutes at a time. It will take more than one half-hour session to do all his homework, of course, but let's start with that. It's reasonable to try to extend him from ten to thirty minutes. (But let's say that he never sat down to do his work, that the starting number was zero minutes. In that case, thirty minutes might not make a suitable target. We'd aim first for ten minutes or so, and then, once he could do that, build up toward thirty from there.) Our basic rule of thumb, remember, is that we begin where he is — not with what we think he can do, but with what he does now. (Yes, I know, *other* eleven-year-olds sit for hours on end and do all their homework, and yes, I know, you feel a bit like you're babying Kevin, but get over it, if you want to solve the problem.) The exact total of minutes we're shooting for at first is not overly important, as long as it's not too demanding.

Let's recognize that setting-up events are crucial here. A setting-up event, as you'll recall, is an antecedent that arranges the environment so that a behavior is more likely to occur. One good example of a setting-up event would be the pre-bed routine we set up for Davey in chapter 3: the calmness and low stimulation of that routine sets the stage for a peaceful transition to bed. Rituals are important setting-up events, so let's work on the afterschool routine with that in mind. Give Kevin some transition time when he gets home from school, a little "free swim" period in which he can wind down. Then, at a prescribed time that's the same every day — let's say 4:00 — it's time to do his homework. You begin with a clear, clean prompt: *Kevin, please start your homework now.* There should be not only a clear regular time but also a regular place for working. If you can dedicate a desk just to homework, that's better than using the kitchen table, because sitting at the kitchen table is a setting-up event for other behavior, like snacking or talking to family members. And what *you* do matters, too. If you take the opportunity of your child's homework time to watch TV or play his favorite video game, that's not helping one bit, is it?

At the outset, you will have to be closely involved to make sure he stays with the job. So for the first few days, after asking him to begin his homework, add, *I'm going to help you.* On the first day or two, you're going to sit with him. You'll try to do the minimal amount of work necessary to help him stick to it. By "work," I mean encouragement and quiet praising, not actually doing the homework for him. In praising him you're not going for a celebratory tone here. Bellowed compliments and thunderous high fives aren't in order. Instead, something more like quiet respect is the key: *Kevin, you're doing your math problems so well. You're sitting here working away, really sticking to it, and look, you're halfway done already.* In other words, praise his success at the *process* of doing the homework (versus, say, telling him how smart he is), since that's what you're trying to reinforce. And don't forget to add a physical component, a touch on the shoulder or a pat on the back, if you can. That strengthens the reinforcement.

After a couple of days, you can begin to fade your participation. Start by arranging to go out of the room — to start dinner, to make a phone call — and come back in, praising him when you do return for sticking to it while you were out. Find reasons to pop out and then come back in to catch him being good. You can also modify the beginning or the end of the homework session. To adjust the beginning, you can try something like, *Kevin, it's time to do your homework. You get started, and I'll come check on you in a few minutes.* Or, if he can't seem to get settled and started on his own, start with him and then modify the end by leaving five minutes before he's done, then ten minutes the next time, and so on. Both of these approaches are likely to work, but choose the path of least resistance. In other words, start with what he can do. If getting settled is his big problem, help him get settled; if sticking to the task once he has started is his big problem, then let him get started on his own but come in to help him keep at it.

A point chart for this activity might be as simple as one point for every ten minutes of uninterrupted sitting and working. So, two points for twenty minutes, three points for thirty, and so on. Put points on the chart and praise along the way — at the beginning, you'll be marking the point every ten minutes, if he earns it — and also be sure to praise him at the end of a successful session. (You may come to believe that the promise of points is carrying the main weight of the program, but that's not true. Really, your praise is more important than ever. Points and praise go together, and remember that when I say "praise," I mean "effective praise": enthusiastic, specific, unqualified, coming as close on the heels of the child doing the desired behavior as you can, and delivered whenever possible via more than one sense — voice plus touch, for instance.) The homework chart should be visible from the place where he does his homework; remember that its presence will act as a setting-up event to encourage the desired behavior. You can set up the usual structure of short-term and long-term rewards. There should be some small things he can earn for a few points. If he can get up to, let's say, four points per day, make the price of the smallest rewards three points.

By the way, I should add that Kevin's homework program worked out well — so well that his parents wanted to apply the same kind of program to practicing the saxophone, which they did with good success.

Involving a Teacher

One other scenario worth mentioning here: a common frustration of parents is that their child comes home and says, *I don't have any homework to do for that class today,* which short-circuits any plans for a program designed to build up a regular daily homework session. One way to work around that ploy is to involve the teacher in a daily reporting routine. The teacher gives a card to the child that lists the day's homework assignment. The child turns in the card to the parents and gets a point on the homework point chart for turning it in.

You can also use the card system, again depending on the willingness of the teacher, as part of a home-based reinforcement program designed to improve behavior at school. Let's say general deportment is a problem. The child would bring home a card every school day on which the teacher ranks him in, say, three categories of behavior: for example, hands to himself (no shoving or hitting), working quietly during desk time, and nice language with other kids (no teasing, swearing, and the like). The child gets a point for delivering the card, then another point or two in each of the three categories, depending on performance (middling gets you one point, excellent gets you two, for instance).

One sample card system might be set up like this:

HANDS TO HIMSELF
1. Shoving and hitting others (no points)
2. Hands to himself some of the time (1 point)
3. Hands to himself most of the time (2 points)

WORKING QUIETLY DURING DESK TIME
1. Very little time working quietly (no points)
2. Some time working quietly (1 point)
3. Most of the time working quietly (2 points)

NICE LANGUAGE WITH OTHER KIDS
1. Teasing and swearing (no points)
2. Nice language some of the time (1 point)
3. Nice language most of the time (2 points)

The teacher marks the card in each of the three categories, and the child gets a point just for bringing it home and turning it in to you. You read the card and award points according to the teacher's evaluation of the day, making sure to praise all success. In the case of a no-point performance in one or more categories, be sure to say, *Maybe tomorrow you will be able to earn points.* All sorts of permutations can work here. For instance, if the child consistently achieves midlevel behavior (the teacher frequently circles the twos on the card) and you want to improve that performance, you might eliminate the point for midlevel behavior (replacing it with praise alone, so that you're now treating it like a step toward the true objective) and award the two points only for a three, excellent behavior. Recently, a teacher doing a home-based reinforcement program with one of the families at my clinic wrote in a four on a child's card to note that the child had an absolutely perfect day. That's fine, and it's worth giving a bonus point for that, but we want to stay away from expecting perfection.

. . .

As a six- to twelve-year-old's abilities develop, and as your child moves out into the world and engages with others more and more, you will be presented with all sorts of situations that are similar but not identical to the examples in this chapter. As you adapt the scenarios here to meet other challenges, keep in mind that the outline of our approach remains consistent:

- Identify what the child does now
- Identify a positive opposite
- Work toward that positive opposite by rewarding behavior that marks progress toward it

The details are full of make-or-break subtleties, of course, and it's all likely to get more complicated as your child enters preadolescence and then adolescence, but the basic approach will still serve you well.

5

Your Preadolescent
Bad Attitude, Bad Language, Home Alone, and Much More

The initial "observe and describe" step in my method is particularly challenging when you're using it to address a preadolescent's behavior. That's because so much of what bothers a preadolescent's parents has less to do with discrete behaviors than with the tone and texture of the child's manner. They complain about touchiness, moodiness, anger, moroseness, and constant low-grade disrespect that periodically escalates to defiance and confrontation. Their child may seem to them to be working up to bigger and more disturbing things, so parents tend to worry not only about present behavior but about what it suggests for the near future as well. They see how today's display of quick temper, low spirits, or misguided independence could soon blossom into full-blown adolescent rebellion: outright refusal to do as she's told, spectacularly unfortunate and perhaps not entirely reversible choices in personal grooming and attire, round-the-clock sarcasm and eye-rolling, and years of making a big show of plainly counting the seconds until he can be rid of his family's intolerable company.

The parents of preadolescents who come to see me often complain about their child's disrespect, precocious flouting of their authority, and growing air of general contempt, but they dwell on their own injured pride. "She's laughing at us," they'll say. "No, it's worse than that. She's *pretending* to laugh at us in this really fakey, annoying way." Or they might say, "He won't exactly stand up to us — yet — but he says things under his breath. At first, we punished him every time we heard him say it, but we had to punish him all the time. The house was a battlefield. Now, we just try to tune him out."

They're not just hurt, they're *mad*. I hear, "After all we do, we don't deserve to be treated like this" pretty often. They're often driving their child to friends' houses, social events, and sports practice; paying for the clothes that must be worn to avoid being sent to social Siberia; and funding music or dance or other activities and the gear that goes with them. And they're trying to keep the channels of communication open, constantly striving to be understanding and forgiving during their child's difficult phase of life. After all they've done, they feel, their child doesn't have the right to treat them badly. It galls them that their preadolescent child wants to be treated like an adult but too often acts like a big, selfish baby. She may be twelve going on twenty-two, but she's also capable of acting like she's seven.

You should not, in fact, have to put up with this conduct. But if you punish every instance of bad behavior, the situation will almost certainly get worse. The best way to change how your child treats you is to work with him on changing his behavior, and we know how to do that. So, I tell the aggrieved parents, let's put your injured pride on hold for a while. Let's try my way for a week or two. To begin with, let's break "disrespect" into behaviors that you can address. The concept of disrespect is abstract, but we can work on specifics, even here.

Let's step back from the injured pose that goes with *After all we've done for you . . .* And let's step back from the temptation of "parenting by revenge." If nonstop punishment would actually change a child's behavior for the better, I would recommend it, but it won't work. In fact, the sternest and most violent punishers, including the ones who cross over into abuse, often have increasingly defiant and aggressive kids. Your parental altruism — that same impulse that causes you to provide regular meals, rides, shelter, and affection to your child no matter how horribly she acts toward you — now requires you to step back from your own sore feelings and take a slightly more detached, more strategic view of her behavior.

A Little Perspective

While I am very sympathetic to parental worries about rocky years with an adolescent in the house — and believe me, the nature of my practice has led me to see the rockiest of the rocky — let me offer two counter-thoughts right up front that might improve your outlook.

First, adolescence does not always live up to its bad reputation. The old notion that adolescence automatically entails storm and stress has been largely overturned by research that shows most children do well in adolescence and do not present horrible challenges or other reasons for parental dread. It also shows that parents can do a lot in advance of and during the teen years to stack the odds in their favor: work to connect your child to the family, help build good values and competencies, and so on. (I'll have more to say about this in the conclusion of this book.) Natural conflicts come up — such as the struggle over how much independence a child will have — but there is much you can do to keep them from turning into crises.

Second, adolescence is not as discrete a period in a person's life as you might think. It's not like your child is fated to lose her mind at a specific age and then regain her sanity at a specific later date, much as it can seem like that sometimes. I was on a congressional panel in the 1980s that was charged with studying adolescence, and my colleagues and I spent hours and hours arguing about a useful definition of the period of adolescence. We ended up casting our net wide, from the age of ten (to catch early maturers) all the way to the point at which a person is substantially on his own (graduating high school, leaving for college, living at home but attending college, and so on). The variation among individuals is great, too. One eleven-year-old might be barely entering preadolescence, while another may already be well into what looks like adolescence. Or the same child may be very advanced in some ways but not in others. The terms "preadolescent" and "adolescent" threatened to collapse into meaninglessness during the congressional panel's discussions. It became very clear that it doesn't really work to just slap an age range on preadolescence and adolescence.

What's *with* Them?

I think it's more accurate to see preadolescence and adolescence as, respectively, the opening and developing phases of an overlapping series of changes that take place gradually as a child moves toward young adulthood. The general changes are fairly obvious: sexual maturity, more time out of the home, more influence felt from peers, friends, and adults other than yourself. But changes are also occurring in the way your child's brain functions. The paths in the brain that control problem solving, planning, and thinking are in transition, influencing how this young person negotiates the world. The risky behaviors that emerge during adolescence, for instance, probably result not just from changing brain function but also, the research tells us, from association with peers going through similar transitions.

In relation to family life and child behavior, there are several potential tension and transition points a family will need to traverse. Here are some:

From being a child (ages 10 to 12 and younger) . . .	To entering preadolescence/ adolescence (10 to 13 and older) . . .
Must have a babysitter	No babysitter — I don't need a babysitter.
No makeup (lipstick, eye shadow)	Makeup, and lots of it
Minor participation in choosing clothing, hairstyle	Deciding what to wear; parents not consulted, except when it's time to buy more clothes
No piercing of anything (except one in each ear, for girls)	Piercing multiple times, ears and elsewhere, girls and boys
Little or no active sex or birth control	More sexual activity and use or possession of birth control
Little or no unsupervised free time outside of the home	Some to a lot of unsupervised free time outside the home — after school, at malls, in the neighborhood, etc.
No cigarettes, drug abuse, alcohol	Exposure to and exploration of some/all
Curfew not relevant	You must be in by . . .

Music not an issue and not loud	Great passion about musical preference, more disputes about volume, content, quality, etc.
Passive on routine decisions (e.g., food preferences, toothpaste preferences, look and feel of bedroom)	Views and preferences on all kinds of things — including posters of celebrities you've never heard of or can't stand, taped to your recently painted walls
Fairly stable moods; occasional irritability traced to sickness, being tired, hungry, etc.	More swings of mood, more seemingly unexplained irritability
A crush, maybe, and comments about a girl/boy, but not much real time spent on this	Feelings of being in love; constant talking, messaging, hanging out
What the family does for dinners, weekends, etc. is fine	The parents of my friends are more interesting or cool, eat tastier foods, have fewer rules
I wish we could always be together at home	I don't want to be like you; living here is a drag
Little or no slang or swearing, beyond some annoying language from cartoons, kids' shows	Swearing and jargon from peers, TV, or music
Little self-reflection or reflection on life	Self-reflection, despair, body-image issues . . . and more intensity about it all

The only way a parent can avoid such transitions is to run away from home. This is not a flippant remark. Statistically, the riskiest period for divorce begins when a child in the home becomes an adolescent (although, doing my duty as a scientist, I should add that no study has yet nailed down cause and effect here, and it could be coincidental timing with an adult's midlife crisis). Parents tend to think of the situation outlined by the table's left column as just how things are — until preadolescence introduces them to the right-hand column, that is. All of a sudden it seems as if this young person who just a few short years ago could not go to the bathroom by herself now has an opinion about everything, and these can be extreme, clear, strong, and nonnuanced views.

So, before we get into addressing specific behaviors, let's consider from a parent's point of view what's different about preadolescents and their situations.

To begin with, many of the changes I described in the previous chapter have continued and become more pronounced as we move into this developmental period. Parents have less control and are more vulnerable. Public embarrassment becomes a more significant issue as more and more of your relationship to your child extends beyond the home. Also, there's far more unsupervised time in the child's life. Because babysitters are becoming a thing of the past, the family increasingly has to deal with what can happen when a child is home alone. And if there's anything dangerous or subject to abuse in the house (weapons, alcohol, cigarettes), the stakes go up considerably. More destructive behavior is also possible. If things get out of hand, a preadolescent can break things, hurt himself, or hurt you.

School is more important than ever, and your child has more work to do, and more responsibilities. But he may well have less interest in it, and less energy to spare for it, than he did before. Peer relations take up more and more of his attention, as well as the lion's share of free time after school and on weekends. At home, parents seem to have less influence than ever, and less control over "reinforcers," the rewards for a behavior that make it more likely to happen again in the future. When your child was younger, your praise, even more than the little prizes you might award, was a very strong reinforcer of good behavior. But as your child approaches full-blown adolescence and begins to claim greater autonomy, your praise temporarily takes on less value precisely because it's coming from you. Your child wants to rely on you less, so she tends to undervalue what you offer — not only reinforcers but also unconditional love, models of good behavior or morality, and all the other parental essentials. Of course, you are more important than ever, too: as your child seeks out and responds to an expanding set of influences, your stability, unwavering commitment, and values serve as a beacon guiding her back to the family. Still, children's assertion of independence and parents' own sense that their word counts for less than ever often give parents the feeling of "losing" their children as they approach adolescence. But it's temporary (parents usually feel that they "get their kids back" when adolescence ends), and you can make adjustments. For instance, you may well find that while your own praise doesn't have the weight it once did, reinforcers that play up to a child's new orientation away from parents and toward others — rewards like movies or pizza with friends, a sleepover, a trip to the mall with friends — may work well at this stage.

You will find yourself moving through an ever more dangerous parenting minefield. As behaviors change and the stakes go up, you will encounter many more opportunities to nag, reprimand, and pontificate. Suddenly you find yourself going on and on about how things were when you were young. How did this happen? You're not sure, but when you find yourself lecturing an eye-rolling thirteen-year-old about the decline of all that is good and true in the world, you have probably just stepped on one of those mines.

A preadolescent may still be a child in some ways but in other ways she's not. Sex and drugs may not be major household issues yet — although we certainly see plenty of both among preadolescents — but they're on the horizon, and at this stage your child may be becoming interested in them. A child's shifts of mood and energy from one day to the next can cause parents to worry that it's a sign she's experimenting with drugs — and of course this may be, or become, an issue they must deal with — but it's also a sign of what's coming. In adolescence, both boys and girls often grow more irritable and variable in their behavior. Boys often grow more aggressive, and girls tend more toward depression and new concerns about body image, although the revelations of widespread steroid use in high school suggest that boys are beginning to catch up when it comes to body-image concerns. Both boys and girls are likely to be more sensitive in general and to react to things that might not have been such a big deal in earlier years.

The research shows a couple of gender-related wrinkles here worth mentioning. Girls who physically mature early in relation to their peers tend to have lower self-esteem and poorer body image, and make more negative statements that locate problems within themselves: *I can't do this, I'm bad at that, It's my fault.* Boys show the opposite pattern. Those who mature early in their peer group enjoy high self-esteem, more confidence, and more popularity. A related body of research shows that among adolescents and preadolescents, girls tend to make many more internalizing statements — seeing themselves at fault and apologizing even for things that couldn't possibly be their fault. Boys tend to make many more externalizing statements: *It wasn't my fault, If you didn't want me to hit you in the face you shouldn't have put your face right there, My mom and dad forced me to shoplift that DVD by not allowing me to buy it with my allowance money.*

The emergence of new issues seems to produce, among other things, many more little household tragedies (but don't call them "little" around a preadolescent): *I can't go anywhere with this hair/these clothes, I didn't make the team, He never even looked at me at the party, I'm the only kid in the world who can't play Machine-gun Safari in Hell III,* and so on.

Pushing the Limits

Preadolescents typically try to expand the limits of their freedom, and these normal moves toward autonomy will lead to clashes with parents. The flashpoints can be as mundane as clothing and personal habits — but seemingly minor squabbles over makeup or clothes are part of a larger process. Your child is developing a new set of wants and "needs" that fall under the parental rubric "You're kidding" — everything from overpriced cool shoes to a passionate wish to diet or lift weights.

Another development you're likely to notice — and resent — is that instead of just not listening to you, which you are getting used to, your preadolescent now listens to other people. Her sources of advice have expanded in ways you're not always comfortable with. Suddenly she's quoting friends, friends' parents, coaches, athletes, rappers, and reality-show hosts — all of whose wisdom seems to have superseded yours in her estimation. And you'll find yourself debating with him about an expanded set of subjects, including his future. There's no more effective way for a child to assert his independence than to shock you by expressing views contrary to yours on the subject of education and career.

It will seem to you that your child's judgment is deteriorating, not improving. That's because it is, but right on schedule. There is a "normal" (that is, common) increase in risky behavior, even among children who have been doing fine in life and who will do fine later on in life. And both boys and girls show an increase in deviant behavior. Even kids who haven't taken risks before may become curious about alcohol, drugs, smoking, or sex, and some begin to experiment with one or all. They may commit minor offenses, like fighting, a little stealing (when your five-year-old pockets a candy bar at the store, it's merely embarrassing; when your thirteen-year-old does it, you may hear from the police), perhaps some property damage. By adolescence, over 50 percent of males and 20 to 35 percent of females have engaged in at least one delinquent act (defined as an illegal behavior), with vandalism and theft the most common. Status offenses go up, too. These are behaviors that are illegal because of age, like underage drinking and sex, and violating curfew.

Even a generally well-behaved child may begin to test the boundaries by skipping a class here and there, turning a sleepover at a friend's house into an unauthorized late-night outing, testing the limits of allowable grooming (if a weird haircut is okay, what about a piercing or a tattoo?), or sampling the endless world of vice available online. I've had a family at the clinic whose eleven-year-old daughter went out with friends and got a tattoo without telling her parents. Some of these risky moves are merely annoying, some present a problem that you can find a way to be understanding about, and some are just plain dangerous or hint at real danger to come. Your preadolescent and her circle of peers are probably not going to have many chances to drink and drive, for instance, but they may have opportunities to ride in a car with others who have been drinking: friends have older siblings, younger kids have older associates they look up to, and one thing can lead to another.

Even as you allow for the natural increase in risky behaviors, you have to decide what's nonnegotiable and then be reliably consistent about enforcing the rules. You can draw the line on some nonnegotiable risks — like, for instance, *We can't allow you to get a tattoo, or to have anything pierced other than the ear. We can talk about it again, if you want, when you're sixteen.* But you also have to consider the nuances of risk-taking. For instance, the research shows that kids who never experiment with risky behavior in adolescence are just as at risk later in life, and in some cases more at risk, than those who experiment a little. Experimentation is normal, in other words. Okay, no tattoos allowed, period, but what about when a good student skips a lesson or a class? Not that you condone it, but draw a distinction between your reaction to such an offense and your reaction to, say, going out and getting a tongue stud without your approval. If your child wants to take aesthetic risks in dress or hair, consider allowing those that have no permanent consequences. You can't make a stand on everything; pick your battles. If you can compromise, try to. (Sometimes this can become elaborate and even sort of funny, such as when parents and daughters get into gory detail when determining just how much makeup or exposed skin is too much.) If your child wants to risk deafness by cranking his music, you might try setting aside a certain time in which it's okay for him to play loud music in the house.

It pays to keep track of your child's friends, too, because peers make a greater difference than ever before, and can push risky behavior toward consequences that get out of hand and prove to be dangerous. And even normal risky behavior — on the level of a prank — also has to be watched and limited because the child can get snared by a system (arrested by the police, for instance) and enter into a series of consequences that takes on a momentum of its own: detention, expulsion, special education. You need to be around, and you need to keep your child involved in the family, even or especially if that means involving his friends with the family.

For instance, girls often go to the mall together, in pairs or larger packs. But sometimes such an expedition leads to going over to somebody's house, where other things can happen, and sometimes the expedition is just a cover for meeting boys, smoking, and other activities you want to know about and regulate. That means you need to be alert: find out who's going, use the excuse of drop-off and pick-up arrangements to check in with other parents, and if your daughter has a cell phone, you can talk to her while she's at the mall. You'll need to check up on her, but reassure her when you do that it's because you love her, not because you don't trust her or her friends. She won't entirely believe you, but that's life. You need to know what's going on in hers.

You may not really be that eager for the company of your child's friends, but it's better to have them in your sight than to have your child absent for long stretches. It might mean that you've got your son and his pals slouching around at Sunday dinner, muttering cryptically to each other about techniques for blowing away enemies in Halo; and yes, it might mean that you find yourself chaperoning the crew to a lousy concert or two. Smile, stay out of the way when you're on his turf, be welcoming when he and his friends are on yours, and remind yourself that he'll be eighteen before you know it.

Family Values

It's distressing for parents to discover that their day-to-day control over their child's life is waning just as the child's penchant for risk and experimentation is gaining strength. But there's another, more indirect kind of parental influence: the relationship and example that has accrued over months and years. How you as a parent have interacted with your child in the past and how you interact now exerts a very important influence. It can be the key to your continuing ability to shape her life and be a meaningful part of it. If you have been nagging, screaming, and punishing heavily for years, that investment will now show compounded interest. Or, rather, your preadolescent will show compounded lack of interest, having become a master of escape, avoidance, and tuning you out.

But, on the other hand, this is a time to reap the benefits of good, positive parenting — and it's never too late for you to work on your own good habits. It is crucial that you continue to emphasize conventional values and activities, which can help a child through even the most difficult adolescence. You have to consistently convey to your child in both word and deed that doing things together with the family (meals, outings, shared projects), attending school, doing homework, having responsibilities around the house, and helping others are valuable and important. The research shows that bonding to conventional values improves a child's chances in the future, like a psychological vaccination that inoculates against the "adolescent flu." In studies, the kids randomly assigned to programs that reinforce such values did better later on, as measured by lower rates of truancy, substance abuse, delinquency, vandalism, and so on.

Different families use different sorts of activities to reinforce desirable values, and any list I make will be partial and mostly by way of example. It might include: regular weekend recreation as a family, and also pairings between a single adult and a single child (a regular Saturday afternoon father-daughter game of pool, for example, or a regular Sunday morning mother-son trip to the coffee shop); family rituals arranged around holidays or seasonal activities; developing competencies together (music, sport, hobby); religious observances; family reunions and other get-togethers of relatives beyond the immediate family unit; volunteering; reading a book in common and discussing it (that is, teach that reading is interesting not by nagging about it but by modeling it), or, if reading is not a family strength, organizing a regular chat about the news that gives a child opportunities to get involved and state her views; subscribing to a magazine that the child might enjoy and commenting on it, leaving it around the house, and otherwise encouraging the child to get interested in it.

Some parents of preadolescents or adolescents who read this list may already be rolling their eyes in a kind of sympathetic anticipation of their child's response to such suggestions. Yes, from the standpoint of a thirteen-year-old who makes a point of being disaffected, many of these examples might seem lame. So, increasingly, do you, just by virtue of being his mother or father. But there has to be some activity on this list, or there are other activities that might easily fit onto the list, that your child may well take an interest in. Getting his friends involved might actually help you strengthen the bonds that keep your child connected to the family. Allow and even encourage him to bring a friend or two to dinner, the batting cage, or the beach. It still "counts" as a family activity if his friend is there.

Look for chances, also, to build or continue building your child's competence — whether it's in sports, music, cooking, or anything else. You can also look for ways to continue some activity of the past but allow the child to select something new to explore, too. If she likes music, then she might want to take up a different instrument or learn to sing. (This is the age, for instance, when all those grudgingly attended piano or violin lessons can pay off in the form of a switch to electric guitar or drums and a sudden passion for practicing *all the time.*) Beyond building competence, such activities require some commitment, another life skill worth developing.

Be more generous about costs when they're associated with family activities or other desirable behavior. If new bike equipment or new painting materials will guide him toward competence and good company, and you have the money to spare, it's probably well spent. Be more stingy, by contrast, about spending money on activities that might place the child in settings that foster deviance and aggression: violent movies, for instance, or video games.

You the parent are more important than ever before, even if it seems your company is less welcome than ever. Persevere in spending more time with your child even though she may often discourage your presence. Be available and around, and try to do regular everyday tasks together every week. Errands or shopping are perfect for this. Even ferrying around your child by car, which can seem time-consuming and annoying, can have the hidden benefit of giving you some time to talk or just to be together. These regular, mundane times are good opportunities for bonding but also for chatting about heavy topics (sex, drugs, and so on) that can come up naturally and without the pressure of a "big talk."

The Art of Compromise

Consider privately (and with your spouse or partner, if you're not a single parent) those areas on which you can compromise and those on which you can't. When you've drawn up a list of areas on which you can compromise, find ways to lengthen it. Try to give more leeway on behaviors or issues that are likely to come and go on their own in the teen years, like disastrous style choices or excessive phone use. When considering your reaction to a potential area of conflict, ask yourself, *Could this make a difference in ten years or will we be past this?*

Pay attention, as a parent, to the difference between consistency and rigidity in your rules and actions. You want to be consistent, but you may have to compromise more. If you find yourself saying, *I did not allow this before and I won't allow it now,* especially as a precursor to punishing your child, stop and consider whether it may well be time to change your policy. Bend a bit more when you can; walk away when you can. If you view your relationship to your child as a series of battles over who is in control, you are far along the path to defeat. Paradoxically, your control and continuing influence will derive from your reasonableness and ability to compromise, so do not mistake these for weakness on your part.

Walk away from battles and return at calmer times for negotiation. When you walk away, resist the urge to lob a verbal grenade as you leave the room. For example, *I can't talk to you when you whine like a baby and sound so stupid.* Frustration may tempt you to say such things to your frequently exasperating child, but when you do, you make it far more likely that you will be receiving more disrespect in return in the near future.

A guiding rule: Praise reasonableness whenever you encounter it. For example, *I like the way you handled yourself today. You came home first and told me what was going on and asked permission. That was good planning and thinking.*

You may long for the days when you merely wished that your child would stay close to you in the grocery store, pick up things from the floor of his room, and use a fork correctly at dinner. This, too, is normal. Those days may well have been easier.

Adapting the Method to Preadolescents

The principles and techniques of the method you've learned in detail in chapters 3 and 4 don't change when applied to a preadolescent. (Indeed, they don't change when applied to adults, as they often are, everywhere from military bases to retirement homes.) But, again, there are significant differences in how you apply them. That's what I concentrate on in this chapter. I'll assume you've got the basics under your belt, and I'll emphasize the adjustments you need to make to fit a preadolescent. Negotiation will be more important than it was when dealing with younger children; parents can no longer impose programs as easily by their authority alone. Some of the reinforcers and points of negotiation will make a parent gulp. At this age, paying for extra cell phone minutes or time with friends may be effective rewards, even if you're not enthusiastic about them.

You probably won't want to use the same kind of prominently posted point chart you used for younger children, but you can certainly still use points if they're less conspicuously displayed. Also, you can feel free to dispense with points and connect actions more directly with privileges: *If you have four days of good homework sessions, then you can go out Saturday,* or *If you call by 3:00 to tell me where you are after school, you can stay out with your friends until 4:00. But if you don't call by 3:00 or don't come home by 4:00, you have to come straight home from school the next day.* In the scenarios that follow, whenever I mention points or a point chart, feel free to substitute this more direct approach to rewarding the desired behavior, if it works better for you.

Praise without caboosing is still important, but tone down the gushing effusiveness you employed for praising younger children. Keep it clean and clear, but no need to oversell. Something simple like, *Now that was really good; you called me just as we agreed and were home on time,* and a muted high five or touch on the shoulder, if it feels natural, is plenty.

Because an adolescent is out of the home and off a parent's screen more than before, you will probably need to employ some novel ways to monitor some behaviors. The cell phone, irritating as it can sometimes be, does give us a valuable new tool, since it makes it much more convenient for your child to call to check in, even if you're at work. You may also find yourself doing more monitoring after the fact, like looking over the results of chores or homework done while you weren't around. Monitoring is crucial; the research shows clearly that less monitoring and supervision are associated with more risky behavior on the child's part. With rare exceptions that I find hard to envision, parents should always know where their child is.

Now, let's get to some specific scenarios.

Bad Attitude

Parents of preadolescents commonly complain about their child's bad attitude, but bad attitude is not always easy to address, in part because it's in some ways hard to define. When you actually sit down and try to describe it as a set of behaviors, you can find yourself lapsing into vagueness. "She's sort of not really there when we talk to her" is how Heather's father described his daughter's attitude problem. "When we do something as a family, she slouches around and makes a big deal of acting like she's not having a good time."

Heather's only twelve, but she's tall for her age and looks older. She has thick glasses and oddly formed front teeth that her parents have been promising to repair; she's concerned about her appearance, and especially about what she wears and how she appears to other kids her age.

If she's vague with her father, she's sarcastic and sometimes just plain mean to her mother. These aspects of her bad attitude can be defined more clearly as behavior. For instance, if her mom says something innocuous like, "Why don't we pick up dinner before going home?" or "Don't forget to tell your teacher you'll be out on Friday," Heather makes a slight turning of the head as if to say no, adding a little vocal click of disapproval, almost disgust, and follows up with a comment like, "That's a dumb idea" or "You don't even know what's going on." She also says cruel things to her little sister, mopes around the house, and rolls her eyes when asked to do anything. Sometimes she seems sad for no reason, just lying on her bed for long stretches, but other times she's irritable and snaps at everyone.

First, as before, we have to translate the abstraction of Heather's bad attitude into specific behaviors, so that we can find positive opposites for them. Once an attitude is expressed as behavior, we can begin to change it. As you define what makes up Heather's bad attitude, I tell her parents, give your descriptions the "stranger test." Would a stranger be able to picture what you mean when you describe these bad attitude behaviors? Sometimes I draw a circle to represent bad attitude and ask parents to tell me what specific behaviors go inside the circle, which some parents find easier to do.

Then, once you've described the behaviors, think about positive opposites. For example:

Bad Attitude Behavior	Positive Opposite
Nastiness (*Are we eating that crap again?*)	Say nice things
Sarcastic tone when responding to parent	Good tone
Slouching and looking away	Stand straight, face who you're talking to
Eye-rolling	Look at me
Little tones, clicks, noises of disgust	Speak clearly and politely
Gestures: elaborate shrugging, waving you off	Show respect
Muttered nasty comments you can't quite hear	Speak clearly, say nice things

(And, in many of these cases, getting Heather to simply walk away silently would be a great positive opposite, highly preferable to many of the bad attitude behaviors listed above.)

The next step is to set up a point system to reward the right behaviors. But now, though, the chart keeping track of points should not be prominently posted, as it was when working with younger children. Even though it might be useful to increase Heather's awareness of the point chart by posting it prominently, I tell her parents, it's better on balance to put it where only Heather and you know about it. Here's why. Posting the point chart conspicuously would make everyone more aware of the chart, but now it has the side effect of embarrassment, which undermines its effectiveness. We take note of the older child's stronger tendency toward embarrassment in other ways, too. For instance, praise and effusiveness are still important and they still work, but we want to minimize the side effect of embarrassment, so we soft-pedal them. For many preadolescents, the very fact that a parent is doing or saying something makes it suspect and potentially embarrassing, so a lighter touch on the parents' part is in order.

Also, as I suggested above, you might find it more effective to skip the middle stage of awarding points with which to buy rewards and just connect desired behavior directly to rewards. You do this, you get that.

I explain to Heather's parents that probably the most effective way to begin, especially if her bad attitude is a major problem, is first to specify a particular period of the day in which to eliminate particular unwanted behaviors. So, for instance, no eye-rolling or sarcastic comments between 5:00 and 8:00 P.M. Once you've eliminated the unwanted behavior during that limited period, you can expand it.

As for ground rules, if you're working on eliminating sarcasm, for instance, you need to make very clear to Heather your standard of judgment. You can explain to her that if you say it's sarcastic, then it counts as sarcastic. Or, if you like, you can decide that if there's any doubt about whether a comment is sarcastic, she should repeat what she said, so that you can decide whether it's sarcastic or not. You don't want to leave too much leeway for her to argue that something she said was not sarcastic, but shaping is not a bad idea here. (For a quick refresher on shaping, see chapter 2.) For instance, if she's constantly making sarcastic comments in an exaggerated nasty tone, a sarcastic statement in a nonsarcastic tone is a step in the right direction, as is a nonsarcastic statement in a sarcastic tone. Or, if she normally shouts, a sarcastic statement in a quiet voice is a step in the right direction. Reward the steps — which is what shaping is — and work toward the whole behavior: nonsarcastic statements in a nonsarcastic tone.

Simulated practice can be a big help in this case. You may find it a little daunting to imagine presenting simulated practice to your preadolescent child, so let me give you a sample. You go to Heather during a calm moment and tell her, *There's a new point chart I want to tell you about. You don't have to work with me if you don't want to* — making it a choice is a setting-up event that takes off the pressure while engaging her interest — *but I have a list here with points you can earn to use on makeup, downloads for your iPod, or a gift certificate for the mall. And if you want we can select a big activity like a concert or a sleepover that you can earn.* This is the "rocket ship to the moon" component for saving up for a bigger reward while earning smaller ones, although she's well past the age at which we'd call it that. *You can let me know if there are more things you want to add. Here's how it works: during the week I'm going to ask you to practice with me on talking nicely. If you practice, you get two points. That's just for practicing at all. If the practice goes well, that's two more points. I will help you to make sure you get as many points as possible.*

Now show her how it will play out. *It'll go like this. I'll say, "Heather, let's practice." Then I come over to you and — this is just pretend — say something to you that might make you a little mad. I'll ask about homework, or about whether you're off the phone yet, something like that, the kind of thing that tends to make you mad. If you immediately start this practice with me right then, that's two points. If you finish the practice, you get two more points. To get those two points for finishing the practice, you will need to answer nicely, with a nice tone of voice. If you make a face, shake your head like you don't want to talk, or say something sarcastic or nasty, you don't get the two points for finishing the practice. But even if you say something like, "No, thanks," or "Can we do it later?" as long as you say it nicely, you get the points.*

Now go right into a simulation with her, and take the opportunity to reverse roles momentarily, like this: *Let me show you. Pretend that you are me and I'm you, and ask me to do something I don't like to do.* Heather says, "Start your homework now because it'll be time for dinner pretty soon." You whisper, not in character as Heather, *Here's an answer that would get you the points,* and then, with a cheery tone and a smile, model a good answer for Heather: *"Mom, is it okay if I take a shower now instead, and do the homework after dinner?" That would earn you two points right there. I used a friendly tone of voice, I didn't say "shut up" or anything like that* (it's good to be specific here, detailing what speaking nicely really means). *Now let's switch back, and you take a turn as you. I'll ask you to do something, and you try to give a nice answer, even if you don't mean it.* (You just gave a good prompt, very close to the behavior you want her to do.)

"Heather, would you come down and help me set the table?" Remember, this is just pretend. Heather, playing along, says, "Okay, Mom, I'm coming." It sounds tentative, and kind of flat, but definitely not sarcastic. So it's time to praise her, and be specific. *That was very good. You smiled, you didn't have your arms folded or look angry. You would have gotten points for that if we had already started the program. Actually, that was so good that let's count it as starting the program and give you four points, two for practicing at all and two for such a good response. We'll practice like this once a day, and I'll let you know when it's coming, so you're not surprised.*

Soon after, add a bonus option: *The points are for practicing, but if you ever act this way in a real situation — say, your dad asks you to pass the food at the table and you pass it politely, and say, "Here, Dad," nicely — then you get six points right on the spot.* Once the program has started, if Heather says something sarcastic, you can calmly tell her, *You could have earned six points then. Maybe next time.* But don't do this more than once a day; otherwise, it becomes negative, a reprimand.

And remind yourself, as often as necessary, that this is all temporary. You won't have to be practicing or even rewarding the behavior for long.

Remember, too, that the early development of a positive-opposite behavior often seems insincere. It may seem that your child's just pretending to be nice to get the points, and not even pretending very convincingly. That's fine, for starters. The basic principle here is to get the desired behavior any way you can, then ingrain it and refine it through reinforced practice. As with a new exercise program, she may at first drag herself to do it, but in time, with enough repetition and reinforcement, she will come to want and need to do it.

As for the mechanics of the reward system itself, we're still working with our basics. There should be regular opportunities for smaller prizes, and periodic opportunities for bigger prizes. The prizes should be appropriate to her age, of course. Smaller prizes she can get with a few points might include extra computer or cell phone time, downloads, renting DVDs, cosmetics, earrings, henna tattoos, and privileges like choosing dinner menus or family activities. Bigger prizes she can work toward might include having friends over, going to a concert, partygoing, expeditions to activities she enjoys, and privileges that signify more freedom for her.

Older kids typically earn rewards that cost more money, which raises for many parents the question: *But are we then just paying our child to be good?* Another version is: *Aren't we just bribing her to be good?* The answer is no. Praise, adjusted to the age group, is still the most important reward, and points and the goodies for which they're cashed in are still secondary to praise. And keep in mind that we just use rewards temporarily, to make reinforced practice as attractive as possible during the relatively brief but intense period in which we're building up a desired behavior into a habit.

Swearing

Jimmy, a fourteen-year-old, particularly irritates his parents with his swearing. He doesn't swear at them, exactly, but he does curse around the house, not so much because he's angry or frustrated but because he thinks of it as a daring, independent, grown-up thing to do. He also curses at his eight-year-old brother, which his parents dislike in particular, because they fear that the little brother will imitate this behavior.

Many parents complain to me that their preteen or teenager swears too much. Often, by the way, it turns out that the parents swear, too, and are modeling that behavior for their child. Just getting the parents to quit often begins to address the child's problem. But in this case the parents don't swear; it's just Jimmy.

If you want to cut down his swearing or cut it out entirely, it pays to first make sure that everybody knows what counts as swearing. If there's doubt, make a list. Yes, of course, some words make that list without breaking a sweat, but others may inhabit a gray area. Does "sucks" count as swearing in your household? How about "damn" or "Christ"? It depends on the household. But if there's any doubt, make a list of words that count as swearing. That will make things clear to all.

You may also need to establish a ground rule about what constitutes *saying* a swear word. For instance, one way to define it might be: *If I can hear it, it's swearing, even if you say it under your breath.*

The other preliminary decision to make is whether or not to have a separate standard for behavior in public. In other words, will you tolerate more — or less — at home than you will in front of people who aren't members of your family, or do you want to establish one rule for all situations?

Once you've made your preliminary decisions about standards, you can proceed with a basic point chart, as we've done before, with points awarded for not swearing — or, thinking positive-oppositely, for using good language. If your child does not swear much to begin with, you can award points for whole days without profanity. But if he swears a lot, you might begin by picking a period of the day in which no swearing is allowed: for instance, that same 5:00 to 8:00 P.M. period we first used for eliminating Heather's bad attitude behaviors. Once your child can consistently get through that piece of the day without swearing, you can expand it.

When in doubt, aim to get control over a smaller time period and extend it later. The research backs up this approach. Parents might argue, *But he still swears in the morning;* however, research shows that it's relatively easier to extend a desired behavior to other situations once you achieve control in one situation. If your child no longer swears in the afternoon, you should be able to successfully extend the program to the morning.

Messy Room

You wouldn't think that a messy room is that big a deal. Compared to the serious crises that bring some families to my clinic — violence, major problems with the law, expulsion from school, clinical diagnoses — the mere fact of clutter or even real filth doesn't appear to merit attention. But a messy room is a typical flashpoint around which household conflicts grow. These conflicts are about things that really matter to kids and parents, like autonomy and respect and the rights of the individual in relation to the family, and they can escalate into serious business. So let's talk about messy rooms.

Picture an amazingly, astonishingly messy room. The new clothes that you bought for your child — the not-inexpensive clothes she relentlessly lobbied for — are carelessly strewn on the floor, mixed in with old clothes, jewelry, cosmetics, empty water bottles, magazines, CDs, DVDs, schoolbooks, magazines, athletic equipment, and less identifiable junk. You have to take the floor's existence on faith, because you literally cannot see it for all the mess in the way.

Now, we can fairly easily apply our familiar method to this problem. Messiness is a habit, a set of behaviors, so it would not be difficult to define a positive opposite of mess-making, set up a system of rewards for cleaning up, and gradually replace that habit with a better one. Having read the book this far, you could set up this program with no trouble.

But let's first ask a basic question: *Why focus on the messiness of your child's room?* There may be good reasons to. For instance, it may be that your child never has presentable clothes to wear because they pile up dirty on his floor, or that his habit of throwing once-worn clothes on the floor forces you to do twice as much laundry as necessary to keep him from looking as if he's been run over by an industrial-strength wrinkler. Or his room could present a real sanitation problem, if there are, for example, dirty dishes or discarded food in there. Maybe there aren't enough clean forks in the house because they're all on his floor, in empty TV dinner trays.

These are significant matters that would need to be addressed right away, but what if the problem is not presentable clothing or sanitation or the household fork supply but just sloppiness? You could fix it, probably, but is it really that big a deal?

When you ask yourself, *Why focus on it?*, a question that comes up much more often with preadolescents than with younger children, you may decide that it's not worth addressing the problem. Or you may find that asking, *Why focus on it?* helps you to narrow down the problem to those elements that really do need to be addressed. Some aspects of a sloppy room may really be nonnegotiable: candles and incense near flammable material, for instance, or food or some other potential biohazard, or, say, the extended family of rats busily erecting a condominium out of DVD boxes on the bedside table. If the mess is dangerous, if there are consequences for other people in the household, then it's certainly worth addressing.

And, guided by your own answer to *Why focus on it?*, be prepared to trade an inessential for an essential. Let her keep her clothes on the floor if she cleans up all of the food mess as soon as she makes it. Let him leave his CDs wherever he likes if he agrees to keep his electric guitar (on which, after he begged for months on end, you spent several hundred dollars last Christmas) on its stand and not where it's likely to be stepped on.

Parents frequently respond to *Why focus on it?* by expressing a worry that if they let their child be sloppy in her room, she will be sloppy everywhere: in her personal appearance, in her schoolwork, in her career. They have fantasies about her getting fired in middle age for having a messy office. But when it comes to messiness, the slippery slope argument is a fallacy. Having a messy room is an identifiable stage that tends to appear in adolescence and then go away. Most people seem to return to or rise to some basic standard of neatness after the messy interlude of the preteen and teen years. Some people are extremely tidy, even as children, and if that's the case with your child, she will eventually come back to that neatness. For those who are not so compulsively tidy, the end of adolescence usually ushers in at least a moderate rise from extreme messiness to normal clutter.

The point here is that if your preadolescent child keeps herself reasonably clean and presentable, and if the problem's not so severe that it's causing other problems, you might consider letting slide the messiness of her room as a stage she's going through. Yes, it may well get worse in the adolescent years. Yes, every parent will always have a story of an adult who's a genuine slob to back up the claim that not everybody recovers from adolescent messiness, but those cases are exceptions. Really, how many adults do you know who have rooms like your kid's? Not many. They grew out of it. So why move heaven and earth — and increase the amount of conflict in the house, and use up energy and goodwill perhaps better reserved for more significant matters — to correct a problem that will almost certainly self-correct?

I realize that parents can have other reasons to object to a child's messy room. It could be that you're very tidy people, and you just can't abide it. That's a legitimate complaint, but recognize that it's not about any abnormal behavior on the part of your child. Be straight about it with your child. Tell her that you can't live with such a mess in the house, and that together you're going to have to compromise on some middle ground between your standards (*No mess ever, anywhere*) and your child's (*Let the clothes fall where they may*). As you work out the compromise, consider that especially if the rest of your house is neat, your child's messy room is an expression of autonomy and independence, normal for her stage of development. You'll want to try to let a little more freedom emerge in your home as your child gets older, and giving her more control of her domain early on is one way to do it. As before, choose carefully the behaviors about which you want to dig in your heels. If messiness is one of them, at least recognize that it may not belong in the same category of urgency as things that can lead to permanent consequences — for instance, those candles and incense right under the curtains.

After School on His Own

On weekdays, Ty gets home before his parents do. He's thirteen, and an attractive child, with a smile and a sparkle that conveys friendliness. He's a few pounds overweight, but his parents do not regard this as a problem. There's not much junk food in the house, so they're not worried about what he'll eat when he's home alone. But they are concerned about Ty being on his own for several hours, and they want him to check in with them. In addition, he has homework to do and a few chores (setting the dinner table is the main one) that don't always get done. His parents want to make sure that he's okay and that he's doing what he should be doing, so they frequently call to check on him and remind him of his duties. Ty, valuing this brief but meaningful daily stretch of being in charge of himself, resents the monitoring as "treating me like a baby" and the reminders as "nagging." The solution, I tell Ty's parents, is to compromise on an arrangement that allows you to check up on him without making him feel that you're clinging to him or infantilizing him.

For instance, you can set it up so that he, not you, makes the calls. He has to call one parent when he gets home, and he should call from the home phone, not his cell phone (if you have caller ID at the office or on your cell, you can make sure of this). You can give this call a stated purpose: for example, he has to tell you what his homework assignments are. Making the call earns him a point on his point chart. Accomplishing his daily tasks while he's home alone — homework, chores — earns him more points. Then he can call when the tasks are done to say that they're done, and he gets points for making that call, too.

When he calls, offer some understated praise for his having called (*It's good you called, Ty; that's just what we agreed on*) and also be sure to give generously of your attention and interest during the call. You're not just checking up on him; if he wants to talk about his homework, his day, whatever's on his mind, this is an excuse to do it. We're always aiming to reinforce reasonableness and engagement with the family, and we're also trying to meet a child's evolving needs, which grow more complex over time. With a younger child, enthusiastic praise *is* attention, but with a preadolescent (and, again, it's hard to pin down an exact age, but I mean when your child has crossed the line to thinking about being cool, referring to friends as primary models for behavior, and so on) you want to lighten up on the effusiveness of the praise and give more attention to what he has to say.

It's not always possible to linger on the phone with him. You're at work, after all. He may call to say he's home, but you're busy. So offer a quick word of praise for having called you, tell him you're busy, and tell him you'll call back. When you do call back (and it's important that you model being as good as your word and do in fact call back), offer another word of praise and ask about his day.

And, as I've said before, resist the urge to be stingy with points. The larger purpose of points and praise and the whole program is to reinforce good habits. Look for opportunities to do that, rather than for reasons not to award points.

Practicing an Instrument

Dina has always been musical. She has taken classical piano lessons for years. Now that she's twelve — and, at least in terms of her social relations and physical maturity, a particularly advanced twelve — she also wants to write her own songs and maybe get into jazz. She still takes piano lessons once a week, and she likes her teacher, but the teacher says that Dina has to practice more. She has talent, but she rarely practices, and when she does sit down, she leaves the TV on and fools around, mostly picking out pieces that are not related to the lesson. Her parents would like her to really practice, even if just for a short while, every day. They don't want to be ogres about it, but they're confident that if she works a little at music now she will reap the rewards for the rest of her life, even if she eventually decides to abandon classical piano for other kinds of music.

As you may have surmised, this is a fairly straightforward matter, the kind of habit-building that my method is especially well suited to achieve. It's a shaping job, technically speaking.

In order to shape good practice habits, you first need to be very clear with Dina about what counts as practicing. For example, she gets a point for telling you her assignment, and another point for sitting down at the piano, then another point for, say, every ten minutes of practicing. You can build in a bottom limit, though. For instance, she has to practice for twenty minutes to get two points; she doesn't get a point at all if she only practices for ten. Also, practicing means working on the assignment, not messing around on the keyboard. If she strays from real practicing during practice time, you can offer one prompt to remind her about the standard for practicing, but no more. After that, she's either going to get the points or she's not. But remember to praise any part of what she did well, whether or not she earns the points.

Antecedents also matter here. Turning off the TV, sitting down to play, running through a finger exercise before she tackles the day's assignment — these are all setting-up events that set the stage for real practice.

Negotiating

Your fourteen-year-old son has a friend who's a few years older and already has his driver's license. Your son wants to go to a big party with his friend next weekend, and the friend says that he'll drive. How to handle this? This is a typical problem, in which two different and often opposed principles come together: the child's sense of freedom and justice (which boils down to *You owe me this*), and the parents' concern about safety (which often takes the form of *Freedom won't do you any good if you're badly hurt or dead, so I have to make sure that you're safe, even if it means making decisions that outrage your sense of freedom and justice*).

You have decided that there's no way your son is riding to and from the party with this other boy behind the wheel. He's a new driver, it will be dark out, there could well be drinking at the party — it's not going to happen. But there's still an opportunity to negotiate, rather than laying down the law. Your attitude should be: *Let's work on it. Let's think of ways that we can make it so you get some of what you want and my concerns are addressed.* Preadolescents and adolescents often present their parents with tricky yes/no scenarios (*Can I drive to the party with my friend or not?*), and the safety-first answer may well be *Not in a million years,* but *Not in a million years* tends to produce escape and defiance, fraying the family's communal bond and, in the long run, leading to more behavior problems. And be realistic. Your son will probably be riding to parties with friends in just a couple of years, which is a lot fewer than a million, so make an investment now in that fast-approaching future. Negotiation is good for its own sake. Parents should look for ways to give up control, and kids should look for ways to address their parents' concerns.

So turn your child's yes/no question into a negotiation: *I know you want this, but I'm concerned about safety, so let's talk about some options. One solution is that you get to go to the party, but I drive you, or I can drop off and your friend's parents can pick up.* But your son doesn't just want to go to the party; he wants to ride with his friend with no adults in the car. So split the desires into two separate occasions. If you're worried about the possibility of drinking and driving, as well as a novice driver driving at night, you can try something like, *I have to drive you to the party, but you can drive by yourself with your friend during the day to the mall, as long as there's no partying. But if there's ever any drinking or drugs connected to using the car, you'll lose the privilege of driving anywhere with him or any other friend without an adult.* None of these is ideal, from his point of view or yours, but they're all examples of compromises between his priorities and yours. And, of course, if it helps to involve the other boy's parents in the deal-making and it's possible to do that, that may give you other options for compromises that are more constructive than either giving in or saying no.

Here, we're largely out of the realm of positive opposites, point charts, and the like. They're not the solution to everything. But throughout the process of negotiation, you should be aware that you're attending to and reinforcing reasonableness whenever you see any sign of it in your child. In fact, during the conversation you can jump momentarily out of negotiating mode to say, *This is good. We're working this out, and we're not arguing about it.* So reinforcement is still going on, even without the usual routines of point charts and so on.

In general, when dealing with a preteen or teenager, you want to express interest in good behavior, attend to and reinforce reasonableness whenever he displays it, and give him autonomy and freedom in the safest possible way. If you still want to catch your child being good, now try to catch your child being reasonable as well. And remember to be reasonable yourself.

The real challenge at this age is to maintain good contact with a child, or to break through and reestablish it. When you're thinking about rewards, try to emphasize prosocial reinforcers — rewards that bring the child into the community of the family, or some other, larger community. So a privilege such as choosing the menu for a family dinner or choosing where the family goes for a weekend outing will reinforce the family's community feeling and reinforce the child's sense of belonging. *We'll go to the game together* is much better than what you might do with a younger child, just letting him reach into a grab bag for his prize. Take opportunities to include the child in the family and to include yourself in your child's world.

Blowups and Everyday Life

Preadolescence will flow into adolescence, and the conflicts of the preadolescent years may intensify. There will likely be moments of total breakdown and crisis between you and your adolescent child —

moments in which, for instance, you say, *You're not going to that party,* and your child says, *I'm going to that party, and you can go to hell.* There may be shouting, screaming, storming out, even physical confrontation. You'll do your best not to let things go that far, but blowups happen in even the closest and warmest families, and adolescence brings them on. When a blowup happens, you're not going to be thinking, *Maybe a point chart would help,* but you can still draw upon the concepts and the method I've been teaching you.

It's not realistic to treat these moments of crisis as immediate opportunities for your child to learn and grow. In the short term, you're just trying to get through the blowup with minimal damage, making sure that nobody gets hurt. Sometimes you do have to let a child storm out and cool off; sometimes *you* have to cool off; and, yes, sometimes the situation gets so completely out of hand that you really fear somebody's going to get hurt (let's say your child is hell-bent on riding to a party with a friend who has been drinking), and you have to do something drastic like call the police. It can happen, and, as I said, in the short run you do what you have to do to get through the crisis. Accept that it will be ugly and messy, try not to do anything unnecessarily dramatic, don't try to clean up the mess until the blowup is over, and resist the temptation to restart the battle when it's winding down. Kids tend to mope a little and then act as if nothing ever happened, but parents tend to dwell on a conflict, replay it, and revisit their hurt feelings and anger. Resist. Even if you were clearly in the right, try to move on.

When the blowup is over and everybody has calmed down a little, it's time to think about what caused the crisis and how to avoid another. From a better-parenting point of view, these moments of crisis are about what's going to happen next (how to prevent this situation from recurring) and about what already happened (what led up to it). Perhaps the most important thing to consider, in this regard, is your daily life with your child. When a blowup comes, everything you did wrong comes back to haunt you: *I've been snapping at my kid and not listening to him, I haven't taught him enough respect for his parents, I've been so inconsistent about rules that he doesn't know where the limits are,* and so on. But, conversely, when you're ready to throw up your hands and say, *I can't deal with this kid,* that's when the accumulated positives of the child's relationship to you can come back to save you. That's the time to reap the benefits of your investment of what I call "quantity time" (which is far more important than so-called quality time), and all of your discussions (even the uncomfortable ones) in which you both listened and spoke your mind, and every life lesson and constructive compromise and simple hug or encouraging word.

All of that steadily built-up groundwork makes you more effective as a parent. If a recent blowup shows you that you need to shore up that groundwork, devote your energy to doing that as a way to strengthen the bond between yourself and your child, which will serve you well the next time a crisis is brewing. And if the groundwork is already strong, be confident that there's a solid basis for your attempts to change your child's behavior (and your own), and get right back to work with your child. Once you've gotten through the blowup, get back to fundamentals. The simple fact of a blowup doesn't mean that all is lost.

To cite an extreme analogy, the research shows us that addicts often relapse, but that the relapse usually isn't the end of the treatment. Most addicts who relapse can still complete the treatment and get better. The relapse is a big fall, a crisis, but you can then get up and work on getting back to a state in which a relapse is unlikely to happen. Similarly, we don't have a panacea that will work in every situation to improve a child's behavior, but the research shows that we do know how to reduce the possibility that the blowup will happen next time. For you, it comes down to good parental habits. That's what you can do.

And remember, too, that explaining things to your child may have some value — it's important to keep the lines of communication open as well — but that explanation has proven to be a fairly weak method for changing behavior. Parents usually believe that everything would be okay if they could somehow make their child see things from their point of view, but it's a fantasy. Almost by definition, an adolescent can't see a situation from her parents' point of view, and vice versa: parents who think that they remember just what it was like to be an adolescent are fooling themselves. Accept that there are going to be fundamental differences in point of view. So even if you could somehow get your child to see things from your point of view, that probably wouldn't change his behavior very much. Rely on re-inforced practice — not explanation — as the strongest method for changing behavior.

But bear in mind, too, that changing behavior is only part of the job. This is never more important to recognize than when dealing with a preadolescent or adolescent. This chapter emphasizes that when dealing with a defiant preadolescent, even while we're working on changing this or that specific behavior, we are more generally working to keep the child in the fold of the family as her freedom grows. You have resources to draw upon in doing that work. Common sense may often be wrong, and science may often seem aloof from the real problems of real families, but we can draw upon the best of both and try to combine them. A battlefield atmosphere in a household makes everything seem more dire and urgent, but we're trying to use the best of common sense *and* science to get you back on the field — not to win the battles but to find ways to engage in fewer of them.

6

Punishment

The Most Misunderstood, Misused, and
Overused Tool in the Parental Toolbox

Some families who come to my clinic are eager to punish and to learn more about new ways to punish. One mom, who was there because her seven-year-old boy had uncontrollable tantrums at home, in the car, in stores, and at restaurants, said in the middle of our first session, "When do we get to the punishment? That's the part I really want." Her son would lose it and make a huge scene over something like what he was going to eat and drink at a restaurant, and she could not regain civility or control. She thought that all she needed was a special new way to punish. Three sessions later, when I mentioned that we were going to talk about and practice time-outs (our first discussion of punishment), she said, "Oh, great! This is what I came for."

This mother was not a bloodthirsty tyrant, but, like many parents, she was far more responsive to misbehavior than to good behavior, and she thought of punishment as the primary way to respond to unwanted behavior. Punishment is the only tool in many parents' toolbox — and they reach for their toolbox only when they see their child's behavior as in need of repair. When we urge parents to catch the child being good, to make a point of noticing and rewarding good behavior, we're trying to correct for the human tendency to give more attention to negative than to positive stimuli. In a number of research studies, individuals who won more than they lost in a game, or who made more than they lost in the stock market, still devoted more attention to their losses. Earlier, I called this the hardwired Eeyore in us all. When it comes to raising children, this inner Eeyore primes parents to ignore good behavior, instead devoting most of their energy to recognizing misbehavior and reacting to it. Far too often, that reaction takes the form of punishment.

Changing this mindset is one of our most important tasks.

Punishment teaches what not to do. It does not teach what to do. Punishment suppresses the unwanted behavior for a moment, but the behavior resurfaces when the opportunity comes up again, since no positive behavior has been developed to replace it. If you punish your child for fighting with her brother, it will indeed stop this fight. The next time there's a conflict between them, though, fighting will still be the first item in your daughter's repertoire, the default setting. You haven't done anything about changing that. Explaining that fighting is bad won't change that state of affairs, either. You have to develop another way of behaving — the positive opposite — to get another response locked in.

So punishment can never be the centerpiece of a program to change behavior. At best, it can be a small but effective addition to such a program. For most parents, who too often turn to punishment as their first and perhaps only way to address unwanted behavior, using punishment properly means fundamentally changing the way they think about it.

If you have a problem with your child's behavior, your first thought should be: *Can I let this go, because it will probably drop out and not be a problem in a month or two? Does the behavior not really do any harm?* If the answer is yes, let it go. But if your answer is *No way can I let this go!,* let the five previous chapters of this book guide you in thinking right away of positive opposites and creating a program (praise, points, other rewards) to shape this positive opposite behavior in place of the unwanted behavior. Both of these responses — *Can I let it go?* and *How can I build up the positive opposite?* — should come *before* thoughts of punishment.

Punishment is a widely misunderstood, chronically misused, and wildly overused method for changing behavior, but when properly employed it can be effective, within limits. So in this chapter I want to talk about using it properly and about why it's so often used improperly.

Multiple Motives Lead to Punishment Myths

Parents don't punish just to change their child's behavior. They typically have more than one motive when they punish. They punish out of a sense of justice, or so the child will learn to respect authority, or in order to be consistent, or to send the right message about what's tolerated, and so on. I understand that all of these motives may be valid in their own right, but let's separate them from the effort to change behavior, which is what this book is all about. When I explain to parents that the research shows clearly that a one-minute time-out is sufficient for changing behavior and that we gain nothing but problems with much longer durations, they respond, "But you can't give just a one-minute time-out for *that*" — when *that* is, say, breaking a lamp, or punching a sibling, or running into traffic. Their sense of justice and proportion is outraged because the sentence doesn't seem to fit the crime, and I understand that.

Right now, I tell them, let's work to change the behavior, and we'll teach the other lessons a different time. Still, I realize that sometimes we have to strike a bargain. If a one-minute time-out would work best to change behavior but the parent thinks that one minute doesn't fit the crime, we can compromise on a ten-minute time-out. I just want the parent to realize that nine of those minutes don't help with behavior change, although they probably don't hurt much either. So, let's regard the first minute of the time-out as sufficient to change behavior, and the nine minutes that follow as a concession to the parent's sense of justice. Of such bargains is a real-world behavior-change program made.

But parents do hold other beliefs about punishment that might actually get in the way of changing behavior, and I want to address them. The main villain is "Spare the rod, spoil the child," a belief that can undermine any program for changing behavior by using positive reinforcement. I'll have more to say later about that one.

Another set of beliefs has to do with using punishment as a teaching tool to inculcate respect for authority or as a way to demonstrate who's in control. I could go on at length to challenge the assumptions behind such goals, but, for present purposes, the greater problem is the means parents usually use to achieve them. More often than not, the parent uses "respect" or "control" as a rationale for harsh, rigid, uncompromising, and authoritarian interventions (does *Because I said so* sound familiar?). Ironically, such interventions have an effect that's the reverse of their stated intent. A parent's measured, nonimpulsive, nonheated responses will earn respect, not the opposite. Using physical power, shouting, and other forceful expressions of authority may oblige a child to comply, but only until the child can be away from the parent's immediate control. Also, the child will become harsh or more harsh with peers, and more "out of control" with other authority figures like teachers and coaches. The harder you press down on the child, the more likely she is to slip from your grasp — your parental influence, or, if you prefer, your "control."

Parents also have a tendency to misrecognize a punished child's crying, wailing, and heartfelt cries of *I'm sorry* as reliable signs that the punishment is working. They aren't. They are only markers of how upset the child is. Don't confuse them with effective behavior change or even with teaching lessons about who's in charge or about justice. And making the child upset might actually get in the way of changing behavior or the lessons you think you are teaching. If you measure the success of a punishment by how upset or remorseful it seems to make your child (have you, for instance, ever said something like, *You better be sorry!* to a wailing child?), you're probably making both of your lives far more difficult and unpleasant than they need to be, and none of this is likely to change your child's behavior for the better.

Effects and Side Effects of Punishment

What happens when a child is punished?

As we've seen, the effect of punishment is immediate but transient. You shout or hit or take something away and the unwanted behavior stops — *hallelujah!* — but the punishment does not make the behavior less likely to recur in the near future. Still, the parent experiences the sequence of punishment and temporary cessation of the bad behavior as a kind of miracle on a less than rational level. Parents feel that punishment is effective, when at best all it's doing is briefly deferring the child's bad behavior. That's at best, but there's also something much more pernicious going on. The parent's behavior is being shaped in a harmful way as she falls into what I described in chapter 1 as the "punishment trap." The parent punishes, the behavior stops. She punishes, the behavior stops. Every time it happens, her tendency to punish is reinforced. Pretty soon, she's punishing more, and more harshly, to achieve the same effect as before.

That's because children have an amazing capacity to adapt to punishment. Typically, a parent has to increase the severity and frequency of a punishment to achieve even the immediate effect it achieved the first time. What worked before may not work as well or at all. The natural escalation of punishment occurs as parents are unwittingly shaped: a little punishment was enough to accomplish the first couple of suppressions of the behavior, but now the child is holding out for more before he shows that same suppression. Children are not doing this in any strategic, conscious way, which we can infer because it's not just humans who adapt to punishment like this. Other mammals do it, too.

For all its limitations, punishment can indeed work, and when it does work that tends to become evident very quickly. If punishment is going to change behavior in a lasting way, you will see lower rates of the unwanted behavior soon. If you do not see a rate change right away, give it up. By "rate change," I mean not just an immediate suppression of the unwanted behavior right when you punish it, but a drop-off in how often the behavior recurs, and thus in how often you have to punish it.

All of these effects are changed if there is a positive reinforcement program that develops the positive opposite. If such a program is in place, studies show that mild and properly used punishment slightly speeds up the process of replacing unwanted behavior with its positive opposite. I'll say more about this in a minute.

Punishment can fail for many reasons. One of them is that the reward for misbehaving is often more immediate and reliable than the punishment. A look at the criminal justice system's normal operation makes that clear. Punishment ought to happen right away every time the unwanted behavior occurs, but the opposite is more often the case. The rewards for misbehavior are immediate, positively reinforcing that misbehavior, and the punishment is more delayed and therefore ineffective. If you steal, you get to have what you stole right away. If you hurt somebody, that person acts submissively toward you right away. You are therefore reinforced in the bad behavior by an immediate reward. If you experience a delayed punishing consequence — three weeks after you steal you are arrested, and then three months later you are tried, and then you're sentenced to some parole time — that punishment is doomed to failure as a method for changing behavior. One must eliminate the immediate reinforcer for the punished behavior, if possible, and that's hard to do.

Or think of the rewards of eating a double chocolate cream pie: the immediate joys of flavor and visual stimulation, a sense of great fullness and satisfaction. The punishing consequences — weight gain, raised cholesterol levels, self-recrimination — are delayed. That's why it's hard for people to control themselves when they eat desserts. It would be much easier for them to control themselves if the rewards and punishments occurred in reverse order: that is, if it took weeks or months for the flavor to reach your taste buds, but within seconds of finishing your last bite of dessert you were subject to instantaneous weight gain, crushing guilt, and perhaps a mild heart attack.

But there's something more insidious about punishment's effect than simply failing to change behavior for the better. Punishment also tends to produce unwanted side effects that have no relation to suppressing unwanted behavior and can make a parent's task far more difficult, if not impossible.

These side effects begin with emotional reactions. A punished child cries, becomes angry, upset, and so on, which will make any attempt to change the child's behavior less likely to succeed. We don't want parents to make the mistake of reading this emotional reaction to punishment as a sign that it is right, just, and effective. When they do misread punishment in this way, they tend to punish in order to produce that emotional reaction — for example, to punish until the child screams, cries, or begs forgiveness. Since there's almost no chance that such punishment will change behavior in any lasting way, what they're doing is equivalent to choosing the dose of a medication by going for the worst possible side effects with no regard to whether it does anything to cure an illness. And the unpleasantness of the experience of being punished drives the child to get away from the parent, so the more emotional the child's reaction, the more he will escape and avoid the parent.

This escape and avoidance, often inspired by strong emotional reactions, is another important side effect. Children tend to avoid interacting with a punishing agent — parents, teachers, whoever it might be — and to minimize the time they are obliged to spend with him or her. This is not good for your relationship to your child, especially if you depend heavily on punishment, and it will undermine even a well-designed program for changing behavior. For one thing, the effectiveness of a parent's praise, which is one of the main tools we use to change behavior, depends in part on the parent's relationship to the child. By driving a wedge between parent and child, harsh and frequent punishment will reduce the effectiveness of that parent's praise as a reward for good behavior. And more generally, for reasons that reach well beyond any program for changing his behavior, we want the child to come to his parents for advice, help, and comfort. Associating a parent with escape and avoidance undermines this.

Physical punishment is likely to lead a child to display increased aggression against you or, more likely, his peers. This can take the form of what's called "modeled punishment," meaning that children tend to "punish" their peers in the way that they are punished. The studies show that children who are frequently hit, in particular, are much more aggressive with other children.

Finally, there's the side effect on your own behavior: you're likely to punish more, and more harshly, over time. When you fall into the punishment trap, your own behavior as a parent is reinforced, and this will keep you punishing, probably on an escalating curve of severity and frequency, even if the child's behaviors don't change over time. The side effects will multiply, and the situation will get worse.

How to Punish

I hope that by now you have newfound respect for how far-reaching and often unhelpful the effects of punishment can be. But that doesn't mean giving up on punishment as a useful tool. It can still be an effective addition to your repertoire of ways to improve your child's behavior. You just have to use it properly and with great care. Let's talk about how to do that.

   1. *Because punishment teaches a child what not to do but doesn't teach what to do, any punishment should be combined with a reinforcement program that encourages a positive opposite or otherwise desirable behavior that competes with the unwanted behavior.* This is the single most critical point to make about punishment. If you punish unwanted behavior without reinforcing its positive opposite, the punishment won't work to change the behavior in any lasting way. However, if you combine punishment with reinforcement of the behavior you do want, that same punishment will be effective. The research shows that a mild punishment will be more effective than a severe one if the mild one is supported by positive reinforcement of a desirable behavior to replace the unwanted one.

   There's a basic tension to reckon with when we discuss punishment. On the one hand, while most parents don't really want to hit their kids, they do tend to believe in some version of "Spare the rod, spoil the child." They believe that punishment is important in its own right and that to fail to punish bad behavior is to condone it. They feel (for moral and other reasons) that they can't ignore bad behavior, either, even when ignoring it would extinguish it more effectively than punishing it would. On the other hand, B. F. Skinner, one of the founding fathers of the study of behavior, famously said, "Never punish." What he meant was that punishment can have negative side effects and that the surest path to changing behavior is to reward the desired behavior — that is, to pursue a program of positive reinforcement.

   Working with parents at my clinic, I find myself trying to navigate between "Never punish" and "Spare the rod, spoil the child." I have to arrive at some kind of compromise between the two extremes with each set of parents I work with, even though in a perfect world I would prefer never to punish and to change behavior just with positive reinforcement. It's clear to me, after more than three decades of working with thousands of children and parents and reading the relevant psychological research, that "Spare the rod, spoil the child" has done infinitely more harm than good in guiding parents' child-rearing practices.

But there's a catch here. It's not true that punishment never effects lasting change in behavior. If two positive reinforcement programs are the same and you add very mild and properly used punishment to one, that whole program is a little more effective than the other. The difference might be slight, and maybe even not worth the bother, but it's there. So why did Skinner, who knew all this, say, "Never punish"? Because, as I've said, punishment usually escalates. Parents are human. They get mad, they allow themselves to be seduced by the apparent immediate success of punishment, and the punished child adapts to punishments and builds up resistance to them — all with the result that even parents who start out punishing mildly tend to punish more and more harshly over time. And once punishment begins to escalate and be applied less and less properly, you lose whatever slight incremental advantage that the punishment gave to one reinforcement program over the other, and the effectiveness of the program that features punishment falls further and further below the effectiveness of the program without any punishment at all.

2. Punishment should be mild and brief. What do I mean by "mild"? Parents' standards tend to be much harsher than science's when it comes to what qualifies as mild punishment. A brief time-out, a gentle reprimand, or even just a warning look qualifies, technically, as punishment. And often that's all it takes, if properly employed. Parental righteousness — acting like Moses chastising the Israelites — doesn't help. As a general rule, if your child is upset, crying, trembling, or startled by your punishment, it was not even close to mild. Take it down several notches. Right now, you're mostly teaching your child how wrath works, a lesson that your child's children won't be grateful to learn from him.

What do I mean by "brief"? An effective time-out for a younger child should last no more than two to five minutes. More is not better, at least when it comes to the usefulness of the time-out in changing behavior. If you're taking away points, stickers, or tokens, and the child can earn five of them in the course of a normal day, then taking away one is plenty. (You may ask yourself, *What good is it if I take away a point and at the end of the day she still has enough points to buy a reward?* But what happened the last time you got a traffic fine? Its effect on your behavior — next time, you're not going to take that right on red when there's a sign that says not to — did not depend on financially ruining you or not allowing you to use your car.)

If you are taking away a privilege — use of a toy, a bike, a cell phone — then take it away for one day and no more. Grounding your child for two weeks doesn't accomplish much. In general, grounding is not a particularly effective punishment. First, the effectiveness of punishment depends on the consequence (the punishment) immediately following the unwanted behavior, so that taking away a bike for a month is no more effective than taking it away for a day. The important part is taking away the privilege right after the offense, not how long it stays taken away. Second, if grounding takes a child away from friends, peers, socializing, and learning something, it can do harm in other ways, and of course it won't constructively address the original offense.

Effective punishment will almost always be much milder than justice would seem to demand. It almost never matches the crime. A two-minute time-out for a five-year-old who hit his sister hard enough to bloody her nose doesn't seem like enough, but that may well be all you need to change the behavior, if paired with reinforcement of a positive opposite behavior.

Let's say your twelve-year-old daughter breaks into school with friends and commits some petty vandalism: she tears down some posters that were created by fourth graders. Your initial reaction is to say, *You're grounded for the semester.* But think again. The actual punishment itself can be mild: no TV for a week, curfew at dark for a week, that kind of thing. Remember, the useful effect of punishment comes from the moment of taking away, not from adding more time after this initial moment. Then you can add in positive opposite behavior: chores at school to help put the damage right, written and personal apologies to the appropriate people. Restitution can go on for longer than a week. Part of her punishment can be to help the fourth graders make new posters to replace the ones she tore down. You're having her perform a positive opposite behavior during the punishment period and then extending it, as you do with a younger child when you have her help clean up the mess she made on the kitchen floor and then help clean up the whole house. You can also involve a twelve-year-old child in setting the terms of restitution. Lay out five choices for her and have her pick the three she will need to perform in order to get back whatever privileges you have withheld. But remember that creating opportunities to practice good, solid prosocial behavior is the goal, not public humiliation.

3. *Do not punish when you are angry.* That way, you're less likely to escalate and less likely to generate the side effects that reduce the effectiveness of punishment. Keep in mind that punishment is not vengeance. Being rational and calm models good behavior for your child. In fact, it teaches a lesson about behavior far more effectively than the punishment does. Being irrational and crazy-mad models behavior, too, and your child will pay close attention to that model. The way in which you respond to difficulty teaches your child how to respond to difficulty.

In response to this guideline, parents will sometimes say to me, "But people get mad in the real world, and my kid needs to deal with that." From the standpoint of changing behavior, learning to deal with people's anger is irrelevant, but I will accept that it's relevant from the standpoint of a child's education in being human. It's a mistake, however, to think that the moment of punishing your child is the particular moment for your child to learn about human beings in general or anger in particular. Do the feedback and message sending later, when it's uncluttered with strong emotions that make you careless and your child less receptive to the lesson. When you get careless, your judgment and your technique suffer. For instance, you find it harder to be specific. You tend to say things like, *You never ever listen to a single word I say!* or *Why are you so bad?* or *Why can't you be more like your sister?* Such sweeping comparative or global statements do no good. If you have to teach a lesson, stick to the specifics: what your child did wrong, why it isn't right. Reasoning with a child in the abstract — *What if everybody did what you did?* — isn't going to do much good either.

Also, parental anger does not really resemble other kinds of anger that a child will encounter in the world. First, your anger comes as a shock and even a betrayal in a way that other people's anger won't. There's nobody else out there who has raised this child, fed her, cared for her when she was sick, and otherwise loved her and met her every superdependent need in the way that you did. Second, social constraints place checks on most angry people your child will encounter; they'll know that she can enlist the help of passersby, call the cops, or sue them. Parents have much greater leeway to go ballistic. Because your child is far more powerless in her dealings with you than she will be with other angry people she encounters, she won't learn much in the way of life skills by coping with your anger. Third, check your own experience: you don't actually know people who were trained to deal well with their own anger by seeing their parents fly off the handle and punish them, nor do you know anybody who has been held back in life by not having such "reality training." Indeed, we're better prepared to cope with the strains of life when parents provide care in ways that no one else could: special attachment, special physical contact, special patience and reasoning. All of our foibles and imperfections teach our children lessons, but don't try to justify your own rage as reality training for your child.

Look, I understand that while it's easy to say, *Don't get mad,* it's sometimes very hard to practice what I preach. When your child pushes your buttons just right — when a little child runs away from you, when an older child swears at you or gives you the finger, when a child of any age says something like, *You don't care about me, you're just selfish* — you are likely to lose it. And who could blame you? It's only human. Mother Teresa herself would have smacked Gandhi upside the head if she was his mom and he acted like that. Children get better at pushing your buttons as they get older, growing ever more expert at making you so mad you can't see or think straight. Some parents will respond by shouting (*Don't you ever talk to me like that, after all I've done for you*) and some will hit, or shove, or manhandle, or come up with extreme off-the-cuff punishments (*You're grounded for six months*) that they can't possibly enforce or, if they somehow can enforce them, will do more harm than good. The blow to your gut from the child's provocation is wonderfully angry-making, and it leads to all kinds of extreme parental behavior in response.

It's hard to step back from such hot emotion, but do step back for a moment with me to recognize that button-pushing behavior depends on the parent's reaction, which is the reinforcer for it. If you can muster the self-possession to be faintly amused by age-appropriate attempts to get your goat, that's the path toward starving that behavior of the necessary reaction that will feed and nourish it. At my clinic, we sometimes train parents to respond to button-pushing behavior with a slight Mona Lisa–like smile that seems to work even better to extinguish the behavior than just walking away. Not getting mad — or cultivating the habit of avoiding a scene when you do get mad — really does set you on the shortest path to eliminating an irritating behavior.

4. *Do not use as a punishment task any activity that you wish to foster.* For instance, never assign reading or writing as a punishment (as in the old schoolroom standby, writing *I will not talk in class* a hundred times on the blackboard), since all you're teaching is that reading and writing are a punishment. In fact, take the opposite approach: make a trip to the bookstore one of the rewards your child can earn with good behavior.

More subtly, try not to use a punishment that will keep the child from positive social contacts with other adults or peers. Forbidding a child from going over to a friend's house might be a reasonable punishment, but if this is a friend whose family demonstrates reasonable behavior and values you'd like your child to emulate, it might be good for him to go there. Do not take a bicycle away, at least not for too long, if socializing with other bike-riders in the neighborhood is something the child needs because she does not get together with friends very much. If the punishment is very brief — no bike-riding for the rest of today, for instance — then this concern is mitigated.

5. *The ratio of praise for the positive opposite behavior to punishment for the unwanted behavior should be very one-sided, like 5 to 1*

— even though I will candidly admit that there's no research that justifies any specific number like 5 to 1. If you're trying to eliminate tantrums, find ways to praise not throwing a tantrum (or lessening the severity of the tantrum) at least five times as much as you punish tantrum-throwing. When parents come back to me and say, *I punish the bad behavior all the time but I can't praise the positive opposite because my child never does it,* I urge them to do simulations. Manufacture practice opportunities for the desired behavior to occur so that you can reward it. Because reinforced practice is the key to changing behavior, creating more opportunities to do the behavior makes a big difference.

6. *If you are punishing the same behavior a few times a day for more than one day, stop and change the program.* Such a steady stream of punishment will not work, will bring unwanted side effects, and makes family life miserable.

A flustered babysitter who was minding the headstrong four-year-old daughter of a colleague of mine reported, "I gave her *ten* time-outs this afternoon and she *still* won't listen." At that point, ten time-outs in one afternoon *were* the problem. Even if the child was inclined to listen at least some of the time, the full-court press of punishment would probably eliminate any such inclination. After ten time-outs in one afternoon, all that could be left between the child and the babysitter was a contest of wills.

Another example is a family that flew into New Haven for treatment at my clinic. They had given their six-year-old son six time-outs in two days for aggressive behavior and were despairing because the behavior was increasing, not decreasing. That's too much time-out, I told them. Let's reconsider our options. One is to increase the let's-pretend sessions in which their son could get stickers or points for nonaggressive responses to cues that would normally lead to aggressive behavior on his part. That was one way to emphasize the positive opposite and reward it, rather than simply punishing the unwanted behavior.

I instructed the parents to do three simulations a day, but if their child wanted to do more then they should do more. Each simulation would earn a point, and the child would get two points for an actual (nonsimulated) time in which he responded calmly to a situation that typically made him aggressive. It was vitally important that the parents give the child credit for handling something well that could have been upsetting. There were other pertinent circumstances. The father hit the child a lot, so the program also included shaping the *father's* behavior to replace hitting with less harsh discipline — first, choosing one day on which he would not hit the child, then, once he had proved he could do that, expanding the no-hitting portion of the week, all reinforced with praise.

We used a similar approach with the son, establishing control over smaller periods of time and building up from there. I had the parents start with a half-hour period in the morning. If their son managed to not be aggressive during that time, he got a point and much enthusiastic praise. We called that period his "big-boy time" and praised him for it. If he was aggressive during big-boy time, then he received no points and no praise. The rest of the day was "little-boy time." There was no need to criticize him or point out to him that little boy time was less appealing than big-boy time; there are few six-year-old boys on earth who wouldn't prefer to be known as a big boy. (Big-boy/little-boy time is not merely some cute psychological ploy — it's a field-tested setting-up event that effectively helps stack the odds in the parent's favor. Put it in your toolbox; it will come in handy.) Once we had control of a brief period, we gradually increased the length of big-boy time until it took up much and then all of the day. When he had a good day, I told the parents, make sure to discuss it with each other at dinnertime in glowing terms: *What a big boy, he's doing so well,* and so on. This is in addition to immediately praising and rewarding the desired behavior.

Finally, there was the rocket ship to the moon. Their son could cash in his big-boy points for rewards as he earned them, but we also kept track of his total points (including those he had cashed in for rewards) on a chart of a rocket ship heading for the moon. When he got enough total points — his family decided on twenty — he qualified for a bigger reward.

These were all ways to put the emphasis on reinforcing the desired behavior and put less emphasis on punishment.

A Common Punishment: Time-Out

The more full and precise terminology for a time-out is "time-out from reinforcement." For a brief period of time, the child does not have access to reinforcers — rewards, yelling, lecturing, any kind of attention at all — that can perpetuate an unwanted behavior. The effectiveness of time-out depends on what happens during time in — a reinforcement program that rewards the positive opposites of the behavior that necessitated the time-out. The point of using the term "time-out from reinforcement" is to keep your focus on punishment as a (minor) element of a positive reinforcement program and to help you move away from thinking of a time-out as giving the child a chance to contemplate his crimes, take a break from an activity, or be distracted from an activity (like throttling his sister). In a time-out, a child is withdrawn from reinforcers for a while, and that's it. If you use time-out to encourage remorseful contemplation of crimes, or to give a child a break from an activity, or to distract him, you will almost certainly use it improperly.

Let me give you an example that illustrates how a time-out's effectiveness depends in great part on what happens during time in. A researcher, building on other studies of time-out, created the "time-out ribbon," a variant intended for a classroom setting. Each child in the class wears a red ribbon loosely draped around his or her neck. When the children behave well, in the normal state, each has the ribbon around his or her neck where the teacher can see it, and the ribbon signals to the teacher that she can call on the child and thus deliver the usual reinforcers, attention and praise. If a child does something inappropriate, interrupting work, he loses his ribbon for a few minutes. While the ribbon is off, the teacher does not look at or attend to the child. When the time-out elapses, the ribbon goes back on and the child is now ready to receive reinforcement again. The richness of the time-in environment, the teacher's enthusiastic attending to students with ribbons during the normal class day, makes the time-out meaningful and effective.

Let's talk about how to administer an effective time-out.

A time-out should be brief — certainly no more than ten minutes. Often, just a minute or two will do the trick, especially for very young children. It should happen immediately after the behavior that made it necessary. If you can, do it on the spot. Too often, parents end up saying, *When we get home from the store* . . . or *When we get home from the playground* . . . , and so on, and such delayed time-outs are not effective. The time-out needs to be directly connected to the behavior that necessitated it.

The child in time-out should be isolated from others, in a separate room or sitting in a chair by herself. Complete isolation is not needed if you feel it would be good to keep an eye on the child — for safety's sake, for instance.

You must remain calm when administering a time-out. It is not decreed in anger or as an act of vengeance. Remember to praise compliance with the time-out: praise for going when asked, praise for sitting quietly, praise for completing the time-out properly.

Do not threaten your child with a time-out: *If you keep doing that you will get a time-out, This is your last chance,* and so on. One warning is plenty. (Remember, warnings lose their effects if they are not regularly followed with the actual event being warned about.) Tell the child which behaviors lead to time-out, and then be consistent about declaring a time-out when such behavior occurs.

If you have to touch, drag, or restrain the child to make the time-out happen, you're doing it wrong and the time-out won't work. This is very important. During punishment, a child will be at least a little more oppositional than usual or may be having a tantrum related to the punishment. This leads to at least slight physical resistance to going into time-out. Stronger physical control by the parent will inspire stronger physical resistance, and things escalate from there. Soon the parent is dragging, pushing, pulling; the child is resisting, perhaps hitting the parent. And maybe the parent is hitting, too. In any case, what's happening is not time-out from reinforcement; it's more like a fight in a bar, and you're reinforcing all the wrong behaviors.

If you declare a time-out and your child folds his arms and says, *No, I'm not going,* and you can't drag him, what do you do? First, give him an extra minute penalty. You can do this twice: up the time-out from two minutes to three, then to four. Then, if that doesn't work, take away a privilege — something significant but brief, like no TV today. Then turn and walk away. Don't give in if he then says, *Okay okay okay, I'll do it,* because then you'd be reinforcing an unwanted sequence. No caboosing, either. Let the consequence do the work. Resist the temptation to add little zingers like, *Next time you better do what you're told,* or *You never listen and now you're paying the price,* or *You really make me mad.* They will not help your child, and they increase the negative side effects of punishment.

Finally, I'll say it one more time: research shows that the effectiveness of time-out depends on the effectiveness of time in — developing the positive opposite of the behavior that causes the time-out to happen in the first place.

Let's consider an illustration. After your child does the behavior that needs to be eliminated or reduced, you calmly go to her and say specifically what she has done and what will happen: *Okay, you hit your brother and you have to take a time-out. Go to your room for five minutes now.*

Will the child go to her room? This is a tense moment. She has done something wrong, and now she's in trouble. If you are upset and she's upset, both of you are likely to take firm positions on going or not going to time-out, and the situation will quickly escalate to a battle of wills.

So, to begin with, stay calm — not just because it's always a good idea to stay calm when punishing (it decreases the likelihood of harsh punishments or escalating the severity of the punishment) but because your calmness will decrease the likelihood of a deadlock of wills. If the child does not go right away, add a minute to the time-out. If she still won't go, you can add another minute.

If the child still does not go, make the decision that the time-out is not going to happen and invoke the appropriate consequences. Inform her of this simply and calmly, and take away a privilege for that day or that day plus the next day: *You didn't go to time-out, so no TV for the rest of the day.* Then quickly walk away. No discussion, no speeches on the order of: *You had your chance and you blew it and now you're going to be very very sorry, my friend, because you could have avoided all this if you had just listened to me* and so on and so on. Also, you might want to spend some time in advance thinking of what privileges to take away that make sense and don't do more harm than good. So don't take away constructive socializing play in the heat of the moment. *You can't play with the neighbors for the rest of the week* will probably do more harm than good, unless the neighbors are even worse behaved than your child is.

If the child goes to time-out either right away or when an additional minute has been added, you praise him for going to time-out. You might say to me, "WHAT?! *Praise* the child while he is going to time-out?!" Absolutely. We want to build compliance whenever it occurs, and especially in difficult situations. We want the child to go to time-out when we tell him to, so we praise that behavior: *Good, you are going to time-out as soon as I asked.* This praise need not be effusive but should still specify what the child did and combine verbal praise with a gentle pat or other contact — if that's feasible, and if the child is not so irate that he's likely to take the opportunity to take a poke at you.

To make time-out work better with young children, we practice it in simulations. Explain to your child how time-out works and say, *Okay, just to practice, let me show you how it works. Let's pretend you did something wrong, like hit your brother.* Now lean over conspiratorially and whisper, *I'm going to ask you to go to time-out now, and you start walking to your room.* Then, no longer leaning over, and in your normal voice: *All right, you hit your brother and that's a five-minute time-out. Please go to your room.* Now whisper, *Go ahead, start walking.* In your regular voice: *Very good. I asked you to go to time-out and you started right away.* You will physically guide the child if necessary, which means walking together with your arm around her, but no shoving. If she goes into time-out and sits down, praise her. If the child stays there, prompted by you, more praise. If she can stay there without being prompted, even more praise. In a simulation, praise should be as effusive as possible, whereas during a real time-out you wouldn't gush so much; you would be more matter-of-fact when praising a child for, say, going into time-out after hitting a sibling. When the simulation is over, you announce in town crier fashion: *Okay, time-out is done,* and offer more praise for having done such a good job. If you have a point system in place, award a point for a successful simulation.

Those are the basics, but some fine-tuning may be necessary.

For instance, here's a case of a competently administered time-out that failed. A mother who came to my clinic grasped the principle of time-out perfectly and used it on her eight-year-old son, Andre. Whenever he shouted something nasty or swore at his sister, mother, or father, she would administer a time-out, which consisted of Andre going to his room for five minutes.

The mother would calmly say, "Andre, that's a time-out for . . ." and she would specify what he had done wrong. If Andre started to walk to his room, the mother said, "That's good, I asked you to go to time-out and you are going right away." So far, so good.

But we checked on the program and saw that over a three-day period she had given six time-outs on the first day, four on the second day, and seven on the third day. This was too much, and indicated that something quite different was needed.

This was an interesting case because the mother was administering punishment correctly, and the child was going to time-out. But the program was weak in developing positive opposites: she had time-out down cold, but time in was the problem. Accordingly, we added practice simulations to the program in which the child was told that he could practice saying nice things to his sister — like *Let's play*, or *I like to play with you*. We started a point chart on which he could earn two points per day (one for each simulation) and a bonus of four points anytime he did not swear when he got really upset in a nonsimulated situation. So we made no change in the time-out procedure itself, but we built up the positive reinforcement aspects of the program of which it was a part. By the third day of this revised program, he earned six points, all from simulations; on the fourth day he got into an argument with his sister and did not swear, and received eight points. (It actually should have been four points, but the parents were so pleased and excited that they bent the rules and double-bonused him.) The program continued uneventfully, now with time-outs averaging fewer than one per day.

• • •

I hope that, after reading this chapter, you'll be very careful about using punishment properly and sparingly. But if you have kids, you're going to punish them sooner or later, and you might as well do it right. It will help to occasionally reread the "How to Punish" section of this chapter — when your child enters a new developmental stage, say, or a new pattern of unwanted behavior. And never lose sight of the homely — and scientifically supported — truth that a good, warm, open, mutually respectful relationship with your child makes all the difference. Don't punish like a wrathful prophet expunging sin; do it as a loving parent committed to developing good behavior.

7

Special Situations

How to Jump-Start Behavior, Work with More Than One Child, and Handle Low-Rate Misbehaviors

What if my child doesn't do the desired behavior often enough that I can reinforce it with rewards? What if the *un*wanted behavior I'm trying to get rid of doesn't happen very often, making it hard to reinforce its positive opposite often enough? What if I have more than one child, but only one really needs the program? What if I want to improve the behavior of not just one child but a group of children?

In the vast majority of cases, the basic approach I have already detailed will give you everything you need to set up a program that will improve your child's behavior. But special circumstances do come up that may require an adjustment on your part. I hear the questions above fairly often; they represent some of the most common special circumstances. This chapter offers you a few special tools that you can use to tailor the basic approach to your situation.

Jump-Starting Behavior

What if my child doesn't do the desired behavior often enough that I can reinforce it with rewards? The answer is "jump-starting" behavior, a one-time strategy to get the child just to begin the behavior or accomplish its initial steps.

Often, the hardest part of changing behavior is getting the new behavior going at all so that you can reward it (or steps toward it) when you see it. That's especially true when there is a sequence of actions that have to be done in order to achieve the desired outcome. To take an adult example, let's say your spouse claims that he wishes to exercise more and has even gone so far as to spend good money on a gym membership, but he never does get around to actually exercising. In this case, "exercising" can be broken into several steps: getting the clothes and equipment together, going to the gym, changing into exercise clothes, beginning the exercise, and then doing the necessary amount of exercise. You could use our ABC's on him. A (antecedents) would include prompts (*Honey, please go to the gym today . . .*), B (behaviors) might include shaping (*. . . even if it's only for a few minutes . . .*), and C (consequences) might include rewards (the nature of which I leave to the adult imagination) or mild punishment for nonperformance (*. . . or I will invite my mother to come over for dinner*). But it might not work. The inertia generated by the number of steps he has to accomplish may well prove too great, and you're not seeing enough of the completed sequence to build it as a habit by rewarding it with praise and age-appropriate goodies.

You might, instead, try jump-starting the behavior: *Honey, I'm going to the gym today, and I'd really like it if you came with me, just to keep me company and check it out. You don't have to work out or anything.* If you can manage to get him there, suited up for exercise, in effect dropping him into a middle step of the sequence called "exercising at the gym," he's more likely to complete the sequence, and you're on your way to a behavior you can reinforce. First you jump-start, then you can shape.

Many of your child's behaviors can be broken into steps and considered as similar sequences. If you want your child to complete thirty minutes of homework, for example, a first step might be sitting at her desk with the book open. For practicing the piano for thirty minutes, sitting down and getting ready to play would be a first step. If you want your child to go outside and play with friends, going outside and making contact for one minute might be the first step. If you want your child to work on a project with you, a first step might be just starting the project with you and working on it for one minute.

After the first step is completed, the child is allowed to stop. You can even say after the first step, *If you would like to stop now, that's okay,* or *Would you like to continue?* Also, you can just remain silent and continue with the activity. The research shows that the likelihood of the child continuing the activity is very high, whether asked or not. Even if sometimes your child elects not to continue the activity, jump-starting can still be highly effective, and its good effects take hold and are maintained after you stop the jump-starting.

Because jump-starting is a one-shot strategy and doesn't involve rewards, it can be perfect for situations in which a child suddenly balks at doing something she's already been doing. You don't want to have to shape and reward behaviors the child has already been doing without special rewards, so jump-starting becomes the tool of choice. At my clinic, we regularly use jump-starting when a child suddenly refuses to come in for a scheduled individual session with a therapist. For instance, a mother who has already been in for a couple of sessions with her daughter calls the clinic to say, "We aren't coming in today because Alexis doesn't want to go, and I don't think I can make her go."

Jump-starting can break this bind. Consider coming in for treatment as a sequence of behaviors: getting into the car, riding to the clinic, walking into the clinic, sitting and waiting for the therapist, meeting the therapist, and so on. Of course, these aren't discrete units — one flows into the next — but for a moment let's think of the whole sequence that way. The research behind jump-starting shows clearly that the further one can get an individual into a sequence, the more likely it is that the rest of the sequence will unfold, without any further intervention on your part. If there are nine steps before the final desired behavior, step ten, the likelihood of getting the full sequence to be completed is increased by getting the person to just do step one. (I won't go into the whole argument for why this is so, but in essence, each completed step in a sequence is not only a behavior but also acts as an antecedent for the next step and a positive reinforcer for steps already taken.) Or forget about step one and drop the individual directly into, say, step three, which will work even better to get her to step ten. If we can drop the child well along into the sequence that leads to "having a therapy session" (our step ten in this scenario), we can greatly increase the likelihood of that therapy session actually occurring.

On the phone, I say to Alexis's mom, *Tell Alexis that she does* not *have to have a session. All she has to do is come in with you. She can stay in the waiting room while we meet with you, and we promise that she does* not *have to have a session.* It's important that we're not lying here. The word "promise" is a special setting-up event, here and elsewhere in life, because it invokes special reactions, including the expectation that there won't be any violations of the promise. You're promising that the session won't be required, that the child will have a genuine choice, not that the session absolutely won't happen.

In this case, Alexis's mom, who is both stretched too thin and an honest person, admits that she's too frustrated and angry to calmly present this to the child, so I have her give the phone to her daughter and I do it myself.

Almost always, when the child hears that the therapy session will not be mandatory, she agrees to come in the car with the parent. I tell Alexis, *We want to see your mom today, but I promise you will* not *have to have a session. You can sit in the waiting room and read or play a game. You do* not *have to have a session.* Any parent reading this example is going to think right about now, *Aren't you just feeding the problem by telling her she doesn't have to have the session?* or *If you give in here, there's a slippery slope that will lead you directly to letting your child run your life,* or *You are sending the wrong message,* or *A parent has to show that she's always in control.*

The conventional parental wisdom, supported by bad advice from experts, is that it's important to win every battle in order to win the war. But that's not true. Let's put aside for the moment the fact that battles and war offer a lousy metaphor for raising a child and concentrate on this: winning the "battles" with your child may be so costly — in terms of side effects and damage to your relationship — that it leads directly to losing the "war." If you are hell-bent on getting your way or preventing your child from getting hers, in every contest of wills between you, you're *more* likely to end up with a child who won't listen to you and who wants nothing to do with you. (And if that's your attitude, there are going to be many such contests of the will.)

You don't have to win every struggle. You can go with, not against, the grain of your child's will and still end up with the behavior you want. Lose the battle *in order to* win the war, if you want to think about it that way.

Another objection that might come up: *What if the sequence isn't familiar to the child? You can drop her into step three, but she won't know that it's step three or how to get to step four, let alone step ten.* But that's not as big a concern as you might expect it to be. Jump-starting may work better if the sequence is familiar, but it will still work if it's not. Even in an unfamiliar sequence, the cues offered by the situation itself — others engaging in the behavior, for instance — act as setting-up events that increase the likelihood that the rest of the behavior will happen. Let's say that the session that Alexis has been resisting is her first. She wouldn't even know what a session consists of, in that case, but even a child who has never been to the clinic before will pick up cues from being there. Children are smiling, people are leaving the waiting room and going into rooms with friendly therapists, and as Alexis gets a bit bored sitting around in the waiting room, she may well come to see these others as engaged in a potentially interesting activity: "having a therapy session," our step ten. More to the point, she will come to see *herself* as already engaged in the initial steps of this potentially interesting activity.

So, Alexis and her mom walk into the clinic's waiting room. They go to the reception window and the mom says, *I'm here to see Susan,* their therapist. Alexis sits down in one of the chairs and plays with one of the toys left strewn on the floor by children who waited there before her. Susan, the therapist, comes out from a side door, says hello to them, and adds, *Alexis, can you sit there while I see your mom?* Mom and Susan go in through the door. The jump-starting sequence is right on schedule: Alexis is at the clinic, which greatly increases the likelihood of her having a therapy session. If she were at home, stewing in front of the TV, that likelihood would be zero.

After a while, Susan comes out to the waiting room again and says, *Alexis, you don't have to have a session today, just as we said, but —* here she pitches her voice a little higher, in a questioning tone — *do you want to come back anyway just for a short meeting?* or *Why don't you come back with me for a little while?* or something like that. Susan's manner and tone are gentle, nonparental. There's not even a hint of authority or "you'd better" in what she says or how she says it. She's giving a choice, and giving a choice — all by itself — is a setting-up event for compliance.

It's been our experience at the clinic that Alexis, who has been relieved of any need to save face by this setting-up event (in other words, it's up to her), is very likely to shrug her shoulders, say, *Okay, sure,* and follow the therapist into the treatment room. From there, they should go right into a regular session — or, at the therapist's discretion, a slightly shorter one. Neither Susan nor Alexis's mother should rehash the earlier problem by saying, *See, that wasn't so bad. Why didn't you want to come to treatment? What was all that about?* Those comments will cue the entire sequence of oppositional behavior that we've just worked so hard to replace with a different, better sequence of behavior.

Now, what if Alexis is one of the rare few who say, *No, I don't want to have my session?* If Alexis says no, the therapist says okay cheerfully and goes right back to talking to Alexis's mother. No *Are you sure?* or *Come on, Alexis, it's just a few minutes.* After two or three more minutes, Susan will come back one final time. She'll open the door to the waiting room, lean in with a smile, and say, *Would you like to come in?* If the child says yes, they go right into the therapy session. If the child says no, Susan says, *Okay, see you next week,* smiles, and disappears. (I haven't done a rigorous study of the success rate of this approach, but I would expect that the numbers come out something like this: 75 percent of the time, the child comes in the first time she is invited to; 10 percent of the time she comes in at the second invitation; and 15 percent of the time it doesn't work.) We coach the parent to let this matter go after the second no from the child. To return to the (deeply flawed) battles and wars analogy, it's much more important to fight this battle *well* than to win it. Letting Alexis have her way this week — and keeping the promise we made not to force her to have a session — is a better investment in eventually getting her through treatment than dragging her kicking and screaming against her will.

What will happen next week? is always the parent's next question. In our experience, the answer is *Nothing special.* Treatment almost always resumes normally. I can think of no instance in which we had to take this jump-starting approach twice with the same child.

Here's a less elaborate example. You want your child to clean up the yard with you. It's filled with sticks, leaves, and the like, and you'd like a little help this Sunday in clearing it. This is a one-shot deal, not a program to develop any special behavior. You don't want to throw a lot of effort at it, but you think it would be good for the child to help out and that it would be good bonding time, too.

You say to your child sometime before the weekend, or before Sunday, in any case, *I would like you to help me clean up the yard this Sunday.* If the child says yes, there's no need to say any more about it. But if the child says no, or whines and tries to weasel out of it, we turn to jump-starting. You say, *Here is what I would like you to do. Just help me for two minutes. After that, you can stop if you like. It will help me get started to have you there.* The child will usually agree. (*Two minutes,* he's thinking. *I can do that standing on my head, so why have a big fight about it?*) If he still won't agree to help, ask again on Sunday morning, just as the therapist asked Alexis a second time.

Once he has agreed to the two minutes, he is further along the sequence to the desired behavior: helping you clean up the yard. Once you and your child start to work, you can remind him, *You only have to help me for two minutes.* This is a great setting-up event for getting the rest of the behavior, because it frames what follows as entirely up to the child. After the two minutes are up, you can say, *All right, if you want to stop now, you can. It really helps that you came out with me. If you want to keep going, that's great, but you don't have to.* So you've kept your promise by giving him the genuine option not to continue. Between these setting-up events and the fact that your child is well into the sequence that leads to helping to clean up the yard, chances are strong that he'll continue to help. And if he doesn't choose to continue helping this time, remember that the way you made the request, kept your word, didn't renege, didn't nag, and didn't undermine your praise by caboosing it with criticism all make it more likely that he will do what you ask next time. Declare eventual victory, and let it go.

Jump-starting increases the likelihood of a desired behavior, especially one that can be described as a sequence of smaller behaviors (as most behaviors can). It doesn't guarantee a good outcome, but you turn to jump-starting when you've hit a wall or a patch of backsliding and are pretty certain that you're not going to get the behavior at all the way things are now. Jump-starting at least keeps alive your chances of getting the behavior so that you can then shape and reinforce it.

Consequence Sharing

What if I have more than one child but only one really needs the program? Consequence sharing gives you a response to this common situation and can help a program to succeed. Let's say you have a six-year-old son who needs a point program to help tone down his aggression, and he has a seven-year-old sister who doesn't need a program. Consequence sharing means that if he does the desired behavior, he gets the reward, as always, but so does his sister. She does not have to do any special behavior to get the reward — she gets it as a consequence of her brother's behavior.

We use this approach only with reinforcers, not punishments, and it's important that you do not take away anything that they were already getting, but add something enticing: fifteen minutes extra before bedtime, a nice dessert — something they both will like. Never set it up so that the "innocent" person not involved in the program loses something she would otherwise get. That would lead to sibling nastiness, while the extra reward strategy usually does not.

One added benefit of consequence sharing is that it offers a solution to the "Me, too!" problem that may come up when one sibling needs a program and the other doesn't. The sibling with the point program is getting lots of praise and rewards, and the other child isn't. That doesn't seem fair to the one who's not involved in the program. The problem emerges most often when the children are close in age (within five years of each other) and young (under ten), and tends to be more significant to the extent that the sibling values the rewards that are used in the program. A twelve-year-old brother is unlikely to become upset if his four-year-old sister gets to reach into a grab bag of fake jewelry, barrettes, and the like. All you need to do is explain his sister's program to him and even enlist him to help in administering points, and that will probably satisfy him. But if his eleven-year-old brother earns a video game that they both like to play, there may well be trouble.

One way to correct the inequity of one child getting lots of rewards — and it's the one whose misbehavior necessitates the program, which doesn't seem fair, either — is to spread those rewards around. The good consequences earned by one child are enjoyed by all, and you can even arrange multiple siblings' programs so that when any one of them reaches a certain measurement mark, they all get a reward. The "Me, too!" effect often obliges parents to develop a point program for the other sibling(s), even if it's not really needed, and you can set up the programs with an element of consequence sharing that allows each sibling to earn something for all.

For instance, one family I know had a fiery, oppositional five-year-old daughter and a more tractable three-year-old daughter. The parents started the five-year-old on a point program for minding the first time when asked to do something, and there was a lot of action: points, praise, small rewards, big rewards, the works. The younger sister naturally wanted her own point chart, so the parents started one for her, on which she could earn points for toilet training accomplishments — sleeping all night with a dry diaper, and so on. They set a policy that when either child filled up her point chart, both children got to make and eat ice cream cones for dessert. This was in addition to whatever prizes each child cashed in her points to acquire. Each child shared consequences with the other child, in addition to earning her own rewards.

But solving the "Me, too!" problem is not the main reason to use consequence sharing. The main reason is that consequence sharing increases the effectiveness of a program. Siblings and other peers end up helping prompt the child to do the behaviors, often with very specific statements: do this, do that, I'll help you. The siblings or peers then help reward the behavior with their praise, even simply by displaying excitement when the shared consequence is earned. And research shows that a child will often value a reinforcer more highly when she earns it for a sibling or peer as well as for herself.

The case of Gary really opened my eyes to the power of consequence sharing. I encountered Gary early in my career, when I was doing research in elementary school classrooms to determine what strategies were most effective in dealing with disruptive behavior. The goal was to improve the level of functioning and cooperation in the classroom. While doing this research, I also helped with individual children who did not respond to a school's attempts to address their behavior problems. At the time, I was working with a special education class of twenty-three boys and girls, ages six and seven, who had been placed in the class because of disruptive behavior problems. The teacher was very good. Rather than attending to and fostering deviance, which is all too common in schools, she deftly used attention and praise to reward good behavior. She had excellent control of the class most of the time, but there was a conspicuous exception.

Gary seemed impervious to her efforts. He was a tousle-haired charmer whose normal expression made him look as if he was about to break into a warm smile, which tended to put teachers (and researchers) off their guard — until they had spent some time around him, that is, and came to know better. He would invariably disrupt the class by taking things from the students on either side of him, writing on their papers (crossing out whatever they wrote, in the middle of a writing assignment), and throwing wads of papers and other things (plastic pencil sharpeners, paper airplanes, paper clips) across the room at others.

The seating was arranged as a U, with the front of the class, blackboard, and teacher all at the open end. Gary sat on one long side of the U and constantly threw material at children across from him on the other side. Much of the deviance occurred when the teacher turned her back for a moment to write on the board, but he would also throw and grab things even while she was looking right at the class. In the back of the classroom was a large mirror, the size of a standard blackboard. It was a two-way mirror: the children in the classroom could see themselves in it, and I, sitting on the other side of the mirror with my graduate students in slightly elevated observation seats, could see the entire class.

To improve Gary's behavior, we tried consequence sharing. The kids were told that Gary could earn extra recess time or a special story for the entire class. On the blackboard the teacher drew up in chalk a chart that broke up the hours between 9:00 and noon (lunchtime) into thirty-minute units. Next to each thirty-minute period was a space in which Gary could earn an X for good behavior during that time.

If Gary earned points for at least five of the six periods, the class would get an extra fifteen minutes of recess or a special story at the end of the morning before lunch. (The teacher had a reservoir of stories that the students found especially exciting. Sometimes she read them; at other times she made them up herself.) Gary could earn points by not throwing things or touching his neighbors' materials. A thirty-minute period had to be entirely free of these behaviors in order to merit a point. (We knew that Gary had occasionally had periods of thirty minutes or longer in which he did not disturb other people, so this seemed like a good place to start in terms of shaping longer stretches of good behavior.)

The program started, and Gary, misbehaving as usual, did not earn the X for the first half-hour period. From that period on, as I and my fellow observers learned with mounting interest (and, yes, amusement), Gary's peers prompted him to behave, especially whenever the teacher turned her back. They did this by putting a finger to their lips to signal *shh*, or by giving Gary a look so that he would not talk. Another child would motion with her head to indicate *Don't throw that.* Another child from across the room ran over to Gary's desk and straightened his materials and put away a toy. It took him too long to get over to Gary, straighten up, and get back to his desk to do it without being seen by the teacher when she finally turned back to the class from the board, but she wisely ignored it.

From my perspective, this was bizarre to watch, but happily so. Whenever the teacher turned her back, all sorts of frenetic activity began, with at least four or five children signaling, smiling, and prompting. Gary's peers — who, you will recall, had been placed in this class because of their own tendency to disrupt class — were on the job almost nonstop. If the teacher looked to one side of the room, a child out of her vision would be holding up an okay sign with one hand to signal Gary, and another child would be motioning *shh*. The funny part was that this spasm of activity, which turned on and off like a faucet whenever the teacher turned to or from the blackboard, was all intended to support appropriate behavior. Once or twice she left the room to chat with another teacher or the principal, who came to the door. When she did this, the room fairly erupted, with all the children working on and for Gary — all positively, all to good effect.

As you might expect, Gary did very well, and the problem was taken care of in a short time. Once Gary was behaving better, we stretched out the minimum time for earning points with good behavior from half an hour to two longer periods: from the start of the day to lunch, and from lunch to the end of the day. Eventually, Gary had to be good all day in order to earn any points. Finally, we got rid of the points and moved to having a reward for the group at the end of a good day — with the teacher praising Gary quietly at strategic moments along the way. After a while, we dropped the program entirely, because Gary's disruptive behavior was no longer a serious issue for the class.

One additional result of Gary's program worth mentioning was that the group's behavior, and not just his, improved. That can happen with this method, even though the primary objective of consequence sharing is to use the group to change the behavior of one individual, not the whole group. The behavior of those who share the reward but are not the target individual is not likely to change as much as the target individual's behavior, because the reward does not depend on their behavior — but they do show some benefits. The research reveals a vicarious reinforcement effect: when the others see someone receive praise and points for good behavior, their own behavior may change to match it. This spread of changed behaviors may not be deep but it can be wide, since it can affect all those who hear and see the target individual receive reinforcement. Hearing a parent or teacher conspicuously praise one child's behavior can greatly speed up the shaping of the same behavior in others. In a classroom, this can be important. Teachers can do a lot of good by going around and praising quietly and individually, but it's also useful for a teacher to look across the room and say, *Maria, it's terrific that you're helping*

Billy work on his project. The vicarious effect will increase the desired behavior in the others.

Now, all this is fairly easily adaptable if you are not a teacher but are coaching a team, teaching Sunday school, volunteering at an after-school homework center, or the like. And it works in a family setting, too. By involving younger and older siblings in sharing rewards, you can solve the "Me, too!" problem, make a child's program work more effectively, and perhaps even improve the siblings' behavior a bit as a bonus.

Group Programs

But what if I want to improve the behavior of not just one child but a group of children? Then you should try a group program, in which the group (which can be as few as two people) as a whole must perform the behavior in order to earn a reward that they share. It can be used in the home for all the children in it, at a sleepover for all the children in attendance, or in the classroom, where the group can be the whole class or subgroups defined by the teacher. A group program treats the whole group as one "person" — the group is the basic unit, not only in doing the behavior but in receiving consequences as well.

For instance, most of the kids in a class are not turning in homework often enough, so the teacher develops a group program and puts a point chart on the bulletin board. On any day that 75 percent of the class turns in homework, the group gets a point — or you can forget points and just award a special experience, such as a movie, extra recess, or a story. After you regularly get 75 percent compliance, you can shape the behavior to a more stringent measure, like 90 percent. This approach brings to bear peer support for the desired behavior, as in the example of Gary above, except now all the kids are influencing one another's behavior. And make sure, as always, that the rewards are "extra," rather than making the class earn (or risk losing) something it already receives.

You have already seen an in-home application of a group program, in chapter 4, when we had to come up with a scheme to get the squabbling sisters Lisa and Christine out of their habit of falling into conflict whenever they were alone together. The program treated them as a single individual, rewarding them both for spending time nicely together. That's a classic group program approach, with rewards given for a behavior that only the group can accomplish. If Lisa's behaving well and Christine isn't, or vice versa, they don't earn the rewards, because if either of them behaves badly then "the group" is misbehaving.

A couple I know came up with a simple but effective variant of a group program for their daughters, ages six and four. The parents wanted to encourage the girls to be kind to each other, especially because the older daughter had recently entered kindergarten, developed her first set of close friends, and started being mean to her younger sister, now that she didn't have to rely on her for companionship. So the parents set out a small, clear glass jar on the kitchen counter and put a red bean in it every time either sister did something nice for the other: said something kind, shared a toy or treat, or just gave her a hug and a kiss when they parted ways in the morning, one on her way to school and the other to preschool. At first, the parents gently suggested opportunities to get another bean in the jar, but after a couple of days the girls caught on and needed little prompting. When the jar was full of beans (and, of course, they praised the girls every time a bean was earned), they took the girls out for dinner and a much prized dessert (apple pie à la mode) at a restaurant they all liked.

The best of all worlds is a combination of group and individual programs. In such a setup, each child has his or her own individual program, but there's also one that treats them as a group. For instance, one family had twin sons who bickered and generally whipped each other into a frenzy. Each child had his own program in which he got points for minding the first time and treating his brother well. The boys' behavior improved, but the parents felt that there was still too much bickering and that they could do better, so they added a group program element. If both kids earned enough points on a given day, an added group reward kicked in, something special (a trip to the batting cage, since they were baseball fiends) that they could only earn in this fashion. The group program element was a good addition here. If you have a group in which everyone is doing fairly well but you want to see better improvement in behavior, adding the group contingency is a good way to do the trick. But if you have a group in which some are doing well and others are not (let's say one brother consistently earned a lot of points, but the other didn't), then sticking to individual programs with added incentives is best.

Low-Rate Programs

What if an unwanted behavior occurs so rarely that you don't have enough chances to reinforce positive opposites? Then you need a low-rate program.

Most of our programs focus on situations in which we want to increase some behaviors (like listening, good manners, and homework) and decrease others (like tantrums, disrespectful statements, and aggression). I stress the importance of having many opportunities for reinforced practice, either because there are frequent opportunities for the unwanted behavior (or its positive opposite) to occur or because we use simulations to create enough such opportunities.

But low-rate behaviors throw us a curve ball. They happen infrequently — once a month or less is our usual rule of thumb — but are significant because of their seriousness. Typical examples of such behavior for older children are stealing, lying about something important, running away, shoplifting, breaking and entering, destroying private or public property, engaging in inappropriate sex activity, vandalizing, or using drugs. However, the behaviors need not be extreme and could include any behavior that we have already talked about, if it occurs infrequently. Perhaps your otherwise well-behaved five-year-old throws a tantrum only once a month, but it's always in a very public situation (like, say, at church), and features loud screaming of curse words and indiscriminate attempts to bite anyone in range. You'll want to do something about this behavior, even if it does occur rarely.

The behavior does not occur often enough to include in the usual point program — because it's difficult to find enough opportunities to reinforce a positive opposite to replace it, and simulations would be hard to set up — but it will still be helpful to provide some consequences. (This is usually a separate program, not connected to any point chart.) Select a punishment just for this behavior. Usually, the punishment is some effortful task, a special chore that the child would not otherwise do. Don't make it cruel or excessive, but it should be a chore that the child will regard as significant. Chores can include scrubbing floors, raking leaves, pulling weeds, cleaning some room or some part of a room (one mother had her preadolescent son clean out and wipe down the shelves of their kitchen cabinets), straightening up the garage, and so on. Think of some task that is tedious — one that the child would not select as something positive to do on his or her own. I recommend a chore of about fifteen minutes for young children of five or six, and about thirty minutes for children over seven. Some parents set up two levels of chores, a regular one and a longer one (thirty minutes for a younger child, sixty minutes for an older one) for different degrees of seriousness in the offense being punished. (Among other things, this gives them more options and also allows them to better satisfy their sense of justice.) Lying or a minor theft from a friend might generate the lesser chore, but vandalism or disrespect to a teacher might generate the more severe penalty.

No consequence other than the designated chore should be used. No lectures, no humiliation, no spanking. Put the weight of the penalty entirely on the chosen task, not on your words or actions. The only exception would be when some person or place outside the family is the victim. In those cases, the child should also be required to meet with the offended parties and apologize. Restitution should be made when applicable (returning a stolen item, apologizing, paying for damage), although the extent of it may be limited by the fact that a child is usually unable to repay extensive damages. In that case, partial restitution may be the only possibility.

The Steps for Designing a Low-Rate Program

1. Be sure you can observe the behavior you want stopped, or can see clear signs that the behavior has occurred. Sometimes the behavior is not easily detected, as in the case of stealing, or playing with matches around the house. Tell your child in advance that you will consider the offense to have occurred if you find signs that these behaviors have happened or could happen — finding objects in her pockets or bedroom that aren't hers, finding matches or even smelling the traces of a match having been lit (or, in the case of one older child at our clinic, smelling the incense that she would light to cover up the smell of burning other things).

2. *Select a chore that is tedious* and *not* something he would like to do during his free time. Do not use as punishment any behaviors that you want your child to like, or that are socially desirable. Exceptionally bad low-rate chores would include reading, writing, or math exercises. We want children to want to write and do math, not to regard them as the nuclear option among punishments. Also, don't pick something you have been constantly reminding him to do but that he never gets done. Don't get this punishment entangled in a separate running battle; you are not trying to accomplish something important in the house here, like finally getting that overdue reshingling of the roof done. Don't mix the agenda. Just pick a tedious job that has some benefit — that is, one that's not expressly and obviously created just to make him suffer. Having him straighten up the garage would be appropriate, if that's not one of his regular chores, but having him dig a big hole in the backyard and then fill it up again would be perversely cruel and therefore not constructive.

It's important to decide in advance on the chore. I want you to have something in your back pocket, ready to go, if and when your child commits a low-rate offense. Parents' tendency, especially for a grave offense, is to improvise drastic, harsh consequences on the spot, when they're mad, and these punishments often do more harm than good. Because we have to rely more on punishment in a low-rate program than we would in the usual points program, and because the punishment is usually fairly significant, we have to be extra careful to make sure that it's handled right. Being prepared in advance and sticking with the penalty you've chosen is a big step in that direction. And don't escalate — don't keep piling on the time it takes to do the chore, for instance. Longer and longer does not equal more and more effective.

3. *Stay calm.* I've said plenty about this in chapter 6.

4. *Before you instruct the child to do the low-rate chore, explain the program to her.* Here's a sample explanation of a low-rate program for stealing: *I know that there are times when you see something you really want and you might just want to take it. There are times I really want something, too. But instead of taking it there are other things you can do. You can always ask for what you want or ask to borrow it. You can ask me to put it on your point chart as a prize. Or you can save for it. I know that you are already doing many of these other things, and that's very good. But when I find that you did take something that is not yours, or suspect you of that, even if you borrow something but forget to ask, I will give you an extra chore. I know you don't want to do any extra chores, and I don't want to give you any chores, so let's stay as far away from stealing as possible.*

5. *Assign the chore immediately,* based on evidence or strong suspicion.

6. *Don't threaten the chore, and no warnings.* Assign it right away. As always, the connection between behavior and consequence should be automatic.

7. *Don't debate or argue.* Tell your child what he did wrong (or what you strongly suspect he did wrong) and calmly assign him the chore.

8. *If your child won't do the chore at first, calmly tell her you won't be able to start the time* (let's say she needs to clean up the garage for thirty minutes, for instance) *until she starts the chore.*

9. *If your child still won't do the chore, give him a choice of either doing it or losing a privilege.* As with the chore, choose a privilege or two in advance, so you don't feel obliged to come up with one on the spot when you're so mad you can't see straight.

10. *If your child complies but in an unacceptable way* — she starts the chore but is angry, out of control, or doing a terrible job on purpose — *calmly stop her and take away the privilege.*

11. Don't forget to praise your child for doing the chore you assign as the consequence for an unwanted low-rate behavior. Praise as soon as he starts the chore, while he is doing the chore, and when it's done. The older the child, the less the need to gush, but do be specific about what you're praising: *You went right to work and did the job well. You really handled a hard situation in a mature way.*

12. Continue to praise the positive opposite of the problem behavior. For example, if you are using a low-rate program for stealing, you want to reinforce your child every time she asks for something, waits to save for something, or tells you that she really wants something. If you are using such a program for lying, you would reinforce your child with praise every time she tells you the truth in a situation in which she would be likely to lie.

A Sample Low-Rate Program

When Matty, an eight-year-old, was told no or got upset, he had severe and dramatic tantrums. He would cry, shout about how unfair things were, lie on the floor, shriek, and otherwise carry on, usually for about ten minutes. The tantrums were routine and happened almost every day — sometimes they were triggered by an occasion as mundane as bath time or bedtime. If he asked for something and was told no, he often (perhaps two-thirds of the time) went ballistic. So far, I'm describing a typical high-rate behavior, for which a variant of the usual point program can be designed. We set up a point chart on which he could earn points for decreasing the intensity of the tantrum. We were very specific. First, he got five points anytime he had a tantrum but spoke in his normal voice, rather than shouting or screaming. He could say anything, but in a normal conversational voice. If he didn't have a tantrum at all, he got twenty points, big hugs, and gushing praise. This was, as I said, a typical reinforcement program.

The low-rate part of the program focused on one element that sometimes came after a tantrum. Once in a while — occasionally, and for reasons that were never clear — Matty would destroy property, usually by tearing or cutting it. He would rip up family pictures, for instance, which enraged his mother (a single parent). Once, he cut the straps off his backpack with scissors, ruining it. The combination of scissors and rage in that incident scared his mother. These were intense and severe behaviors, but they occurred infrequently, making it hard to reinforce positive opposites. The behaviors just did not come up often enough, and they did not happen every time he was upset. Matty's mother's response to this destructive behavior also needed improvement. Prior to starting the program, she would hit him, yell, and impose harsh punishments — like not letting him play soccer, which he loved to play, for a week — and he would show virtually all the negative side effects of punishment that we have discussed. The regular, high-rate program we began helped her to handle his tantrums well, without losing her cool, but when Matty destroyed property, she got so mad that she lost her ability to do the program.

So we devised a low-rate program. Whenever Matty damaged anything in the house on purpose, he had to do a special low-rate chore: stacking logs in the backyard. The family had had a large quantity of logs dumped in their yard to fuel a wood stove, so there was plenty of work to do. His mother decided that twenty minutes of stacking logs was the appropriate penalty. Fifteen would have been fine with me; but she insisted on twenty and it was not worth the additional argument — my children are not the only people who don't always listen to me.

Over the course of a week, the tantrums decreased in intensity. For the first eleven days of the high-rate program, he did not earn the big twenty-point reward for no tantrums at all, but he did adopt a normal tone of voice when he got mad, and earned the five points that way. After a few days of this, his mother explained to him (at my urging) that he could earn five more points (for a total of ten, if he also used his normal voice) if he explained what was making him mad and did not blow up, and if he did not lie on the floor during a tantrum. Over the next three weeks, his tantrums decreased further.

During this time, he had two destructive episodes, the low-rate behavior — once he threw a knife at the floor by his feet, and once he threw a ball across the room and just missed a lamp. Each time, he had to do the low-rate chore, stacking wood.

By the third week, he was earning the twenty-point no-tantrum prize and not engaging in any destructive behavior. By week four or five, his mother switched to simply giving him a special treat on the weekend — a video game or movie rental, or a family activity.

I told Matty's mother to keep the low-rate program in effect for at least six months after the last destructive episode. At that point, she and Matty could renegotiate — but we both expected that it wouldn't be necessary.

While we do not know everything about the role of the low-rate program in improving his behavior, we can say a couple of things about it. First, it helped his mother to calmly administer consistent, nonharmful punishment. Second, it helped to embed the low-rate program (which, after all, consists of little more than punishment) in the high-rate reinforcement and shaping program that taught him some positive opposites to the frequent tantrums that also seemed to trigger the less-frequent destructive episodes. And, of course, what we can say most certainly is that his behavior improved — so much so that his mother ended the regular program after about a month and didn't have to use the low-rate penalty after that.

8

Troubleshooting

When an appliance doesn't work properly, you reread the owner's manual and make sure that you followed all the directions properly. If that doesn't solve the problem, you look in the back of the manual in the section headed "Troubleshooting." The first thing it says there is usually something like, *Make sure that the appliance is plugged in, and that you have turned it on.* Sometimes, the problem's that simple. Sometimes it's a little more involved. With my method, too, often there's something very basic that requires a simple adjustment, but sometimes troubleshooting can be a little more involved. Either way, this chapter helps you make adjustments in the program to increase the likelihood of getting the results you want.

Am I saying that your unique, precious, and ever-so-human child is like a toaster? I am not. I'm saying that the method for changing behavior I've been explaining to you in this book is more like a technology than it is like a theory or an opinion. It's a scientifically tested means to accomplish predictable results. Because science offers concrete guidelines for how to change a child's behavior, it can also offer concrete guidelines for what to do when a program is not working well enough. This kind of precision is rare in the field of psychology. For decades, most providers of most therapies assumed that when the patient did not get better, it was because something was wrong with him. He was resisting the therapist, for instance, or not doing what he was told, which was taken as evidence — in a less-than-scientific way, of course — that he had a real problem and needed help. The problem was assumed to be inside the patient. Psychiatry and clinical psychology have long histories of blaming the patient — or, at their worst, the patient's mother.

Even today, even at our most scientifically precise, we can't always or even often locate the exact source of a behavior problem. Is it genetic? Is it the result of early childhood experiences? Is it made worse by adults' responses to it? Sometimes, it's all of the above. But we don't have to know exactly why a child has tantrums, or why a child lies, in order to change that behavior. We know how to change behavior for the better, regardless of its exact cause, and our best bet is to just go ahead and change it. Instead of treating the child as if there's something wrong inside her that needs to be fixed, let's treat the *behavior* as the something wrong, and address it directly. In practice, that means locating the problem in the relationship between the child and the situation around him, in how he interacts with other people and things, which might well include flaws in the therapy or how it's delivered.

My method, like much of the best current thinking and research on children's conduct, emphasizes what can be done — in the home, especially — to alter behavior. When such alteration happens, there's a curious tendency among parents to see the change as having happened *inside* the child. The parents say, *My child is a different person now,* or *She has become a caring person, and now it's easier for us to love her again.* What really changed, of course, was behavior: fewer and less intense tantrums, reduced aggression. Anything else that has come of that change — less conflict, less opposition, more compliance by the child — can be traced to that external change, usually a result of adjustments in the ways that parents prompt, attend to, and reward or punish behavior. Our research shows that when a child's behavior improves, the parents' levels of depression, anxiety, and stress go down, and families get along better. Are those changes happening inside the various members of the family? Perhaps, but the action that's making the changes happen — and therefore the action we can adjust if it's not working right — takes place *among* them, out in the open on the level of behavior, where we can get at it and make changes in it.

So when a program doesn't work as well as it should, first we ask, *Are we doing it right?* Then, if we can't find a problem in how we're delivering the program, we ask, *Do we need to change the program to better fit the situation?* Only after we've asked and answered these questions is it meaningful to look at the child to see if the problem lies there. This troubleshooting chapter offers guidelines for parents who have started a program, aren't satisfied with the results, and need to make adjustments.

When You Need to Troubleshoot

How can you tell that the program's not working as well as it should be? Here are five scenarios that call for troubleshooting:

1. No change in the behavior is occurring.
2. Change is occurring but is too slow or too small. For example, it's hard to see much progress after a week, or the number of tantrums decreases but the ones that do occur are still intense, and the child still runs the household with the threat of them.
3. The behavior problem that you're working on has gotten worse; the program seems to have had no effect or even made things worse.
4. Change occurs but is not enduring. You stopped the program and everything went back to where it was, as if you hadn't done the program at all.
5. Change occurred when and where the points were given (for example, after dinner at home), but the problems still happen outside of this context (at school, at grandma's).

At my clinic and when working with parents outside it, I have seen all the situations outlined above. By far the rarest is number 3. I have seen children's behavior deteriorate rapidly for all sorts of reasons —

bad combinations of medications, disastrous family conditions such as the death of a parent, psychiatric conditions — but I have seen only a couple of cases in which we started a behavior-change program and the behavior got worse. In each instance, something else major was going on in the home. In one case, the parents were physically abusing the child while doing the program; in another, the parents said they were carrying out the program but we could not establish that they really were. Backsliding as a result of the program is very rare. So are situations in which perfectly implemented programs do not lead to the level of change needed.

Common Problems (and Quick Fixes for Them)

Before we get into details, let's check for two common problems that can hamstring a program but are relatively easy to fix. These are the equivalent of not plugging in or turning on the appliance.

First, are you indiscriminately throwing rewards at all behavior? Parents can fall into the habit of saying, *If you do X, you'll get a prize* whenever they want the child to do something, even if it's not something they're working on in the current behavior-change program. They shoot from the hip all day long, coming up with new requests and behavior-reward relations on the fly. *If you go upstairs and get me my slippers, I'll give you a sticker,* for example. Or *I'll give you two points if you are quiet for the next thirty minutes and let me take a quick nap.* This improvised scheme will not work very well for very long — and may even be aversive, leading the child to escape from, avoid, and not respond to the program — because it violates some of our basic principles. Remember, we want to establish consistency in behavior-reward connections. We want to work toward weaning the child from rewards, so that soon he will comply without rewards or with just mild praise as the reward. We want the child to know ahead of time what the behavior-reward connection is — so it's not constructive for the parent to keep improvising new behavior-reward connections on the fly. And we want to stress reinforced practice; that is, multiple opportunities for the same behavior to occur. So resist the urge to come up with new reward schemes on the spur of the moment. Stick to the program, and make sure to explain clearly in advance to your child the system for earning rewards, so that you are not winging it all day long.

Second, are you giving too many reminders? Here's a rough rule of thumb to go by: if you say it twice (the initial instruction plus one reminder), that's reminding; if you say it three or more times, you're nagging, and nagging can undermine the program. I'll explain why. We have discussed using clear, specific prompts, which are statements to get the behavior going: *Please go pick up four toys from the floor in your room and put them away in your toy box*. Prompts initiate a behavior, and the prompted behavior must then be reinforced: *Great, you picked up the toys right when I asked. This is wonderful!* But if you keep up the usual parental patter of reminders, your prompts will soon exert little effect. Repeated reminders will not help the behavior to occur, and because each command that doesn't lead to the desired behavior weakens the link between the antecedent (your prompt) and behavior and consequence, they can actually hurt by diminishing the power of your words to get behavior to happen. More prompts mean that fewer of them will be followed by a behavior you can positively reinforce, thereby weakening the child's responsiveness to *any* prompt from you. And, as anyone who has been nagged can tell you, nagging increases the chance that the child will escape and avoid you.

So, first, check to make sure that you're not throwing around too many rewards and reminders. If that doesn't solve the problem, we can move on to check other things.

Troubleshooting the Basics

Okay, you've determined that you're not throwing rewards at too many behaviors or nagging your child; or you've fixed those problems, but you're still not getting the results you want. So let's go to our checklist for troubleshooting. In the vast majority of instances, a change in one or more of these areas will dramatically alter the program's outcome. Check and change, as necessary, in the following order:

Check Your Prompts

Are you providing prompts right before you want the behavior to occur? Prompts can include verbal statements, notes, messages, gestures, guidance, and help (doing part or all of the task with the child, at least at first). Reminders that are distant from the behavior in time are less effective. Especially at first, say, *Please clean up your room* right before you want the behavior to happen. Later, when the behavior is well developed, you can add the phrase *later today* or *when you get home from school,* and eventually work up to not giving any reminders at all. We're aiming to achieve a state in which a messy room is itself the prompt to clean up. But in the beginning stages of developing a behavior, prompts ought to occur in close proximity to the behavior. Remember that prompts alone will not establish a behavior. Prompted behavior must be reinforced with praise, and sometimes with other rewards as well. See the section below on consequences, "Your Reinforcements," for more on that.

Is the Behavior Bar Too High?

Are you expecting too much good behavior? The most frequent culprit leading to program failure is a parent expecting too much of a desired behavior — for example, the child must do *all* of her homework, clean up *all* of her room, or behave well *all* day. This unrealistic expectation causes a lot of almost perfect or pretty good behaviors to occur without praise or other rewards, and will lead to the good behavior dropping out. In effect, not rewarding good but less-than-perfect behavior equals ignoring it ("extinction" is our keyword for this), which is the opposite of reinforcing it. Shaping is the troubleshooting strategy here. Provide reinforcement for smaller steps along the way to the goal. Never demand perfection in performance. Children, like parents, can't meet this standard. The place for perfection is in the Olympics, where training is aimed at that level, and even then it rarely occurs. If the child is not performing the behavior, break it down and provide reinforcement for small parts of the behavior.

For example, instead of awarding your child ten points for cleaning her room, give "partial credit": two points for some cleaning, five points for pretty good cleaning, and ten only for almost perfect. If the child earns high points, ratchet up the praise: *I can't BE-LIEVE you picked up everything! A-MAZING!* Now go get your spouse and bring him into the room and enthusiastically show him, in front of your child, what a great job she did.

You can also use shaping in how you reinforce the positive opposite. For instance, you can estimate how much time usually goes by before the child engages in the unwanted behavior, and then extend it. Let's say your child usually gets into an argument with his brother within five minutes of sitting down to dinner. Now provide the reinforcer for not engaging in the behavior for that usual amount of time plus an extra amount. For example, the child can earn a reinforcer (praise, points) if there's no argument within seven minutes of sitting down to dinner (set a timer to make it clear to all). If you can reinforce this behavior with praise and other rewards for a few days, you can extend the time for earning the reinforcer: eight minutes, ten minutes, the whole meal. Then, as the positive opposite behavior (getting along at the dinner table) gets more established, you can taper off to just praise, then eliminate the rewards entirely.

Do the opportunities to do the desired behavior occur often? Our approach depends on reinforced practice — multiple opportunities for the behavior to occur and then be followed with reinforcement. If the behavior is not occurring, then we resort to simulations — practicing the behavior in the home under conditions that are purposely very artificial. This is exactly like airline pilots training in a flight simulator, in which they practice and practice behaviors that we want to be sure they know well. With your child, arrange an opportunity once a day to practice the behavior when everyone is calm. The child can earn a point as you practice the positive behavior you want. As more practice of the behavior occurs, even under pretend conditions, the likelihood of the behavior occurring during the day by itself is much higher. When the behavior does occur, either in simulations or real life, you support it instantly with praise. When the behavior happens in real life, include in your praise a specific recognition of that fact: for instance, *That's so great that you stayed calm and didn't shout when I told you you couldn't go to Tara's house after school. And we weren't even practicing!* Also, while you praise behavior that is prompted, you ratchet up the praise even further when the child does the behavior with fewer or no prompts. So, for instance, you add something like . . . *and you did it all on your own! I didn't have to say anything at all. That's great!* Remember that the end result we're shooting for here is that eventually the child will perform the desired behavior without being prompted or rewarded for it, so greater praise for unprompted or less-prompted good behavior encourages important steps along that path.

Your Reinforcements: Praise and Points

Let's move on to checking consequences. First, are you sure that you're praising the behavior every time or almost every time it occurs? Occurrence of the behavior is directly proportional to the percentage of times you reinforce the behavior. At the beginning of a program, praising the behavior every time is better than almost every time — or, more precisely, praising it 90 percent or 100 percent of the time is better than 60 percent or 70 percent of the time. In real life, 100 percent is not feasible, but when programs are not working, I often find that parents are closer to only 25 percent.

Second, are you providing effusive praise even when you also award points? Be careful of a dismissive tone in your praise (an absent-minded *Good, good*), don't give it short shrift if you are in a rush, and don't convince yourself that "effusiveness is not really me." We are not asking you for a personality change or long-term bout of mania. Take the enthusiasm up a notch, and be sure to give a little hug (for a younger child) or high five (slightly older) or *Way to go!* with a big gesture for an adolescent who is too cool to be hugged or patted.

Third, is the praise immediate or very near that? After the behavior occurs, it must be praised immediately to maximize change, especially when the behavior is just beginning to develop. If you cannot be there, try to find other ways to make your praise immediate. Have the child phone you after she completes homework, feeds the pet, or prepares part of the meal. Immediate praise by phone, even without the chance to add a touch or smile, is better than delayed praise in person.

A small adjustment to more immediately connect reward to behavior may be all that's needed. This was the case with a four-year-old child who wanted to eat only bread, refusing to taste the main course or vegetables. His parents wanted him at least to sample more foods, so they set up a program in which he received two points, marked on a refrigerator chart, whenever he ate some of each of the three foods provided at dinner. The child sampled a few more foods at the beginning of the point program but soon went back to all bread, all the time. Getting points didn't entice him, even if he could trade them in for rewards. So we ended the refrigerator point chart and switched to a simple grab bag. The parents put little trinkets on the gumball-machine level — little toys, rings, a bottle of bubble-making liquid — in a paper bag. If the child sampled two or more foods, right after dinner he could reach in the bag without peeking and pull out one item and keep it. The effect was to make the rewards more immediate than the point system, and from then on the program worked well.

Fourth, are the back-up rewards for points — the prizes and privileges your child can "buy" with those points — varied enough, so that some can be earned each day and others after saving up for a couple of days? And are the rewards good enough? Is the child using the earned points to buy them? If not, add a couple of back-up rewards, and devote some more thought to what your child's preferences would be for such rewards. Do not assume that you need to spend more money to make the rewards better. Privileges, opportunities for choosing how to spend time, what to eat, when to go to bed, what the family does in its leisure time . . . there are many options for coming up with more various and enticing rewards that don't cost more.

Changing the rewards made the difference for Carmen, a twelve-year-old who had a reinforcement program to get her home within one hour after school let out. She wanted to hang out with her friends, but her parents were (rightly) concerned about unsupervised time and not knowing where she was. So she would earn points whenever she came home within an hour of school letting out, by 3:30 on the kitchen clock. The points could be exchanged for more cell phone time, more computer time, and staying up later than usual on Friday or Saturday. The effects of the program were mediocre until Carmen's parents and I realized that there was a better reinforcer available to us: namely, time out of the home with friends, which was what she really wanted in the first place. Remember, involving children in selecting reinforcers tends to increase their acceptance of the program and improve its effects. We adjusted the program so that she could come home by 3:30 to check in, earning her the right to go out again and rejoin her friends for half an hour, *or* call home by 3:30, reporting in by phone, to earn the right to stay out with her friends for half an hour longer. If she failed to come home or call in on time on one day, then the next day she would have to be in the house by 3:30 and stay in. If she was in by 3:30 on the punishment day (and her mother praised her for that: *You had a responsibility to be in on time and you met it, that's really good*), she would regain the right to go back on the program the following day. We also added a new reward. She could fairly easily earn the privilege of having friends come over after school and spend an hour with her at her home.

These small adjustments led to major changes. Her behavior improved immediately, and she reported in or came home on time four or five out of five days each week. In time, the program continued to work at this level even when she did not use the time that she had earned to have friends over. Also, when she came home, she did not always go out again. She might talk a bit with her mom, hang around the kitchen, start a little homework, or call a friend. The increase in casual mother-daughter time was good for both of them. Even as the program continued, Carmen would sometimes just come home, and sometimes she would call to say that she was coming home, rather than staying out. So the program produced the behavior we wanted, and, more subtly, it led to Carmen willingly spending more time at home and strengthening her connections to the family.

Finally, is the child earning enough points but unable or unwilling to spend them? It's true that some children do fine by saving up their points and not spending them too often, and in that case, if their behavior is improving, you don't need to force the issue. But not spending the points becomes a problem if the child's behavior has not changed enough. A program can fail if the link is broken between earning points and using them. If that's the case, we want to encourage the child to spend points so as to earn more. Make the rewards more tempting or more varied. Read on below for more on spending points.

Troubleshooting the Scrooge Scenario

In a point program, points are exchanged to buy the prizes and privileges that children covet. The act of spending the points has two important effects. First, it keeps up the value of the points themselves; they are a currency, and they have value for your child because they can be used to buy things he wants. Second, spending points keeps your child working to get more points, if they are valuable to him, and working to get more points leads to reinforced practice, which is one key to our program.

So it can be a problem when a child accumulates points but doesn't spend them. It does happen. Children differ in their attitude toward the points they earn, just as adults differ in the way they treat their money. Some adults spend the absolute minimum to maintain their daily lives, preferring to hoard the rest — in the bank, in the mattress, wherever gives them the most satisfaction. So humans vary in their saving and spending practices. But in a points program, we want the child to earn and spend, and thereby stay motivated to engage in reinforced practice.

If your child accumulates points but rarely spends them — our Scrooge scenario — first check to make sure that there are five or six good rewards that can be purchased with those points, and that at least some of these rewards can be purchased with only a day or two's worth of earned points. If this is all right, and the child's behavior is improving, allow the hoarding to continue. Let it go, and don't change the program, since the program is working. Apparently, the hoarded points have value enough to your child to reinforce the behavior you want, in the same way that a business mogul may be motivated to make money long past the point that she can realistically spend most of it on things that make her life more pleasurable. The money becomes primarily a way of keeping score of her success. If that happens with your child's attitude toward points, just make sure that you're accompanying the points with lots of good praise, but no further special procedure is needed. Your child may well grow up to be a saver, not a spender, and that's not a bad thing.

But if the child's performance is not so good — if behavior's not improving or has reached a plateau at a mediocre level — we want to encourage spending. The easiest way is to add a rule to the program that does just that. For instance, you can specify that the child must buy at least one reward every other day, or by the end of each week. The exact time period is not so critical. I have used both the every-other-day and end-of-the-week variants, depending on how many points are accumulating. Again, institute this new rule only if points are accumulating *and* the behavior is not improving at an acceptable rate.

An example: Henry, a seven-year-old, was earning points each day for talking nicely to his sister and not disrupting her things (taking items from her dollhouse, knocking down the stuff on her dresser, and so on). Each time he spoke agreeably to his sister during breakfast or dinner, he earned two points. By the end of the first week, he had accumulated thirty-eight points out of a possible forty-two (he could earn a maximum of six per day). However, he had bought nothing with these points. His parents were concerned, but we decided to wait it out and see what happened. The same thing happened in week two, so that now he had accumulated seventy-three points and spent none of them. Henry's parents added an enticing reward or two to the menu of back-up reinforcers, but he still hoarded his points and refused to spend any. We took another look at the program. Henry's parents were praising good behavior and awarding points properly, and Henry's performance was almost perfect: he earned almost all the points he could earn, and his behavior toward his sister had improved to the point that it could be called normal. He and his sister were two years apart in age, so some squabbling was natural, and they did squabble from time to time, but with the program in place, the tension between them went down to an acceptable level.

What was going on? It seemed Henry just liked to pile up points. That was incentive enough for him, even without using them to buy prizes or privileges. To allay his parents' concern, and to take advantage of his pleasure in accruing points, we asked Henry's mother to ask him if he would like help making a graph to keep track of how many points he had accumulated. He loved the idea. (I would like to add that he grew up to be chairman of the Federal Reserve, but he hasn't grown up just yet.)

The lesson here is that when you see you've got an effective reinforcer, which in this case was the sheer accumulation of points, then use it. Find a way to integrate even more of it into the program, which is what the graphing accomplished. We faded the program by week four, getting rid of points and shifting to a graph of "great days" — that is, he got a "great day" rating when he was nice to his sister at breakfast *and* dinner, *and* didn't maliciously mess with her stuff. Eventually, everybody lost interest in keeping the graph going, and the program faded out. We checked back six months later, and the new behavior had held up: Henry's treatment of his sister was no longer a problem in their household.

Another example: Crystal, eleven years old, was on a point program to help her complete her homework assignments. She got two points for starting her homework, one point for every ten-minute period of doing homework (up to forty minutes), and extra points if she completed her work within the time period. She did well the first day and earned points, but not so well the next day, a zero-point day. Over the next few days, her performance fluctuated between earning three points, which was mediocre, and six points, which was good. We looked to make an adjustment to improve her consistency. She was not spending the points, so we checked on the quality and quantity of the rewards to make sure they were enticing enough to encourage spending. We added some opportunities to buy a little makeup and things for her hair, which she liked a great deal, and then we told her she had to buy something — to spend some points — at least three times per week: Monday, Wednesday, and Friday. The changes led to consistent performance in homework: five or six points every day for the next six days. We are not certain whether the better rewards or the requirement to spend points did the trick, but the combination got the consistency of performance we were looking for.

Check Each Other

We've gone through our checklist of basics; now it's time to take a look at consistency. If there are two (or more) parents or other adults in the home, work together to be sure you are administering the program similarly. It's unlikely that you will both be on the same page, at least at first. In working with families to change the behavior of children, I have seen inept and skilled spouses, grandparents who get it and those who don't, couples or extended families displaying wildly different levels of ability to administer the program — all in the same home, and all having received identical training in our sessions. If there's one thing that psychology can say for sure about human beings, it's that individuals differ. Give two, two thousand, or two million individuals the same training, instruction, or medicine, and they will not all respond similarly.

This is important for our program, because inconsistency in carrying it out can undermine its effects. At the beginning of the program, it is better to have one parent administering the program well — or the program administered well for part of the day — than to have inconsistencies across several people and time periods. The initial task is to get behavior change under some circumstances — in the mornings, say, or with just the father or mother in charge. Once you develop the behavior under even very narrow circumstances, which is the hard part, it is easier to extend the program to other people, settings, and times of the day.

A Couple of Common Questions, Quickly Answered

What if I relapse into yelling at my child, or hitting? Have I undermined all of my progress? No. It's like going off your diet and eating a whole cheesecake, or breaking your vow not to smoke. What do you do now? You get back on your diet; you abstain again from smoking. If you can't quite stop smoking entirely or eating the occasional entire cheesecake, you can at least cut down, or eat smaller cheesecakes. You'll still be healthier. When it comes to yelling at and hitting your children, your objective is none, but even cutting down some on these behaviors will have a positive effect on your family life. I've worked with scores of families to entirely eliminate harsh physical punishment by the parent, but I've probably worked with more families in which we've reduced heavy spankings (that is, the parent losing his temper and going off our program) from an everyday or four-times-weekly occurrence to an aberration that happens once a month or so. That's not perfect, but the imperfect change — reducing spankings considerably — is still an important one.

What if the program is suspended? What if my child goes to camp, or I have to go away for a few days? Go ahead and temporarily suspend the program if you can't do it well. Doing the program partially and well is always better than doing it always and poorly. If you have to take a week off, take it off and then get back to it. If you can only do it properly on weekdays, take weekends off. It would be better to do it exactly right all the time, but the program will still show useful results if you do it most of the time, as long as you can do it at least pretty well when you do it.

Advanced Troubleshooting

In chapter 7, you learned about some special tools that can be used to address situations in which you're faced with not enough behavior or more than one child. They included jump-starting behavior (getting the child to begin the behavior or accomplish its initial steps), consequence sharing (in which peers share in the rewards if the child does the behavior), group programs (in which the group as a whole must perform the behavior in order to earn a reward that they share), and low-rate programs (for changing unwanted behavior that happens only occasionally). Each of these tactics can be employed in a troubleshooting situation, too, since each can increase the effectiveness of a program that's not working well enough. But this news comes with a warning: I do *not* want you to think that if a program's not working, you should automatically add a special tool. Not at all. If a program's failing because it's poorly administered or designed, adding consequence sharing or another special tool to it isn't going to help. So I'm returning to the special tools last in this chapter, to emphasize that you must check the basics first. But the special tools from chapter 7 do belong on the list of troubleshooting options.

For instance, jump-starting can be useful if a program is not working well because you're expecting too much good behavior, and therefore not getting enough repetitions of the desired behavior to reinforce. While shaping would be our main strategy for fixing that problem — rewarding partial behaviors that lead to the one you want — you might start by just concentrating on getting the first part of the sequence in order to jump-start it. Let's say you want your child to clean his room. You could say, *Please go to your room and pick up the toys on the floor and put them away in the toy box* (a nice, specific prompt) while you are both standing in the living room, but if this doesn't produce the results you want, it might be more effective to walk with your child to his room, stand in the room with him, and then give the prompt. The reason has to do with jump-starting. Going to his room is an early step in a sequence that ends with him cleaning up his room.

Or if you have two (or more) children with separate points programs and you're not seeing enough progress, you might decide to add a group program element to the mix in the form of an additional bonus that kicks in on any day on which both children earn ten out of a possible twelve points. That kind of incentive might be just the enrichment of consequences (another reward) and antecedents (the two siblings urging each other to behave well so they can earn the group reward together) that's needed to put them over the top.

And so on. Consequence sharing may be the answer to a situation in which one child causes most of the problems but you need to involve other children who are present, or a low-rate program might be required if the behavior you're trying to address doesn't decrease in severity but drops off in frequency to the point that you can't reinforce its positive opposite often enough, even with simulations.

So I do want to refer you back to the special tools in chapter 7 as potential troubleshooting aids, but only with the understanding that you consider them last, after you've checked that the program is plugged in, turned on, and properly operated.

9

Your Child's Wider World

You have set up and followed a program for changing your child's behavior, and it's gone pretty well. Your child isn't perfect (news flash: he never will be), but the incredibly frustrating and household-racking problems that inspired you to start the program in the first place have been reduced to something approaching normal, age-appropriate behavior. It's time to ask yourself, *Is the behavior where I want it to be, realistically?* If the answer is no, you continue with the program, troubleshooting where and if necessary, until the answer is yes. Once the answer is yes, it's time to consider the next — and, we hope, final — question: *How do I ensure that the improved behavior lasts and extends to other situations?*

There are three objectives to keep separate here: 1) getting the behaviors you want (which the previous chapters have covered), 2) getting the behaviors to endure after the program has ended (the technical term is "maintenance"), and 3) getting the behaviors to extend to all the situations in which you want to see them (the technical term is "transfer"). Number one, of course, matters most. First you get an effective program going to improve the behavior, and don't worry at that point about sustaining and extending the improved behavior. We only turn to maintenance and transfer once the program is working.

These latter two overlap a bit, so it makes sense to deal with them together in this chapter, but they represent two distinct objectives, which we'll need to tease apart and deal with individually as we proceed.

Good Behavior for Good

Let's start with questions you might have — questions that parents often ask once the first and most important step, consistently getting the behavior they want to see, is completed: *I can get my child to do what I wanted, but will it last only as long as I'm giving rewards for it? What good is the program if that's the case?*

It is true that if you begin a program and get a child to do this or that behavior, but for only a brief period (a few days, or a week), and then end the program right there, the behavior will probably revert to the original levels. You will probably lose whatever gains you temporarily made. But when programs are in place for a little while longer — I cannot name a single magic length of time here, since how long is long enough depends on the individual and on how the program is administered, but the critical period appears to be a few weeks, up to a month or two — and there is sufficient opportunity during this period for reinforced practice, good behaviors often are maintained after the program ends. My own research on maintenance of improved behavior has focused on follow-up one and two years after treatment, and it shows that the positive effects of a program continue.

That shouldn't be surprising. In everyday life, we know that once behaviors are developed, they are often sustained and extended without any special effort on anybody's part. When behaviors are performed consistently, they become routine, locked in, and not very dependent on moment-to-moment rewards. Almost all child, adolescent, and adult behavior shows this. Our behavior during work, exercise, self-care, family routines and rituals, and social encounters (like the standard *Hi, how are you?* and social smile) becomes fairly or completely independent of immediately rewarding consequences. This is what we mean by "habit," and it's important. A deep body of research tells us that behavior in general can become free of whatever antecedents and consequences may have been used to develop it, and that's the case as well when it comes to the kind of program I describe in this book. When your three-year-old daughter is twenty-three, you will not be giving her a sticker and a high five every time she uses her spoon and not her hands to eat cereal. The behaviors you build up with a behavior-change program enter the large class of nonrewarded behavior that is well maintained without special attention. In other words, you may not have to do anything special at all to sustain and extend a new behavior.

Of course, new behaviors that fail to maintain themselves are also part of everyday experience. Behaviors that we very much want to develop — regular reading, learning new things, practicing a musical instrument — are often not continued after the removal of strong controlling antecedents and consequences. Even good math students will often stop doing math in the absence of homework assignments and exams. Even gifted musicians who enjoy playing their instrument will often stop practicing if parents stop reminding them to and rewarding them for doing it. Like behaviors that continue, behaviors that fail to continue are part of everyday experience. (Our criminal justice system, for instance, has never come up with a cost-effective, politically acceptable way to sustain noncriminal behavior in those who have committed crimes.)

But when it comes to children's behavior, we don't have to content ourselves with simply hoping for the best. Hoping for the best isn't good enough for parents, and it isn't good enough for researchers, either. Psychological research conducted over the past twenty-five years or so has produced a set of reliable techniques one can use to make sure that the behavior continues after the program is withdrawn, and that the child performs the behavior consistently in different contexts.

The most important way to make changes endure is to do the program well in the first place. It may require no special strategies beyond the simple application of good techniques the first time around — sound ABC's, and sticking consistently to the program for a few weeks — to make the behavior endure.

A behavior developed through reinforced practice and many practice opportunities is often maintained. What typically happens, in my experience, is that we design the program and the parents carry it out, we tinker as needed to make sure it is working, and the program goes on for a few weeks. The behavior change occurs, becomes fairly stable, and proves satisfactory to all parties, and the program tapers off. Once the positive opposite behavior has largely replaced the problem behavior, no one has much incentive to bring the program back, and there usually is no need to unless we see a little relapse.

This happy sequence is the norm. But if you slack off in the initial program, you will see little behavior change at the time, and it may be harder for you to sustain the behavior when and if you finally get it. In other words, if it's at all possible, you should have the pedal down to the floor at the beginning of the program and keep it down for a lap or two, which means doing the program right and doing it consistently for two or three weeks or a month — however long it takes. You can ease off for a half lap at that point, then coast completely to the finish line (more on that shortly). Part of doing the program right in the first place is using praise heavily, along with points and rewards, so that praise and attention constitute as much or more of the consequences as points, other tokens, or the rewards they buy. Relying on praise will help a program's good effects continue long after the program itself has been abandoned.

Also, a child's improved behavior is often maintained because the *parents'* behavior is different after the formal point program ends. It's not just the child who learns; often, parents' command of the ABC's of behavior has drastically improved. They may well have taken up some good parental habits that extend beyond the program. Specifically, they are not so likely to foster or exacerbate problems with harsh commands, endless reprimands, caboosing, or corporal punishment. They're specifying exactly what behavior they would like and offering more specific praise for that behavior when they see it, using nonnagging prompts and trying to identify and reinforce positive opposites.

More generally, a change for the better in a child's behavior changes his or her environment, which can mean a more relaxed household in which parents are more likely to support and sustain the child's improved behavior with their attention and praise. Neither parent nor child may even realize it, once the formal program is over, but reciprocal influences can maintain both the child's and the parent's improved behavior. Our research consistently shows that implementing a program does change the family environment beyond the ABC's. Relationships improve, the family functions more smoothly as a unit, and family life changes in ways over and above the technical details of implementing a program.

Fading the Program

There are ways to reduce the program — called "fading" — so that, by the time you abandon it, discontinuing the program does not make much difference anyway. By then, the behavior no longer depends on the A's, B's, and C's that developed it. Fading has been well studied; there's a solid research base that tells us what works.

1. *Make the reinforcers more intermittent or more delayed (or both).* When you're developing the behavior, it's important to reinforce all or almost all instances of the behavior that you see. As the behavior develops, give the reinforcer for larger chunks of the behavior, so that there's less direct connection between performing the behavior and getting the reward. For instance, instead of awarding points each day for twenty minutes of homework, do it every other day. The child gets the same number of points, but she has to perform up to the standard for two days in a row to get any points at all for those two days. If she gets five points per day for those twenty minutes, she can get ten points on Tuesday if she did the required amount of homework on both Monday and Tuesday. (Remember to praise her on Monday, even though you don't award points on that evening.) But if she slacked off on Monday *or* Tuesday, then she gets no points for *either* day.

Then, after a week or so of this, you can go to just giving twenty or twenty-five points at the end of the week if most nights — let's say four out of five school nights — meet the homework criterion. Don't insist on perfection, but you can build in a bonus for perfection. For instance, she gets twenty points for four good nights of homework in a week, and a fifth earns her a five-point bonus, for a total of twenty-five. But if she does only three nights of homework, which falls below the minimum standard of four good nights per week, she gets no points at all for the week.

The delayed program probably would not work as an initial way of changing the behavior. It would be too sporadic; the connection between behavior and consequence would be too tenuous. But as a way of maintaining behavior, it's great. Soon, after maybe a couple of weeks of awarding points just at the end of the week, the program can probably be dropped entirely.

2. Use a leveled system. Another way to fade the program and maintain behavior is to introduce levels into the program and to have the child progress through these levels. The final level is no program, when the behavior can be maintained without any special attention to it.

The first level is the regular program we have been describing in previous chapters. After behavior stabilizes, the child progresses through additional levels, with incentives to move on to higher ones. The minimum number of levels is two; when we do employ a leveled program, we usually go for two or three levels. As the child progresses to the next level, the consequences for behavior are more delayed and intermittent, exert less immediate control over behavior, and are not connected to specific acts during the day. The child's incentive to move from one level to the next is that he can get access to new rewards and more freedom — more choice, more independence.

We used a simple two-level version of a leveled program for a six-year-old boy named Jake who was prone to tantrums. At level one, Jake earned points each day if he handled *No, you can't do that* or *It's time to go to bed* calmly, without crying and arguing. He could earn two points for a reasonably peaceful bedtime. If he had no tantrum when his parents said no during the course of the day, he received two points for each instance of that, too. Because he was in the habit of asking for special foods, privileges, expeditions, and shows on TV almost every day, requests to which his parents frequently said no, he had lots of opportunity to practice responding calmly to not getting his way. There was a point chart on the refrigerator, and at the end of each day, if he had enough points, he could buy all sorts of rewards, including a pick from a grab bag, a special healthy miniature candy bar, and so on. Early in the program, we had practice simulations during the day to accomplish the reinforced practice and get the behavior going. After a week, we reduced the simulations to only two practices a week. The tantrums were lessening in intensity, and most of the time he had no tantrum at all.

We added a second level. We kept the first level just as it was, but, in addition, we told him that any time he had two perfect days in a row with no tantrums, he would earn himself off the program. That was level two. On the day after two perfect days in a row, he would not earn points, but he could choose any of the rewards (without paying with points) and could stay up fifteen minutes later (a new reward, available only at this level). If the next day continued with no tantrum, the level-two conditions would continue for another day — because the second and third perfect days in a row would, of course, meet the criterion for two perfect days in a row, and so on for another day and another and another, as long as he kept up the no-tantrum string. Any day he had a tantrum, we went back to level one. We called level two the "big-boy level," which gave it an air of challenge for him — a setting-up event to increase the likelihood of the behaviors. Jake was at level one for the first four or five days, went to level two, stayed there for a couple of days, had a tantrum and went back to level one, earned his way back to level two with two perfect days in a row, and from that time on remained pretty constantly at level two.

Soon there was no more need for the program, but of course his parents could always return to it if necessary.

Transferring Behaviors to New Situations

Parents sometimes tell me they're concerned that developing a behavior under the unnatural circumstances of a well-structured point program has no bearing on the real world — where, typically, people do not lavish effusive praise, specify exactly what the praise is for, give an enthusiastic high five or hug, or mark up points on a refrigerator chart. When parents tell me something like this, I take it to mean that I have not conveyed the point. We never intend these programs to be forever. We do not need them to be. And of course they're unnatural.

But they're also temporary, even though their results aren't. Then the parent asks, *If I do all of this at home, will the behavior carry over to school and lessons and the school bus, and all those other places?* That's the crucial question when it comes to extending a behavior to other settings. A similar question applies to other people: *If I follow the program with my child, will the better behavior carry over when he's with his dad, grandparents, teachers, coaches, strangers, and everybody else who's not doing the program with him?* For convenience's sake, I collect new settings and new people under one heading: new situations.

First, I should point out that programs often do not require special strategies or techniques to extend the behaviors to new situations. There are three points to make here.

Sometimes transfer to other settings is not necessary. Sometimes, programs are devoted to changing behavior in one setting only. For example, I have seen many children who do well at school but not at home, and vice versa, in relation to a particular problem: arguing, fighting, destroying objects, poor peer relations, and so on. Here the program focuses on the problem in the setting where it occurs, and once the problem is resolved there, the program is over. There is no need to worry about a new or different setting in which the behavior is not occurring.

Some programs, by their very nature, inherently apply to many settings and the presence of many people, so we need not worry specifically about extending the program. Stealing is our usual example. Some children do just steal at home, or in stores, or from friends, but many who steal do so in multiple settings: from a store, from their mother's purse at home, from a classmate's locker at school, and the like. So a program to curb stealing is inherently designed to change behavior in multiple situations, although the rewards are delivered at home. There's no special concern about extending the effects of the program to new situations. Doing homework, too, inherently involves two settings — home and school — and there is usually no special concern about extending to another setting.

Often, improvements in behavior automatically transfer to different situations. Controlling tantrums at home usually reduces tantrums in other settings where the parent may be present (like grocery stores) and where the parent may not be present (like school). As with maintaining behavior, extending it to other situations often occurs on its own, but of course we won't settle for hoping that it will.

Different Settings, Different People

When you set up a program, you have to decide not only what the desired behavior is but also where and with whom you would eventually like it to be performed, and what the conditions are under which it should be performed. If the answer is *Everywhere and with everyone,* that's fine, but just give a few examples of what you mean. For example, a mother tells me, *I want Joey to show respect to adults — first to me, of course, but also to his dad* (who is not in the home) *and to his teachers, and his grandfather, and the neighbors, and people on the subway.* In other words, she has several different settings and groups of people in mind. It is best to think about this and to state the objective clearly at the beginning of the program, but at that point you don't do anything about reaching that objective. The first task is always to get control of the behavior, even if it is for a brief period of the week (one day, for instance) and under very narrow circumstances (before dinner, with the parent present).

When the behavior is developing and shows reasonable progress, now you can ask, *Has the behavior changed in the range of situations in which I want it to happen?* The answer might well be yes for one or more of the situations. But if the behavior has not transferred to all of the settings or people you would like, then extend the program to one or two other situations that have not changed. Research shows that when the program is continued in one or two other settings, the behavior very soon generalizes to all settings in which it can be performed. Similarly, when it comes to transferring the behavior to situations in which other adults are present and you are not, if the improved behavior only occurs in your presence, have one or two other people administer the points on an occasion or two.

The procedure is called "training the general case," which means that by diversifying the program to a few new situations, you train the child to do the new behavior in *any* fresh situation. How many times have you reminded your child to say please and thank you? Ideally, if sometime later in this century we figure out a way to offer affordable travel to Mars, she'll be saying both to the flight attendants on the rocket. You won't have to be there to prompt her or award points for it, and you won't have to have coached her to say it when in outer space. Teaching her to say it at home, at the playground, at other people's houses, and when her Aunt Stella is babysitting might be enough to teach her to apply it to any fresh situation that might come up. She will then be ready to import the habit into situations you never trained her for or even dreamed of.

In order for the behavior to become generalized, how many situations must you train for? Determining this is the tricky part. No one knows for sure, but the answer seems to be only a few.

To take an example of parental, rather than children's, behavior, when we train parents at my clinic, we train them in the sessions at our office, but our goal is to ensure they carry out in real life the behaviors we're teaching. So very early in treatment, we praise them in the sessions for doing things right (good prompts, for example) but also have them implement the programs at home. This is not just to accomplish the obvious goal of changing their child's behavior at home but also to make sure the parents are doing the desired behavior in real life as well as in our sessions. We praise them for what they say they did and what the charts show they did, and when we call them during the week to ask them what they did, we praise the good parenting behavior that they report. If there is a spouse or partner, we train both to praise each other for the desired parenting behaviors (*Nice specific prompt, honey*), so it is not just the therapist providing praise. These are examples of introducing different settings and people as part of training to develop a behavior so it will extend outside of the original situation, which was a session at the clinic with a therapist.

When it comes to different settings and different people, one important decision you'll find yourself facing is between extending your program to a new situation and taking a break from it instead. When your child is going to be with an adult other than you for a few hours or away for just a day or two, it would not be bad to simply suspend the program. It's important to do it correctly and well, even if for only part of the day or the week, rather than doing it all the time but unevenly. It is fine to take little breaks from the program if they are brief and planned. The distinction that matters is between taking a planned break and being inconsistent in administering it. If you're consistent, a vacation should not be a problem.

Consider brief breaks from the program as little tests to see how the program is going and if behavior is maintained or extends to slightly new circumstances. If the program has been in place for only a week or two, don't expect much. If you've been at it longer and it's going well, the behavior will soon be performed without a special program, and it's fine to see if this will occur by suspending the program or weaning from it.

There's a continuum that runs from extending the full program into a new situation, on the one hand, to dropping it completely for a vacation, on the other. Often, you'll be somewhere in the middle. You could, for example, suspend the points for a certain period and say, *See if you can still do behavior X even without a chart. Boy, that would be great.* If you're going to be apart from your child, you can add, *Call me if you do it* (or *I'll call you to check*) and then during those calls, praise the child for thinking about it or trying it or doing it. The program is partially suspended because you are away and no points are being given, but you can still praise long-distance by phone.

Let's consider some common situations — babysitters or nannies, daycare, school, coaches, vacation, and joint custody — that raise questions about maintaining behaviors you want and transferring them successfully to your child's wider world.

Babysitter for the Evening

You and your spouse are going out. Should you keep the program for your child and go through all of the points business with the babysitter? Generally, unless the program's focused on a behavior that may occur (or can only occur) during the time you're away, you should just let it go.

But let's say you have a bedtime program for your child, along the lines of the one for Davey in chapter 3, and you've had a good first week and want to keep the momentum going. You have been giving points to your child for going into his room, putting on pajamas, and getting into bed, and the program has been working pretty well, with points earned on most nights.

It would be fine to just skip the program tonight, but you decide to keep it going. Keep the instructions to the babysitter to a minimum; she doesn't need a crash course in the whole method. Tell her to give a gentle prompt at 7:30: *Please go to your room, put on your pajamas, and get into bed.* Tell her not to nag, force, or argue with your child, but she can remind him (once) that in the morning his parents will give him points as usual if he goes to bed on time. When you get home, she can tell you if he went to bed on time (and stayed there — you have been deducting a point for getting out of bed more than once). In the morning, you can give points based on her report.

But it would also be all right to tell your child, *You're on your own for bedtime tonight. I'll bet you can't go to bed on time when Mom and Dad are not here* (said playfully, as a gentle challenge, with no hint of needling or threat). Then ask the babysitter to remind him just once to go to bed at the usual time. When you return home, ask her if he went to bed and if he came out more than once. If he did anything right, even part of it, effusively praise him and give him any points he might have earned, and do it first thing in the morning. In this scenario, you need even less involvement from the babysitter.

Daily Babysitter or Nanny

If you have a regular babysitter or nanny with daily responsibility for your child in your absence, it would be useful for her to continue the program in some form. It's not mandatory if you can still do the program consistently and well when you're in charge of the child, but it would help your child make progress. When you're deciding whether and how much to involve this caregiver in the program, consider some basic questions. First, is she willing and able — cooperative enough, flexible enough — to do the program well? Second, does the behavior you're working on occur, or is it likely to occur, during the time when the caregiver has sole oversight and you're not there? The stronger your yes to both questions, the more likely it is that she needs to be involved.

You have at least three options for how you continue the program on the babysitter's watch. One is to continue the full program — points, praise, time-out, and so on, exactly as if you were there. Another is an abbreviated or simplified program, concentrating perhaps on one key behavior. Or you can just have the babysitter report to you, using a three-by-five index card in the way that you would have a teacher or coach report to you on your child's day: rating the child with a 1, 2, or 3 on one or two specific behaviors, which you then reward with points and praise when you get home.

When you're developing a behavior in your child, it's okay and maybe even desirable to confine the program to times when you're around. This is especially critical at the beginning, when slipshod efforts by the adults are almost guaranteed to produce slipshod results in the child. If you want to continue the full program when you're not around, you'll need to train the babysitter in proper praise, how to award points, and so on. In most cases, you can't just hand her this book and say, *Here, read this by Monday.* You'll probably need to instruct her yourself in the key points of the method. Understandably, many parents do not want to go through all that, so they use the second or third options, the simplified program or report-card scheme, either of which will do nicely.

The main thing is to figure out how much the babysitter can do well and work around that. In one family I worked with, the parents had two boys, seven and ten years old, and a live-in grandmother who stayed at home. The grandmother had care of the children from when they arrived home after school until the parents returned from work at about 6:30. The parents wanted the boys to play nicely, even if separately, and not to get into arguments over TV and computer games, as they often did. The grandmother screamed at the boys when they argued — which, the mother noted, was exactly how the grandmother (her mother) had disciplined her when she was a child. She and her husband did not want the boys to be screamed at; this concerned them as much as the boys' arguing. So they wanted the program to change the grandmother's behavior as well as the boys'.

The grandmother did not believe in praising or rewarding children, convinced as she was that it would just spoil them. She believed in screaming, basically. So the mom and dad took the pressure off her to maintain discipline by asking her just to tell them at the end of the day if the boys had argued over anything, the definition of arguing being raised voices. If grandma said no, the boys received a point on their Brothers Chart on the refrigerator, a group program. The responsibility removed from her was transferred to the point program, through which the boys could earn extra computer games and movies with points on that chart. The points they earned and spent also went toward a larger cumulative prize (the "rocket ship to the moon" wrinkle): a comic book of their choice, which they could buy over the weekend. The parents added one more excellent feature that may or may not have been necessary. They agreed that they would separately call home one afternoon per week — so, on two out of every five school days there was a call home — to talk to each boy, ask if they had argued, and praise them over the phone if they had not.

The end result was a much calmer home. The grandmother grudgingly conceded that "something totally changed the boys," but steadfastly argued that "it probably wasn't the program." The main thing is that it worked, even if she claims to remain unconvinced. We managed to involve her in the program without going beyond what she was willing and able to do.

Daycare

Daycare providers can be helpful allies in administering a program, as in the case of Grace, a four-year-old we recently saw at my clinic. She was not toilet trained, and when she came to us she was having "accidents" at daycare almost every day, usually between noon and 2:00. We started Grace on a routine of practicing going to the toilet when she was at home. She went in, undressed, sat down, and stayed on the toilet for a few minutes. When she came out, her parents praised her, put points on a chart, the usual. Grace didn't have to actually use the toilet to get points for practicing; she just had to go through the regular steps of going to the bathroom.

But the accidents usually happened at daycare, so we needed to extend the program to include it. Her daycare provider readily agreed to help out. They practiced once per day, between 11:30 and noon, and sometimes a second time in the afternoon. We told the provider that she could do the second practice session if she wanted to and had time to do it, but no more than that. More practice is good, but we didn't want her to pressure Grace. She had several kids to keep an eye on, and too many practices with Grace might well have put a little stress on the provider, which could lead to a slightly harsher tone of voice, greater irritability, and other such setting-up events for opposition and resistance from Grace. So we agreed with the provider that one practice a day was great, two was even better, but three was too many.

When it was time to practice, the provider went over to Grace and said, *Let's go to the bathroom.* She took Grace by the hand (a good way to do this, since holding her hand is a setting-up event for cooperation) and they walked to the bathroom, where Grace went through the same routine as she did during practices at home. The teacher praised her for going into the bathroom (complying with the request) and for sitting on the toilet.

The provider marked a three-by-five-inch index card every day, noting whether Grace practiced. Each afternoon, when Grace's mother picked her up, the provider gave the mom the card. If Grace practiced at daycare when the provider said to, she received double points. We wanted the same behavior to be worth more at daycare, because that's where the accidents were happening. If she ever pooped in the toilet at daycare, she got triple points, and on the way home the mother and Grace stopped to pick up a fast food dinner for the family, or just for Grace.

As of this writing, we've effectively ended the program because Grace reliably uses the bathroom at daycare and doesn't have accidents anymore. She practiced at daycare four of five days during the first week of the program and on all five days the second week; she began actually using the toilet during some of these practice sessions. By the next week, she was initiating bathroom visits herself. The provider praised her whenever she did, and her mother made a huge fuss when she picked her up, giving her praise and points and special rewards. At this point, Grace usually goes to the bathroom at daycare on her own, but if she doesn't initiate a visit, the provider announces, "Does anyone have to go to the bathroom?" and that's enough to prompt her to do it. Her mother and the provider periodically remark on what a big girl Grace is and how grown up, but not even this will be necessary for long.

What if the daycare provider is not so cooperative? It's a rare situation, since they're usually willing and able to help a program succeed, but it does come up from time to time. In such cases, we have to work around them. In Grace's case, it would mean no program of practice visits to the bathroom at daycare, but her mother could still give her points and praise when she picked her up if the provider reported no accident that day. A parent could practice the bathroom visit with Grace in the morning or in the afternoon when she gets home from daycare. If the parents' schedule allowed, they could also temporarily cut Grace back to half a day of daycare, having her at home to practice bathroom visits during the noon-to-2:00 P.M. danger time, until she had more reliable self-control in the bathroom.

School

Back at the end of chapter 4, I gave you a scenario for involving a teacher in a child's homework program or in a program for a child who has trouble keeping his hands to himself. That's where I introduced the basic scheme of having the teacher — or daycare provider, or coach, or babysitter, or whoever the responsible adult might be — fill out a card that the child brings to you. The card can simply list the required homework, or it can rate the child's behavior for the day. You can then award points and praise at home, which includes a reward for bringing the card home at all, even if the behavior that day doesn't earn anything further. That's our basic model for involving a teacher.

Teachers are generally responsive to requests to help with our programs, but they have a lot of kids to attend to, plus administrative and professional duties, and you can't ask for a great deal of personalized service. So ask for as little effort as possible on the teacher's part. That's the beauty of the card program, which is often a hit with teachers. It's very effective, but it doesn't take more than a moment or two for the teacher to do her part. When you do ask for the teacher's help, remember that she is not the enemy, and she's not your employee. The teacher's on your side but very busy; so *ask* for help. Most parents — and this cuts across social class, at least in my experience — give teachers a lot of attitude. A wise parent can take advantage of this situation by being reasonable. And praise the teacher for talking with you, being available to help, and actually sending the card home or otherwise doing the program. They're human, and you're asking for behavior from the teacher, too, so reward it. Don't be stingy with your praise, and remember to be specific, whether you're doing it by e-mail, by voicemail, or in person.

Coach

One of the children we saw at the clinic, a nine-year-old boy named Jackson, shouted most of the time. After a few phrases in a normal voice, he would crank up several decibels higher than normal. His parents had his speech and hearing checked, but all was normal. Jackson consistently got in trouble for his shouting, despite the fact that the content of what he said — bellowed, really — was not a problem. He was not provocative, nasty, angry, or anything else like that. He was just way too loud, and it happened everywhere: at home, at mealtime and in sibling play with his eleven-year-old sister; at school, during recess, but also in class activities in which children worked together; at swimming lessons, which he had one day after school, plus a weekend group swim; and in the car, traveling with parents or friends.

We devised a fairly standard program. Jackson had a point chart for talking softly when playing with his sister or eating meals at the table. There were three situations per day — breakfast, pre-dinner play time, and dinner — and during each period he could earn zero, one, or three points, based on whether he shouted a lot (zero points), some of the time (one point), or not at all (three points). We used simulations, too, to create more opportunities for reinforced practice. The program worked predictably, with checkered performance in the first few days. Meals were fine, but when he played with his sister, he consistently earned zero or one point for the first week. He improved over time, and soon the shouting in these at-home situations was virtually eliminated. But he wasn't making the same progress in the car, at school, or at the swimming pool.

We turned to the pool next because it was the most urgent situation: the coach wanted to kick him out of the class. We called the coach to get his view of extending the program to the pool. He wanted Jackson to quiet down, but he wasn't very forthcoming about helping us accomplish that goal. To be fair, he just wanted to coach swimming, and he was reasonable in expecting families to deliver coachable children to him. We could work around him, though, so we moved forward with transferring the program to swimming. During swim time, Jackson's mother stayed in the bleachers, which were filled with waiting parents and siblings. There was a big clock on the wall that proved useful in marking out time periods. Jackson could earn three points for each fifteen-minute period of not shouting; zero points for that period if he shouted a lot, one point for a little shouting, and three for none. The unhelpful coach would not let Jackson's mom go over to the boy and use verbal praise, be close, be specific, and so on, so nonverbal praise had to be the immediate reinforcer. We work with what we've got. When he had a nonshouting or not-much-shouting time period, she would stand up with a huge smile and extended arm, making an okay sign.

The program at the pool was carried out twice per week. Jackson's shouting at the pool had already declined by the second time we did the program in week one. We extended the program to the car, where shouting was controlled immediately. The program was *not* extended to school, but the behavioral gains *did* extend themselves to school. Jackson stopped shouting there, except at recess as part of normal games. (Kids do shout. We weren't trying to turn him into an unnaturally quiet child.) Other situations where we knew of shouting but could not easily work on it, like the school bus, also reflected the change. We have no idea why Jackson shouted in the first place, but it was readily controlled by our basic ABC's, and we found it easy enough to extend the program to a few situations, after which the improved behavior generalized itself to all situations. The usual rule is that changes in additional situations are more rapid than in the original situation. Extending the program to one or two other situations will bring the desired behavior up quickly not only there but in others beyond them as well.

Now, if the coach had been willing to help with the program, here's how we would have involved him.

First, he gave feedback and comments to all the kids as part of the practice, anyway, so we would ask him to make a point of praising Jackson two or three times during the lesson when he caught him being quiet or talking softly. He could just lean down to Jackson between exercises and say, *Jackson, the way you're talking, nice and soft, that's great,* and give him a thumbs-up or an okay sign. Even if it meant that Jackson got a little less coaching on his backstroke in the short run, it would be good to have the coach reinforcing the desired behavior.

Second, it would be ideal if the coach was willing to use an index-card program like the one we use with teachers. As it was, the mother would go in to see the coach and do a verbal version of the index-card report. The card method would be better, though, because the card itself functions as a setting-up event. It cues both child and adult to focus on the program and do it well.

Vacation

The family outing this year includes a thirty-minute ride to the airport, a four-hour plane ride, and an hour-long ride to the hotel — lots of opportunities, in other words, for you to be glared at, reprimanded, or even kicked out of an airport, airplane, or cab if your child is out of control. You're worried about that because your eight-year-old child has meltdowns when she does not get her way. You read in some parenting book that you should take a lot of toys, books, DVDs, and so on to keep her distracted and occupied. Distraction has its place and can be useful, but it does not teach the desirable behavior. Its usefulness is limited to getting you through situations that occur infrequently and in which getting through it is all you need to do — for example, a medical test for your child that is mildly painful or stressful, or a long car ride that would be hard on anyone. In the case of predictable meltdowns, distraction is not likely to work. We have to teach new behaviors, and distraction techniques will never do that.

Then there's the related issue, of which as a parent you are well aware, that children often become irritable when they are tired or hungry. Adults, too. Biological conditions like hunger, fatigue, and heavy stimulation are internal setting-up events for problem behaviors in all of us. Again, rest and food, like distraction, can be useful in counteracting these setting-up events, but they will not teach desirable behaviors.

So you're ready for the trip. You've got toys, books, DVDs, a few bottles of water, and a snack — and let's also add to these a vacation point chart. (One parent kept it on a clipboard, so she could move it easily from car to hotel and back again.) This is like the chart you would use at home, with two exceptions. First, the behaviors may be different. Keep it simple and choose just two, and choose them with peaceful vacationing in mind. For instance, your child can get points for playing nicely with her brother and for being calm when mom or dad says no. Second, the rewards are different. Choose events that can be earned every day — a certain food, a TV show, a rented movie at the hotel, a later bedtime, a choice of activity for the next day. You can reward the behaviors directly (*If you play nicely with your brother and stay calm when mom or dad says no, you get to spend an extra half hour at the pool*), or you can use points that your child cashes in for prizes, as long as she cashes them in regularly during the vacation. It's fine to award points, but you can't wait to put them on the chart at home in a week and then exchange them for prizes, since delayed reinforcement makes a program ineffective.

And remember, as always, that your praise carries much of the weight of a program's success. You're not on vacation from praising your child for doing the behaviors you want her to do.

Joint Custody

I have seen many joint custody situations, and there is no one answer to the question of what to do about administering a program in two different homes. In order to come up with an answer that suits your situation, consider three factors that influence the decision: How often/long is your child in the other home rather than yours? Is the behavior as likely to occur in the other home? And how good are the prospects for cooperation and communication between you and your ex (and your ex's new partner, if there is one)? There are other dimensions, to be sure, but let's start with these as we take a look at a couple of scenarios.

Traci, a ten-year-old girl, has a homework program in which she can get points for starting her work and working for thirty minutes, with a bonus for telling and showing her mother exactly what she's done. (It's good for your child to talk to you about her homework, since talking as part of the learning process improves retention, comprehension, and language. Also, in a general sense more related to our method, it allows you to reinforce the habit of sharing information and treating you as an educational ally, not just an enforcer.) She has a standard point chart, and her mother is great at praise. The mother has primary custody, but Traci spends two nights of every week at her dad's apartment. The homes are close to each other, a little over a mile apart, but, still, this less-than-optimal custody arrangement means that Traci's life is disrupted every week.

Among our options would be to set up something like what we would use with a teacher in school: have the dad complete a card that tells Traci's mother that Traci started her homework and worked for thirty minutes (or not), and send the card home with Traci so her mom can provide points on the main chart. But the dad insists on having his own program for his daughter. So over the phone we develop an easy-to-implement homework program for Traci when she's at her dad's. The nights at his place are Thursday and Friday; one could argue that Friday is not a homework night. We decide to take advantage of Friday night. Rather than using points, we ask the dad to choose a privilege for Friday night that he can provide or withhold based on Traci's homework behavior on Thursday. If on Thursday Traci starts her homework and works for thirty minutes and tells her dad what she did, then on Friday they can do one of three things: go to a movie of her choice, eat at a restaurant of her choice (just diners and chain restaurants, nothing fancy), or have a friend come over for a few hours (or go to a movie with Traci and her dad). If she doesn't have homework that Thursday, we allow her instead to read a book or a magazine (her dad has *Time* and *National Geographic*), and this counts if she reads for thirty minutes and then describes what she read to her dad — which is all very good for reading, general education, and verbal skills.

A second scenario: We have a similar family at the clinic, with a five-year-old boy who spends every other weekend at his dad's place. The father and mother have a very adversarial relationship. Dad wants no part of the program, and in fact thinks that a special program for the child's tantrums is not needed because the problem behavior is the mother's fault. This is a common situation, and it's not our business to argue with the father about it. Also, we know that arguing will not be an effective way to change his behavior, and that it would be a setting-up event for resistance and noncooperation from him. The boy is there only two weekends per month, and it's unlikely that we can get the father to do the program well, so let's suspend it on those weekends. There's no program at all while the dad's the custodial parent.

Surprisingly perhaps, we have had divorced couples, with one or both of them remarried or re-partnered, and both the mother and father come to the treatment session. They want to be consistent, to have a seamless program in their joint custody, and genuinely want to do what is best for the child in relation to our program. I'm struck by how often the divorced couple seems to get along wonderfully well in our session, even though their prior comments about the divorce suggest that this wasn't always the case. When everyone's willing, we have the program as usual in the primary home in which the child spends more time, and have the parent in the other home provide a card each day with a 1, 2, or 3 checked on it. The child takes it back to the primary home to turn it in for points, as we would do when working with a teacher.

Of course, some divorced couples do pick at each other during a session at the clinic. Often, it takes the form of the father telling the mother something like, *If you would get tougher with him, he wouldn't have such a tantrum or hit his sister. It's got to be you, because I don't have a problem with him.* In cases in which the father has primary custody, we often see the roles reversed: the noncustodial mother says she has no problem with the child and accuses the custodial father of spoiling or babying him. It makes sense. The parent who's in charge of the child more often is much more likely to make requests and to be saddled with regularly handling the hardest day-to-day behavioral issues — homework, chores, and the like. We do not get involved in such family arguments, but just remind the parents what we are here for and that we have to stop the session immediately if their relationship issues keep getting in the way. In 99 percent of the cases, this takes care of it. When you're trying to figure out how to extend our program between two households, you'll probably need to find a compromise between the desire to help your child (which you share with your ex, no matter how bitterly you may be divided now) and a realistic assessment of how much cooperation is possible.

You Already Did the Hard Part

When maintaining or extending the results of a program, keep in mind that doing the original program — getting the behavior, reinforcing it, stabilizing it so it happened consistently in the original situation — was the hard part. The research on maintaining improved behavior and transferring it to other situations tells us clearly that you don't need to go through all that again. Although the numbers can't be guaranteed, a general rule of thumb is that if it took you three weeks to get the behavior at home, you can probably extend it to school by starting up a program there for a couple of days or a week. You're building on the original work, not replicating it.

When the body of techniques for changing human behavior first emerged in the early 1970s, continuing through the 1980s, objections came up as soon as the first successes were announced. The objections usually went like this: *Yes, you can change this or that behavior or problem, but it may not be maintained or carry over to other situations.* Many of us thought this was a curious reaction, just on the face of it. The new approaches had accomplished dramatic and unprecedented changes in behavior, in diverse populations that had been considered intractable (including children with intellectual or developmental disability and adults with severe psychiatric disorders), and now they were talking about the next problem? *Sure you've found a cure for child leukemia,* the naysayers seemed to be naysaying, *but what about all those adults?* The concern was still valid, but, hey, allow us a moment of celebration for the initial victory in accomplishing something that other approaches had not been able to do at all.

As I've noted before, though, the hardwiring of the human brain favors Eeyore rather than Pooh, so greater attention to weaknesses and problems is natural. The technology of behavior change was in its nascent phase, and, to be fair to the critics, it was unclear back then that behavior could be maintained after treatment and could carry over to other situations. But the field has largely consigned this doubt to the past. It *is* clear now that behavior can be maintained and transferred. We know how to do it. The problem is that conventional wisdom and popular opinion in this matter have not always progressed far beyond where they were in the early 1970s, when the great wave of breakthroughs in research into human behavior began to appear. Nor have most child-rearing experts devoted much effort to teaching parents how to sustain better behavior. So I feel that I'm writing against the grain of your expectations in telling you about the good prospects for maintaining and transferring improved behavior. It's eminently worth doing, though, especially since I'm bringing good news.

10

Parenting Stress and Household Chaos

I have tried to walk the line between the ideal and the real in presenting my approach to changing children's behavior. You now should have a sense of how to administer a program under ideal conditions. Especially in the program's initial phases, that means making an effort to do everything as well and as regularly as you can: ensuring that there are many opportunities for the desired behavior to occur, attending to and reinforcing the behavior, being specific in your prompts and praise, displaying enthusiasm whenever it's called for, remaining calm at all times, and so on. But we're all imperfect, and our busy, complicated, stretched-thin lives do not often allow for ideal conditions or perfect execution of a program. Real parents often have jobs and other responsibilities that affect their ability to administer a program. They get sick, they get mad, they get divorced, they have to be elsewhere for large parts of the day. You should take heart in knowing that even if you have one or more of these stressors in your life, you can make progress with a program if you can be at least pretty good some of the time.

Still, the basic point holds: when you're trying to administer a program for changing a child's behavior, life frequently gets in the way.

So let's talk about the stresses that child-rearing typically puts on parents, the effect of those stresses, and what might be done about them.

Parenting Stress

Your body and mind are powerfully affected by how you respond to the world around you. In a stress reaction, neurotransmitters in the brain and hormones trigger all sorts of changes, including increased heart rate and blood pressure, tensing of muscles, and other responses that prepare you to be alert and to take action, if necessary. Normally, there's a quick reaction, followed by recovery. And stress is not automatically negative, since many of life's most exciting and stimulating events induce a similar reaction. However, if there are too many quick reactions or when there are chronic sources of stress, you remain on alert in a hypervigilant state for too long, which can lead to mental and physical health problems — from more colds to serious diseases, from anxiety to suicide.

Stressors that produce these physiological and psychological reactions range from important but infrequent low-rate events, such as divorce or loss of a job, all the way to chronic stressors that are always with you, like a physical disability or psychiatric condition. In the middle are episodic events, periodically recurring, such as bouts of depression or a period of heavy work at your job. Stressors can be positive as well as negative, and many come in mixed packages. A wedding or the arrival of a baby, for example, brings both great joy and new cares.

The hassles of daily life are stressors experienced in smaller, regular doses, such as dealing with a child's problems at school, handling the details of child care, managing schedules, arranging for rides, and so on. The accumulation of these minor stressful events, even though none by itself may be a major shock to the system, can take a toll on mental and physical health. Stress in all its forms, from the most momentous once-in-a-lifetime event (*Triplets?!?!*) to the most mundane little hassle (*For the thousandth time, I've got to fix that screen door*), is a normal part of life that can influence child-rearing. Parenting stress, the range of pressures and worries that comes with the role of being a parent, is often significantly influenced by your own expectations, beliefs, and sense of your duties as a parent, and by your child's reactions to them.

One important thing to understand about stress is that the event itself — the stressor — is only part of the equation. An individual's perceptions and attitudes contribute to how the event is experienced (as positive, neutral, or negative) and the extent to which it acts as a stressor. Think of a roller coaster ride, which can be an exhilarating experience for one person, a difficult and frightening experience for another, and a boring nonevent for yet another. Stress is not just a function of what kind or how many stressors come at you in life; it's also a function of how you handle them.

A child's obnoxious behavior, to take a relevant example, will vary in its stress value to the parent. Do you see the child's behavior as willful or manipulative on her part, for instance, or as part of normal child development? For one thing, if it's the former (willful and manipulative), the child is at greater risk for physical abuse. I have seen a couple of parents who beat their infants or toddlers because they "cried too much." It turned out that there was nothing special in the amount or intensity of the crying, which could be tied to being hungry, or needing a diaper changed, or teething. A crying child, especially your child, is a universal source of stress, but different people in different situations will react differently to that stressor.

These days, more couples are having children after being in their careers for a while. This makes the birth of the child and the early years a little more stressful than usual, as parents have to coordinate family life around two careers. The child must fit into reasonably well-established lives, whereas in years gone by this was less likely to be the case, because the child was in the picture earlier in the marriage and exerted a greater influence on how the rest of the picture shaped up. For two-career families, the routine challenges and responsibilities of raising children — coordination of meals, transportation, daycare — can be especially intricate and stressful. And if you add just one other item to the mix — the need to care for a parent's parent for a little while, the loss of a regular babysitter — the whole system can be greatly strained, which not only produces new stressors but can also increase the stress value of even the most common hassles.

Whether you're part of a two-career, one-career, or no-career family, the pressure as well as the joy of new and changing demands as your child grows can be inherently a little stressful. Parents worry about welfare, safety, schooling, babysitting, and their own parenting skills, but they also worry about what will happen next. It's not crazy or uncommon to wake up in the middle of the night in acute distress over 1) the baby's cough, and 2) how to pay for the baby's college education. There's also a little extra anxiety associated with the first child, as demonstrated by a few too many calls to the pediatrician and subjecting the first babysitter to a security screening worthy of a nominee to head the FBI. In the Web cam age, you can now even try to address your worries about your child during the work day by checking up on her from the office. But this response to a typical stressor — having to be away from your kids for much of the day — may also *increase* stress: *Why did the babysitter put her to sleep on her stomach? And where is that babysitter? Is she taking a nap, too? How do you get this %@#*! Web cam to track to the left? Uh-oh, here comes my boss.*

Becoming a parent at all is stressful. About 10 percent of new mothers and about 4 percent of new fathers experience serious clinical depression after the child is born. There's more marital conflict after the birth of the child as well. These reactions do not rise out of nowhere. Any early signs of depression or marital discord before the birth are more likely to make these reactions more salient after it. The child's arrival increases the pressure on a household, revealing and deepening preexisting cracks and tensions.

The medical and psychological conditions of having a child, especially any complications (preterm, low birth weight, physical or psychological abnormality, disability, a chronic health condition), also increase stress on the parent, which in turn influences parent-child interaction. For example, increased parenting stress often makes parents less responsive and infants more fussy and distractible.

Parents also respond differently to different sorts of problems their children might have. They tend to be most acutely stressed by what are called "externalizing problems," those that affect others by disrupting the environment, such as oppositional behavior, aggression, or hyperactivity. By contrast, "internalizing problems," with their focus within the individual, such as anxiety, depression, and withdrawal, tend to be noticed less by parents and teachers, and therefore bother them less, and so are less likely to cause parental stress, even though they can become serious. Both externalizing and internalizing problems can range from very mild to very serious, but the externalizing ones tend to get the attention.

Effects of Parenting Stress on Parent and Child Behavior

Parenting stress has been well studied. The research shows that parents who are more stressed in relation to their parenting role are

- More likely to be harsh and authoritarian in their interactions with their child
- More hostile and aggressive in their statements
- Likely to rely more on corporal punishment
- More reactive (they're less able to let things go)
- Less emotionally involved with their child

This list translates into A's, B's, and C's in ways that undermine a parent's effectiveness.

Consider the differences between a stressed and a nonstressed parent asking a child to put on a coat. The stressed parent speaks sternly, with a harsh tone, furrowed brow, arm almost fully extended, with index finger pointing to the coat closet: *Put on your coat so we can go out.* The parent's manner presents nothing but setting-up events that will greatly increase the likelihood of noncompliance (the child simply not doing what he's being told to do) and oppositional behavior (refusal, whining, a small or large tantrum). A non- or less-stressed parent will make the same statement in a more empathetic tone and with less confrontational body language. It's a much more effective antecedent, and therefore much more likely to get compliance. Throw a "please" in front of the statement and we have gone from a weak pop fly to a home run.

Stress also affects a parent's reaction to a child's behaviors. It takes a lot less misbehavior to set off a stressed parent — and, it's important to note, a given parent will react differently on more- or less-stressed days. A child's routine behaviors are more likely to elicit a negative comment from a stressed parent. Here I'm talking about accidentally spilling food or drink, taking too long to get out of the car or get ready to leave the house, dawdling over brushing teeth — things like that. More severe behaviors, such as hitting a sibling, staining a tablecloth, or tearing clothing are likely to inspire a more severe reaction from a more-stressed parent.

Finally, there's the effect on the delivery of consequences. More-stressed parents are less able to praise and more readily prone to punish and react negatively. The more stressed they are, the more they are on the lookout for deviance rather than for good behavior. That is, they are more prone to attend to misbehavior and not attend to good behavior. Stressed parents also punish more, and more harshly. You're having a bad day, your child is getting on your nerves, she crosses the line in some trivial but last-straw kind of way, and you find yourself hauling off and slapping her for an offense that on a good day you would barely notice. When it comes to consequences, as is the case for antecedents and behaviors, a reciprocal process develops in which the parent's reactions make the child's behavior worse, which in turn contributes to further stress on the parent.

This reciprocal process can mute, mitigate, or flatly undermine everything positive that I ask you to do in this book. Very stressed parents who come to the Yale Parenting Center and Child Conduct Clinic have honestly reported to us that they cannot do the program, but what we actually see is that they have an unwitting and unintentional but nonetheless systematic program in place that *maintains* their child's deviance and defiance. For stressed parents, not being able to follow through and do our program usually means, instead, doing many things that are counterproductive to developing good behavior in their child. When their parental habits — like overreacting — make life more difficult for themselves and their families, those habits tend to be errors of commission. For nonstressed parents, by contrast, not doing the program typically means nothing worse than bumping along like the rest of us, probably raising kids who turn out all right, not doing any flagrant damage but also not necessarily taking conscious, programmatic steps to develop the behaviors they'd like to see in their child. Their parental habits, when they make life more difficult in the household, tend to be less harmful errors of omission. That is, even if he or she can't get it together to do the program, the nonstressed parent can still practice the kind of child-rearing that most of us experienced as children and now practice with our own children.

Effects of Stress on Attachment

Attachment is the bond between parent and child established early in life. From the parent's perspective, a good, strong "secure attachment" (the term used by psychologists) includes perceiving the needs of the child, responding to them, and providing a caring, warm, soothing relationship. The parent's behavior is predictable and dependable in providing necessities like food and comfort. This type of parental reaction helps the child develop. A child with a secure attachment can better cope with anxieties of life (such as early separations from the parent) and, more generally, will display better social, emotional, and behavioral adjustment over the course of life.

Parenting stress disrupts the development of attachment. A harsher, more authoritarian, more hostile, more aggressive, more reactive, less emotionally involved parent who's more likely to rely more on corporal punishment will find it harder to establish a secure connection with a child. And, of course, a parent's attachment history with his or her own parents is relevant here. So are the child's individual traits. An infant with an easy temperament who is adaptable when presented with some change in routine (like being handed to other people) makes everything easier for the parent, but a child with a more difficult temperament will increase the parent's stress, which may well further disrupt attachment.

Parental depression is also related to stress and has significant impact on child-rearing. Depressed parents are more likely to be reactive, hostile, and overly controlling in their interactions with their children. They are also more withdrawn. All of this interferes with attachment and affects a child's adjustment more generally.

In short, parenting stress, parental depression, and later child behavior problems are all intertwined.

What to Do About Parenting Stress

When we work with parents at the clinic, one of our goals is to cope with, better manage, and reduce parental stress. There are several facets of life in which you can do something about stress, and as is the case with investments, it is wise to have a portfolio with at least a few of these.

- *Social supports.* Spending time with friends and relatives, with and without the children, can reduce stress. Of course, some friends and relatives can be stressful in their own right, but having some time free from specifically child-related stress is important.
- *Time for yourself.* Plan some time in advance. Even a fairly brief regular break from family life, by yourself or with a friend or friends, can make a big difference in your life.
- *Time with your partner.* Schedule these in advance, if possible. For example, every Saturday you and your spouse give the children early dinner, set them up with a movie, and tell them they cannot interrupt your dinner.
- *Quality time.* Nonrushed time with your child in an outing or family activity.
- *A less programmed life.* It may actually take more planning, and you'll be moving against the grain of our increasingly overscheduled family culture, but you may well find that you can reduce stress by reducing the number of scheduled activities in your week. You and your family may need more down time, and you may well have to program that down time in advance.
- *More family time that is routine and ritual.* One popular option is a special meal during the course of the week, a special Friday dinner or Sunday breakfast that becomes dependably regular.

- *Participation in some group activity that makes you part of a community:* a hobby, arts, religious services.
- *Psychotherapy.* If depression or stress get too bad — if your functioning as a parent is significantly impaired, and the solutions you can pursue on your own don't do enough to address the problem — then you need to consider seeking professional help. I will have more to say about this option at the end of this chapter.

Stress Research and Family Stories

My method is effective even in highly stressed families. The research shows that clearly. However, those highly stressed families encounter more obstacles than other families in even coming to treatment. They have higher rates of canceling sessions, not showing up, and dropping out of treatment before we finish. All of this makes sense. When a family is juggling — or feels like it's juggling — too many balls and just barely catching them, coming to the clinic just seems to add another ball or two to the mix. It's another transportation headache during the peak afternoon hours of logistical hassle, a day of the week on which they must rush to throw together a delayed dinner after treatment, and so on. Throw in a car repair, a sick child, and maybe a single parent's extra-crazed schedule, and we have changed the game from juggling to standing in front of an out-of-control tennis ball machine and trying to catch the balls as they rocket past at unpredictable intervals. Of course they skip treatment and drop out more often.

So parenting stress affects a family's ability to do the program or even to try to do the program, and it has also been clearly established as an influence on child-rearing. My colleagues and I decided, therefore, to add a component to our treatment at the clinic that focused on parenting stress. We interspersed individual sessions for the parent who was more involved in the care of the child (in two-parent families) or the sole parent/guardian in single-parent families. These sessions identified stressors (for example, no time for myself or my spouse) and gave concrete assignments in conjunction with the parent's ideas (such as a coffee klatch with a neighbor, go out one night a week with a friend). The parents who received this stress-management intervention, not surprisingly, showed greater progress in improving their children's behavior and reducing their own depression and stress.

My method works, in large part, because parents do the ABC's properly and in a systematic way, but, as we've documented in several studies, it also leads to reductions in parenting stress. Doing the program right and feeling less parenting stress reinforce each other. We often see parents' stress levels go down early on in the program as the introduction of a systematic approach and some new skills (how to give specific prompts and praise, for instance) lessens their sense of being under pressure with no tools at their disposal other than those that make the problem worse, like punishment. As stress goes down, the parent administers the program better — issuing fewer commands, using a less harsh tone, and so on. And as the child's behavior improves, some major stressors are removed from the parent's life.

Some stress is so great, though, that it needs attention before treatment. Sometimes, a family coming to us has a parent so obviously stressed and depressed that the first priority is to get the parent into treatment, which sometimes includes hospitalization for suicidal behavior. Sometimes, the stress can be traced to basic living situations that have to be addressed before we can begin effective treatment. In one extreme case, a mother called our clinic and wanted treatment for her seven-year-old son. He was very disruptive, refused to go to school, and fought endlessly with siblings. She told us that everything in her life was out of control. She and her four children had been evicted from their apartment and were living full-time in her car — a large car, she noted, as if that made it much easier. With these living conditions, she was under so much stress that there wasn't any point in starting treatment until we could help her get better housing and food for her family. So we worked on that first. Once these basic life issues were addressed, we could work on her son's behavior problems.

More typically, a thirty-five-year-old mother, Marya, a single parent who worked as a paralegal, came for treatment of her eleven-year-old son, Darryl. It was just the two of them in the home. Marya worked at a high-powered, high-pressure law office, she frequently worked overtime, and she had complex afterschool-care plans for Darryl. He had to be driven to his afterschool program on some days and driven home on others. Making this arrangement work, which included cooperating with the person Marya hired to do pick-ups and transfers and babysitting, was complex and difficult. When Marya got home, the babysitter left, Marya made dinner, helped Darryl with homework, got him to bed, handled the mail and cleanup and other household business, had a glass of wine, went to bed, and started up again the next day. This life was very stressful even on a good day. Marya came to us because they started having too many bad days. Darryl was getting in trouble at school, he was placed on detention at home for three days, Marya had to hustle more babysitting, Darryl went back to school but got sent home again for provoking a fight, and so on. The school was now calling Marya regularly at work. She came to the clinic visibly distraught; she was one of the parents who arrived asking for better punishment techniques.

We began our regular work to set up a program to deal with Darryl's aggression and oppositional behavior, but also devoted a few sessions to addressing Marya's stress. We identified the stressors, brainstormed possible solutions, and tried one or two of them. The first of these sessions focused on back-up plans for child-care help, including carpooling with someone else at school so Darryl could go to a friend's house two afternoons per week. This adjustment eased some of Marya's tasks and squeezed in a little more time for herself. We also discussed the importance of her conveying to her bosses at the law firm that she could not work overtime. In addition, we asked her to select some activity she could do to make her day a little less stressful. We settled on eating lunch with someone at the office. Marya was always invited out but usually said no and ate at her desk. The small adjustments to aid her own situation that came out of these sessions were huge hits. She loved them and felt very relieved. The program for Darryl also went well, the level of stress in the home was greatly reduced, and the relationship between mother and son improved.

Another family that came to the clinic was composed of a twenty-eight-year-old mother, Liz, a nurse's aide; a thirty-four-year-old father,

Alexai, who drove a local truck route; and their four-year-old son, A.J. Liz worked a full nursing schedule, made dinner, took care of the house, and was entirely responsible for their child. Not surprisingly, she felt seriously stressed. In one of our brainstorming sessions with her, she said a little time for herself would be good. She thought shopping one evening with a neighborhood friend would be great and would fit her schedule. She meant just window shopping; money was tight in her household, which was one of the major pressures on them.

But Liz felt that she could not ask her husband for a night out. It just did not fit with the roles in their relationship, she said. In the session, therefore, the therapist and Liz practiced asking Alexai for the night out. The therapist first played Liz's part, addressing her as if she were Alexai; then they talked about what was said; then Liz repeated the therapist's little speech back to the therapist as if she were talking to her husband. They practiced some more, refining the speech. Liz went home that night and gave the speech to Alexai. She would like some time out, and would he please take care of A.J. for that evening. She would be out from approximately 7:00 to 9:00, if that was okay. After all this buildup, Alexai anticlimatically shrugged his shoulders and said fine. After the first Tuesday evening expedition, Liz was much happier and less stressed. She did not take this little two-hour break as merely a night off or time for herself. These evenings had much greater significance for her. They showed that her husband cared about her, that he was willing to share in child-rearing, that he could change. She did not take all the Tuesdays to which she was entitled but did periodically go on a Tuesday evening outing for at least a year and a half.

Household Chaos

Household chaos contributes to children's misbehavior. It's related to other influences, like parenting stress, but also makes its own unique contribution to behavior. Lowering chaos and related stress won't solve your children's behavior problems all by itself, but it will make you more effective in carrying out a program that will change their behavior, and it may give your children a stronger base upon which to build their relationship to you and their own sense of security and confidence.

How do we know all this? Household chaos, believe it or not, has been studied by scientists, who define it as a set of conditions: a household high in noise and activity and low in regular activities, routines, and rituals. It's a matter of degree, of course. All households with children in them can feel chaotic at times. So when we talk about household chaos as a condition, we mean a little more movement and activity around the house; a little less knowledge of where everyone is or what they're doing; more decisions made on the fly about meals, transportation, and other logistics; a little less predictability when it comes to even the most basic activities.

Chaos is related to other harmful influences on family life and a child's behavior. So, for example, people living in overcrowded homes tend to experience more chaos. Granted, such families generally have less money, more stress, job insecurity, poor health care, live-in relatives, and so on, but chaos is not merely one among such factors. Chaos cuts across all of them, and *also* across social class. It's present in uncrowded, financially secure middle-class and wealthy homes, too. I have learned that you can actually hear chaos over the phone. When I call a parent in a chaos-filled home from my clinic, the experience is almost stunning and more than a little sad. When the parent answers, the background noise is so thick and vibrant that it sounds as if somebody, perhaps the director of a new reality show called *Families Gone Wild*, had gathered everyone in the home and instructed them to cut loose on cue. There's shouting, a cacophony of video game noises, rapid-fire requests from a child to the parent to whom I'm speaking, a crying infant, an adolescent yelling. Everyone in the home is on edge, almost as if they were exposed full-time to the piped-in sounds of fingernails running down a blackboard. I grow anxious even writing this description. Serious household chaos definitely passes our "stranger test" — even someone who knows nothing about the people who live in that home can see, hear, and feel it.

Parenting stress, depression, poverty, and chaos are related, but researchers are able to study chaos under conditions that separate it from these other influences. This matters because the research shows a relationship between household chaos and oppositional and difficult child behaviors in the home. More chaos tends to equal greater difficulty in the child; the relationship is not trivial.

Do problem children make a home more chaotic and is *that* the problem? That's half of it. Chaos contributes to problem child behavior and problem behavior contributes to chaos, but the chaos in the home is the major source of influence in the two-way relationship. And when you put chaos together with parenting stress, which tends to lead to parenting practices that can increase oppositional behavior, the results are often particularly bad.

Reducing chaos and parent stress in the home is likely to lower the level of oppositional behavior, because chaos and stress are setting-up events for actions by the parent (overreacting, harsh comments) and by the child (more oppositional behavior) that boil up to a high level of emotional heat and conflict. Improving a child's behavior will reduce chaos and stress, as I've demonstrated in my research. If there are behaviors to develop or get rid of, we still turn first to reinforced practice and our program. However, reducing the chaos and stress in the household by other means can also help, even if it's not likely to solve the problem all by itself. Even minor reductions in chaos and stress can allow the parent and the child to avoid provoking each other and therefore work more effectively on improving behavior — by delivering ABC's better, for instance, or doing simulations better.

So, in addition to working on the child's behavior, we can work on changing the tone of the home. Effecting even a slight change can make a big difference in the outcome of our program.

Bringing Order to the Household

Science shows that there's something you already do that, if done slightly better or more, can go a long way toward reducing household chaos and related stress. The main recommendation coming out of the research is to develop more routines: regular, repeated, predictable, reliable activities that individuals in the home usually perform as a group.

Most of these are daily activities, but they can recur over any period, as long as they're regular. Daily and weekly activities might include, for instance, eating any meal together (including special meals like Sunday dinner, Saturday pancake breakfast, Thursday night seafood, and so on), watching TV, going to some event (a game, church, and so on), weekly pizza night out, or an afterschool pattern of behavior (say, a parent-child snack during which you chat for fifteen minutes about school or friends). More intermittent are holiday routines — a special birthday tradition, family Thanksgiving traditions, a big picnic on the Fourth of July or Labor Day. These activities don't need to be unvarying, and if there is a base of several routines then changing any one or two once in a while is of no consequence. But, in general, the greater the regularity, the less the chaos.

The research emphasizes instituting some select routines rather than trying to rigidly structure every facet of family life. To my knowledge, what you might call "the Goldilocks point," the point at which chaos tips into order and vice versa, has not yet been determined, but one can usually tell the difference between chaos and order nonetheless.

We emphasize all-family activities, in particular, to combat the general sense of household chaos, but routines for the individual child can be good, too. A set bedtime, a standard pre-bedtime sequence, some familiar Saturday morning or Sunday evening activity that begins or ends the weekend, walking the dog, a regular chore like doing the dishes, accompanying a parent on some regular errand . . . they can all act to reduce chaos. Try to create a mix of types of routine: some for the family, some for smaller groups within the family (depending on how big the family is), some for individuals.

If you think back to your own childhood, routines tend to be memorable and to organize memory, often fondly so, even when there was nothing special about them. I have a friend who as a child used to accompany his father to buy produce at Italian markets on Saturday mornings. It was a chore, basically, and the little boy's services were not really required to restock the household's supply of eggplant or potatoes, but the rich smell of spices in the stores and the sound of people speaking Italian (including his own father, who rarely spoke it at home) live on vividly in his adult memory as the feel of a time and place. My friend recalls that he was sometimes bored on these expeditions, wishing he could be home watching monster movies on TV or playing with his brothers and his friends, but the visits to the markets with his father helped give shape and rhythm to his week, and they gave him a chance to spend some time with his father, who worked long hours and was rarely home during the week when the kids were awake.

Routines bring with them other positive attributes. For instance, they give individuals a special role. Mealtime is a classic example: who sets the table, who sits where, who clears the table, and so on. These roles and activities reduce chaos but also increase communication in a positive way. Routines can also provide a structure for specific behaviors. At meals, to continue the example, a family "works" on manners, discusses values, retells the stories that give shape to its image of itself, and otherwise goes about the business of reminding itself that it is, in fact, a family. The routines of mealtime can act to bring together these positive influences. Another example would be a weekly trip to the public library, which not only helps give shape to a child's week but also can teach her to value books, reading, public institutions, and time spent with the parent who takes her there.

How Much Order Is Too Much?

You might plausibly ask, *Isn't it possible to have too much order? Couldn't that turn into a problem, too? Don't too many families already have overscheduled lives these days?* Yes, of course, but remember that I'm talking about trying to bring some order to households in which individuals — both parents and children — can barely identify and play their roles because life is so disorganized, unpredictable, and disorienting. A child unmoored from security by serious household chaos is not going to become some kind of robot if his parents add a few regular routines to his life on the order of walking the dog every afternoon, an afterschool snack with dad on Wednesdays, an hour set aside for homework before dinner on weeknights, and a drive with mom to visit grandma at the rest home every other Saturday.

But, yes, as with any human endeavor, occasionally someone will take the useful and usually constructive principle of greater routine a bit too far, into unhealthy regimentation. One family I worked with, in which the father was a corporate executive and the mother a part-time attorney, had almost every hour programmed for the two children: a nine-year-old boy and a ten-year-old girl. The kids had the usual school and afterschool routines, and then some lessons, but our first clue that this household had perhaps taken the notion of order too far was that each child had a checklist — not a point chart, just a check-off form — to monitor his or her room cleaning, homework, taking laundry downstairs to the basement, practicing (the son played an instrument, the daughter took ballet), and the like. During the weekends, the children were allowed one hour of TV, some homework time, an activity, and that was it. Everything else was heavily scheduled.

So virtually all of the kids' time was structured, and the parents' expectations for performance were also very high. They pushed the kids hard to do very well, all the time, at homework and music and dance. The combination of heavy structure and uniformly high standards for achievement produced a kind of hysterical parody of order that had some of the same stressing effect as household chaos. With everything having a clearly demarcated time, duration, and deadline, no one was ever relaxed. There is a lot of order in a space shuttle launch, for instance, but also great tension. If one little routine goes wrong, the whole mission — which, in the case of a family, is to achieve a tenable daily life, not to mention a decent future — may have to be aborted. You wouldn't want to endure that kind of tension every day of the week. In order to keep their routines running on schedule, the parents were constantly prompting behavior, making demands, rewarding or punishing — they were just *on* the kids all the time. The boy, especially, responded with tantrums, overactivity, and a truly astonishing amount of shouting. You met him in chapter 9: he's Jackson, the boy who shouted at home, in the pool, at his sister, everywhere, at everyone, almost all the time.

In addition to working with Jackson and his sister to support positive opposites of their problem behaviors, we came up with a shaping program for the parents as well as the kids. Our basic goal was to get the parents to chill (another ultratechnical psychological term). To that end, we created a new category, "off-duty time" — a term the mother, whose professional life was measured in billable minutes, liked and fully understood. There were no activities on Thursday afternoon or Saturday morning, for instance. During these two-hour blocks, the parents gave no prompts, made no demands, and made no statements (either questions or praise) about performance or achievement.

This easing of regimentation altered the tone of the home for the better, and there's a lesson here not only in balance and moderation but also in the principle of a U-shaped relation. Let me explain. Most of the time, we think about cause and effect as a linear relation. That's because it often is. If you do X, Y happens. If you do X a lot, Y happens a lot, so more X equals more Y. It works for, say, pressing on the gas to make your car go fast, or drinking alcohol to get drunk, or the correlation between high cholesterol and the risk of heart disease. But some relations are U-shaped. One of them is that between cholesterol and the risk of stroke. People with high *or* low cholesterol have a higher risk of stroke, and those in the middle have the lowest risk. It can be the same with routines. Chaos (not enough routines) and regimentation (too many routines) can have a similar negative stressing effect on a household. Regimentation is much rarer, and most households could use a few more routines, but we have seen a few cases of it at the clinic, and it can be almost as debilitating as chaos. One way to guard against regimentation, as you introduce more routines into your household, is to make sure that you include some all-family time, and not just a series of things that the kids need to do, and make sure that there's down time built into the day and the week.

Investing in Routine

Sound research, some of it very new, demonstrates that more routines (within reason) and reduced household chaos relate to these positive changes:

- Better performance in school — fewer academic problems, better performance in reading
- Fewer disruptive behaviors at school
- Reduced exposure of adolescents to risky situations, because

parents monitor their children better and/or have them engaged
in more constructive activities

- Greater stability in family life

I would expect that routines and reduced chaos also make children
feel safer, less anxious, and more able to cope with their own stressors. I have not conducted or found research to conclusively support
this leap, so at the moment I can call my expectation no more than
that. There are other such probable benefits of routines that have not,
to my knowledge, been studied. (Household chaos is a relatively new
area of study.) So, while I'm extrapolating beyond the research, let me
add to my list of expectations about what further studies will tell us.
Having a better idea of what's going on in the household and what
comes next probably reduces stress and tension for all individuals in
the home. Parents and children can devote less energy to improvising
the logistics of their day and more of it to positive, structured interactions: more talking, more problem solving, more conveying of values.
Finally, routines are an investment in the future because they help
build relationships in ways that should make difficult times less difficult. Children whose families have invested in good routines are
more likely to approach their parents and seek them out in times of
crisis or before a crisis arises. They're the opposite of children who are
punished too much, who escape and avoid their parents.

Seeking Professional Help for Yourself

Stress can be hard on a parent and family, no matter where it comes
from: within the parent, a strained relationship between parent and
child, a chaotic household, a difficult life situation that extends beyond the household, or all of the above. This book is about working
on the child's behavior (which also means, of course, working on the
parent's behavior), but that emphasis should not exclude the possibility of working on the parent's well-being.

Psychotherapy is suited for handling stress, life crises, and the like,
and not just for mental illnesses. It's the option for seeking help that I

wish to discuss here in greater detail, although, as I already noted, you would do best to develop a whole portfolio of ways to reduce stress.

If you feel on edge, depressed, and stressed about your child or your parenting, you might want to seek professional help. How do you decide that you need such help? Sometimes it's obvious that you're in trouble — you can't get out of bed to go to work, or you're crying all the time — but often the situation feels less clear-cut. It may help to think of stress as rain. When things are going all right, it's no more than a light drizzle, with occasional heavier showers. You've got your umbrella and raincoat, and if you get wet anyway, you can towel off when you get home, or maybe stand next to the radiator or in front of the fireplace for a while, and feel reasonably dry and comfortable. The umbrella, raincoat, towel, radiator, and fireplace represent your normal recuperative routines: a good night's sleep, a talk with your spouse, a contemplative walk with the dog. Usually, these are enough to re-equip you to get out there and do it again. But when you're feeling the stress more powerfully, the drizzle feels more like a monsoon, and you can't seem to get dry, no matter what you do. You're shivering and miserable, and it looks like it'll never let up. In other words, your normal recuperative routines aren't meeting your needs. You may try other such routines, but they may make the problem worse. For instance, you're drinking more alcohol, or at least your spouse says so, although you say you aren't. Or you're more vocal — maybe too vocal — at work, complaining and coming into conflict with others. Has something changed in how you're coping with stress? If the answer's yes, that might be a warning sign. Then ask yourself if the results are keeping you dry enough, so to speak. If the answer is no, then you might need some help.

On a good day, child-rearing is a challenge and can wear a parent thin. Contemporary life wears you even thinner with unreasonable work schedules and the logistically terrifying transportation schedules that come with often highly programmed lives in which children have activities before, during, and after school. Also, unlike years past, it's less likely that parents can call upon support from within the family — live-in grandparents who can help, or a spouse or partner who doesn't have a job to go to. All of these conditions can make contemporary life more stressful and child-rearing more difficult. Add a scoop of guilt on the part of one or more of the parents, and a topping in the form of an occasional crisis or deadline at work, and we have a problem, which can show up in all sorts of ways — from colds, anxiety, or a little more drinking or smoking, all the way up to seriously pathological behavior. One way in which the problem shows up is in parent-child interactions.

For your own mental health and for the social, emotional, and behavioral good of your developing child, it is not only acceptable to seek professional help, it also may be beneficial and well advised. Professional help might focus on managing stress, anxiety, or depression — three of the most likely needs. There are effective and brief psychotherapies (and medications, too) that can work wonders. Psychotherapy can be especially useful to help temporarily with stress. There are many situations in life in which additional support can be of great benefit. They can be very serious one-time jolts to the system — such as a member of the family receiving a diagnosis of a serious disease — or they can be ongoing situations that strain coping, such as taking care of an aging parent.

You may be thinking that this view of psychotherapy — as a temporary treatment to re-equip you to deal with parenting stress and do my method better — makes it seem like just a Band-Aid or a crutch. Don't say "just." Sometimes a Band-Aid or a crutch is exactly what's required to get you well. If you've got a cut on your hand or a sprained ankle, you could do worse than a Band-Aid or a crutch, two great inventions for helping people weather a health problem and recover from it. Similarly, if you're overwhelmed by parenting stress, psychotherapy may help you regain your equilibrium.

11

Beyond the Method

The method for changing children's behavior presented in this book can be applied to a great range of behaviors, from the everyday to the extreme. We know that for a scientifically well-tested fact. But there are limits to any approach, even a flexible and broadly applicable one. It's a big world out there, and human beings — even small ones — can be very complicated. So it's worth devoting this final chapter to considering what you should do in the unlikely event that having followed the program properly, you don't see good results. What's the relationship between my method and other approaches, such as addressing behavior problems with medication and changes in diet? When should you consider seeking professional help for your child?

When and Why the Program Doesn't Change Behaviors

You might follow the program correctly the first time, or find an error in your program and troubleshoot it properly, and it still might not work. The chances of this happening are relatively slim, yet the possibility exists.

The techniques we use at my clinic have been proven effective in dealing with the usual everyday child-rearing issues. But it's important to remember that our success rate of about 80 percent has been achieved for the most part in treating the toughest cases: the extreme problems of children referred clinically for oppositional, aggressive, antisocial, and violent behavior. "Success" means that families who come to the clinic with severe children's behavioral problems, and often with stress and household chaos as well, show great changes at home and at school. Most of these families have problems you would regard as far worse than whatever you're dealing with. They come to us because of serious fighting, apocalyptic tantrums, destruction of property, that kind of thing, and often they come to us because their child has been suspended from school or because their child's behavior has occasioned visits from the police or to the emergency room. One of our children, who became angry at his mom on the way to the clinic, tore out the ceiling lining of their car — all of it. When angry he would also systematically seek out his mother's oldies-but-goodies cassette tapes and break them. Another girl was so mad at her mother that she waited until her mother was sleeping and then jumped up and down on her chest, breaking three ribs. I'm telling you this to give you a sense of the severe behaviors that our sample group presents to us. The behaviors you're dealing with will probably not present as great a challenge.

So I can say with confidence, backed up by copious research, that my method will be successful most of the time and for most families. It offers a first and best intervention that you should employ before thinking of moving to more costly or invasive interventions — which may well have side effects, involve professionals, or cost a lot of money.

But we must also recognize that no treatment works every time and for every person. It's true of aspirin, chemotherapy, and antidepressants, and it's true of my method. But I can say at least this: we know this approach usually works to change behavior, and that when it doesn't work at first we can usually troubleshoot effectively to make it work, which means that you have much more control over the success of the therapy than you do when dealing with, say, medication or surgery. Doing the program right usually leads to good results; doing it sporadically or inconsistently usually leads to sporadic, inconsistent results. That doesn't mean that it's always your fault if the program doesn't work, but you can have a relatively greater effect on making changes in your child's environment, changes that will produce good results, than you would with almost any other treatment.

Research shows that parents and teachers often jump too swiftly to the conclusion that the program won't work for a particular child, when in fact troubleshooting can almost always turn an ineffective or less-than-ideally effective program into a success. So it's critical to troubleshoot the program first, and not conclude prematurely that it just doesn't work with your kid. That said, it is true that on occasion a particular behavior in a particular child is *not* influenced by the environment. In other words, it happens from time to time that it doesn't matter how good or how bad your prompts are, or how regularly you reward the desired behavior — the child still has tantrums or whatever the problem behavior in question might be. One cannot always tell by looking at the behavior whether it's one of these rare cases in which the environment's influence is weak. The same problem — tantrums, in this case — can occur for different reasons and vary in its responsiveness to what you or anybody else can do to affect it.

To take an extreme example, I have seen uncontrollable tantrums among children with rare genetic diseases that also feature major physical anomalies in organ systems, facial features, and growth patterns. The disorders can include psychological characteristics expressed as behavior, such as uncontrollable tantrums. Management of these often can be improved slightly with our usual techniques for changing behavior, but sometimes those techniques don't work. The behavior is so heavily determined by the genetic disease that it seems impervious to changes in the ABC's — changes, that is, in the environmental factors under parents' control in everyday life. More intensive treatment is needed, and even that, too, may be no guarantee of change.

Or consider headbanging behavior in children, which was once mistakenly thought to be maintained by the social attention it received from others. Parents, teachers, and others were thought to contribute to headbanging by giving their attention to a child who was hurting himself. (If you don't know what headbanging usually looks like, close your right hand to make a fist and pound your head on the right side, so that the heel of your hand — not the pinky-first part you would use to pound a table — hits slightly in front of your right ear, just on the hairline. Do it a few times, and throw in a few lefts. Picture a child doing that a lot.) It was reasonable to expect that concerned adults, instead of saying, *Are you all right?* or *Please don't do that*, might do better to ignore the behavior, starving it of attention — the strategy called "extinction." But that expectation did not pan out. It turned out that the self-stimulatory aspect of headbanging, the vibration and sensation of hitting, somehow reinforces the behavior. The attention of others doesn't matter very much in this instance. The lesson for us, in this context, is that reinforcers may be unexpected and not easily controlled, the consequences we expect to eliminate or sustain a behavior may not do so, and what we think of as a reinforcer may turn out not to be. A program could fail because it can't control the consequences that are critical to success.

I mention these examples because they convey that our procedures are not a cure-all for any type of problem that shows up in behavior. Usually the approach can help change everyday and even extreme behaviors, but not invariably.

Now, if you do the program right and it doesn't work, please don't jump to the conclusion that your child has a serious disorder. And in the likely case that there is a disorder involved, it might be something rare but not particularly serious that we can find ways to work around.

In some cases, not all of the usual consequences work to reinforce good behavior. For example, a very small fraction of children do not respond to praise as an effective reinforcer. In such cases, we can often turn praise into a reinforcer by pairing it with delivery of tokens, food, or other things that do function as reinforcers. Also, over the course of our treatment sessions I have repeatedly seen a child become responsive to praise, especially when it's given often and combined with warm physical contact.

Similarly, in some cases a typical punishment doesn't work as a negative consequence. I recall one little girl who regarded a time-out as a privilege, not a punishment. Her program wasn't working at all, mostly because she was receiving the supposed punishment as a reward. Once we switched over to using time-out as a reward, her program became much more effective and she made good progress.

Here I feel it necessary to make a distinction I haven't yet made in this book: between a reward and a reinforcer. I've used the terms more or less interchangeably so far, but this discussion obliges me to split a hair. Technically, a "reward" is defined as something the child will like and value. A "reinforcer" is defined as a consequence that when given contingently (that means the child gets it if and only if he does the desired behavior) increases the likelihood of the child doing the behavior again in the future. There's a large area of overlap between rewards and reinforcers, but not all rewards are reinforcers and not all reinforcers are rewards. The nonoverlapping portions can be critical. For instance, to take an adult example, if you ask teachers to list things they'd like to get more of in exchange for doing their jobs well, they'll mention vacation days, breaks during the day, and, of course, money. Teachers value these things, which makes them rewards, and they might well perform a particular behavior (say, teaching in a certain way) in order to get more of them, which makes them reinforcers. But studies show that there's another important kind of reinforcer that teachers rarely identify or claim to value: praise from principals and students. Such praise affects teachers' behavior, so it's a reinforcer, but they don't ask for it because they don't consider it a reward on a par with the others.

The point is that in some cases your child may not share your view of what constitutes an effective reward, reinforcer, or punishment. Or he may share your view, but even if you both agree that it's a reward it still may not function as a reinforcer. If the program's not working, you may want to consider such a possibility. And yes, in some rare cases you may have to conclude that you just can't come up with consequences that have the desired effect on behavior.

I remember one such case involving an aggressive thirteen-year-old girl who was referred to me after she beat up a few boys her age. We developed a program to reinforce positive opposites. The teacher sent home a card with her each day, awarding zero points for aggressive behavior, one point for no aggressive episodes, and two points for positive interaction with peers. We had all sorts of appealing rewards she could buy with points: time at the mall, gift certificates at a music store, and sleepovers with a friend. The program wasn't working, but, not wanting to be premature about declaring failure, we went troubleshooting. After making sure the basics were all right, we added consequence sharing, and that helped a little, but the results were still unsatisfactory. We tried other things, but made no further progress. The program just did not work, and I still can't say why, not for sure. Maybe she had a unique resistance to reinforcers and punishment. Maybe the submission she inspired in others by being aggressive reinforced her misbehavior so powerfully that it trumped everything we could throw behind the positive opposites. As I said, we're not sure why the program didn't work, but this particular child just didn't respond in the way that most others do. Like a pack-a-day smoker who lives to be one hundred, it's rare, but it happens.

When a program's not working, though, it's usually not because there's something unique about the child or because the program failed. It's far more commonly the case that the parents or other adults just can't do the program properly for some reason. Often, it's a practical issue, like the familiar situation in which a single parent has to work long hours, the child's at home alone too much, and there's no real time in which the parent and child can interact. This situation can indeed undermine a program's ability to change behavior, but it would be wrong to say in such a case that the program failed. It may have been impossible to do the program properly, but it didn't fail. The distinction is important, because if you can find a way to do the program properly — shortening work hours, more help with child care, and so forth — there's every reason to believe that you can improve your child's behavior. Don't conclude prematurely that there's something about your child that makes him or her immune to the program.

Medication and Diet

Parents who come to my clinic frequently ask about medication. Is there something we can prescribe that will solve the behavior problems they're grappling with? Less frequently, they ask the same question about diet. Can they make a change in what the child eats and drinks — less sugar, for instance — that will make him less disruptive, calmer, less out of control? I can understand why they ask. In our culture, we put a lot of stock in the silver bullet solution: the single fix, often with a high-technology component, that makes the problem go away all at once in a puff of smoke.

I have no general position for or against medication, nor do I regard medication and the proper use of the ABC's as in competition with each other. Medication, like diet, surgery, or remedial reading, can be very effective if used properly to treat a problem for which its use has been proven effective by scientifically reliable evidence. Specific medications provide specialized tools that can be used to address certain behaviors, and in some situations a medication can be the tool of choice. But these situations are limited, and medication is *not* a treatment of choice in addressing the disruptive behavior problems we've been discussing in this book. Nor is diet very relevant to treating these behavior problems. If medication or a change in diet were treatments of choice and the research backed up that conclusion, I would strongly recommend and endorse them. I have no investment in one tool over another. I try to use whatever the research, not just my own opinion or experience, tells me will work the best.

For now, though, let's ask the more general question that medication and diet bring up: where to begin in deciding how to treat your child?

Can Medication Help Address My Child's Problem Behaviors?

It depends on the problem. Currently, medications are not available or approved by the Food and Drug Administration for oppositional, aggressive, and antisocial behavior in children, or for problems that emerge in normal child-rearing. There is one exception. Professionals recognize stimulant medications (methylphenidate and amphetamines) as the treatment of choice for children with a diagnosis of attention-deficit/hyperactivity disorder (ADHD), which is characterized by symptoms such as inattention (a child makes careless mistakes and is easily distracted, for instance), hyperactivity (fidgeting, squirming), and impulsivity (blurting out answers, interrupting others). This recognition is based on strong scientific evidence. Even so, few professionals view medication as a satisfactory treatment, because the positive effects of medication — improving a child's concentration and reducing overactivity — occur only while the child is on the medication. Also, the long-term effects of medication are not evident. It makes no clear difference in adulthood whether one had one's hyperactivity medicated in childhood. As with any medication, there are side effects — affecting, for instance, growth and sleep. And, as with any treatment for any problem, treatment with medication does not always work. That said, medication often does work for hyperactivity, and it's the treatment of choice.

Many children who are hyperactive are also aggressive and oppositional. Medication is useful to reduce the hyperactivity but does not usually affect the other disruptive behaviors. The reverse is true, too. If the child is very aggressive and we control the aggression with my method, that may not reduce overactivity. Children sometimes have both types of problems at the same time. It is important to get expert advice on the matter of medication, especially because some schools loosely refer to children as hyperactive and strongly encourage their parents to seek medication to control their child's behavior. In many of these cases, this is an unnecessary measure. The children are not impaired and not abnormally active, and they don't need medication. These children can be readily managed by parents and teachers without medication, as we have done in homes and in schools for thirty years.

One tricky aspect is that stimulant medication improves the concentration of children and adults whether or not they are hyperactive, which is why stimulants have become the steroids of academia, widely abused on the occasion of exams by students who do not suffer from ADHD. So if a teacher or pediatrician tells you that your child is hyperactive and ought to be on meds, and the child is not at all hyperactive but you let yourself be convinced nonetheless to approve the meds, your child's concentration will indeed improve with medication. That doesn't mean he should be taking it, though, or risking the side effects. A parallel example: Even if you're not afflicted with a disease that dangerously decreases your muscle mass, taking steroids will help you increase that mass. That doesn't mean you should take steroids, and the fact that they "worked" doesn't prove you needed them. Nor was there good reason to risk the side effects.

If your child's school tells you that your child is hyperactive, or if you see signs of it yourself, seek expert advice from a pediatrician, psychologist, or child psychiatrist. If they do recommend medication and you choose to use it, monitor its effects closely. If the child is also oppositional or aggressive, research shows adding a program like mine to the medication can help.

But, I will reiterate, there is no medication, approved or pending approval, known to alter or intended to alter the kind of problems I address in this book, including

Not complying with parental requests
Having a bad attitude
Speaking offensively or harshly
Breaking things
Having catastrophic tantrums
Showing disrespect
Being careless in playing with siblings
Stealing
Arguing
Lying
Hitting peers, parents, teachers, or principals
Confronting others
Bullying
Finicky eating
Playing disruptively with peers
Not sharing
Not engaging in self-care (bathing, brushing teeth, getting dressed)
Not going to bed on time
Breaking curfew
Not letting parents know where you are
Not taking medicine
Not socializing with other children

In these and countless other cases of everyday — and not so everyday — behavior problems, medication is not very likely to help, and it might well hurt. And there's no medication that builds good habits.

What About Diet and Nutrition?

In the last few decades, there has been a spate of research in response to the worry that diet and nutrition cause behavioral problems in children, especially at school. The two main suspects, among many, were sugar in cereal and various dyes in foods. Obviously, good nutrition is essential to child development, and we know now that the consequences of nutrition run deep in families. Recent research even suggests that the nutrition of grandparents can affect the development and lifespan of grandchildren. So the issue is not whether nutrition is important or worthy of very careful deliberation by each family. Of course it is.

However, in relation to the problems listed above, changing a child's diet is not the answer. If a teenager's bad attitude, a toddler's playing with matches, or a child's morning tantrums when told to get ready for school could be altered by what we feed them, I would be hawking the preferred foods from a booth on the front lawn of my house. As a rule, there is no diet solution to the behavioral management problems we are discussing. "Sugar high" is not the issue.

This is not to discount diet-behavior connections within the larger realm of mind-body connections. For example, a small amount of lead in a child's diet over an extended period can lead to hyperactivity. This is not the usual cause of hyperactivity, but it is one cause for a small number of children. Or a child may have a very special allergy that is difficult to identify, and the allergic reaction could include irritability and oppositional behavior. So, I'm not saying that diet never *ever* plays a role in behavior problems. These and other examples convey what *can* happen and what does happen occasionally, but they are not the rule for hyperactivity and anxiety.

Be skeptical about nutritional solutions to social, emotional, and behavioral problems. They may not do any harm, but they may not do anything to solve the problems either. But yes, by all means, make sure your family eats well.

Seeking Help for Your Child

In changing children's behavior, as a general rule, we want to start with interventions that are the least invasive and costly in terms of restriction of the child's freedom (or yours), side effects, risks to the individual, time, and money. You don't place a child in long-term psychotherapy or a psychiatric hospital because he swears too much or has tantrums. You don't use medication, either — not only because these approaches have not been shown to be effective for swearing or tantrums but also because they bear other costs in time, side effects, stigma (at school, for instance, where regular trips to the nurse for medication can inspire comments from peers, different treatment from teachers, and the like), disruption of the child's and the family's life, and more.

As a point of departure, ask two questions in selecting interventions for yourself and your children.

First, is there evidence to support the efficacy of the treatment? Most therapies have no solid scientific evidence to show that they work. Make sure you are getting one that has been studied. See the end of this chapter for further advice on how to do that.

Second, is this the first place to begin, or is a less costly, less invasive, less restrictive alternative available?

Deciding when to refer a child to treatment is challenging for two main reasons. First, many people have psychiatric disorders or close approximations of them and yet are in the world, moving through normal life. Research consistently shows that one in five children, adolescents, and adults meets the criteria for at least one psychiatric disorder. This is a conservative estimate, because there is no clear-cut point that defines most disorders, and people who "just miss" meeting the criteria still have short- and long-term problems. With such a large proportion of the population meeting the criteria for psychiatric disorders, we must look not just for symptoms but also for signs that they interfere with the individual's functioning in the world. This is why impairment and dangerousness are among the decision-making criteria I list below.

Second, as part of normal development, many problems come and go routinely. Lying, stealing, stuttering, tantrums, oppositional behavior, anxiety and fear, sleeplessness, and excessive crying all emerge for many children as part of normal development. They can become significant problems, even for children who make up the "normal" sample (those not clinically referred for the problem). They're not trivial. If they were to persist, many parents would no doubt seek help for their child. But these behaviors tend to come and go without being treated by professionals, sharply decreasing after a brief peak.

- *Lying.* Studies show that approximately 30 to 40 percent of ten- and eleven-year-old boys and girls lie in a way that their parents identify as a significant problem. This age seems to be the peak, and the rate of problem lying tends to plummet thereafter and cease to be an issue.
- *Inability to sit still* is a significant problem for approximately 60 percent of four- and five-year-old boys, but decreases as they age.
- *Whining.* Approximately 50 percent of boys and girls who are four or five years of age whine to the extent that their parents consider it a significant problem. This too decreases with age.
- *Fears.* Before the age of five, the large majority of children go through phases in which they experience fear and anxiety. Common fears include darkness, monsters, small animals, or separation from an adult. Just because these fears occur in many children does not mean they are minor to the children experiencing them. They worry, cry, and lose sleep. Fortunately, most children lose these fears over time.
- *Delinquent acts.* By adolescence, over 50 percent of males and 20 to 35 percent of females have engaged in one delinquent (illegal) behavior. Typically, this involves stealing or vandalism. For most children, it does not turn into a continuing problem.
- *Stuttering.* Approximately 2.5 percent of children under the age of five stutter. The vast majority simply stop stuttering on their own, without treatment.

The normal course for all of the above problems is to decrease significantly or disappear entirely over time. The challenge is deciding whether to intervene professionally. Let's say your child is of just the "right" age to be afflicted by fears. That would argue for just comforting your child and waiting to see if the fears drop out on their own. But what if the child's anxiety really means he is crying all night, cannot go to daycare or school, and cannot be easily comforted by a parent? If things are that bad, you should consider seeking professional help. Let's consider some general criteria to help you make such decisions.

Some Help with Signs and Signals

How does a parent or teacher know when to seek help? Most parents have worked out a rough routine for deciding when to take a child to the doctor for a physical ailment. A sniffle and cough, by themselves, probably don't qualify. But add a fever and a rash, and most parents are likely to decide that this is something for a medical professional to look at. Add a stiff neck, and even the do-it-yourself holdouts may well call the doctor. You plug the data into your rough decision-making routine and out comes a judgment. That's how you make your decisions when it comes to physical health, but deciding when a person has the mental health equivalent of a high fever that requires a visit to a professional is not so clear-cut a process. The data are less precise, since there's no psychological equivalent of a thermometer, and in this area of health care, most parents tend not to have decision-making routines as ready to hand. But there are criteria you should look for to decide whether professional help beyond this book is needed. Look for any one of these:

Impairment. Does the child's behavior interfere with meeting the usual role expectations at home or at school? Many children (and adults) have anxiety, fears, and tantrums, but does the problem interfere with going to school (or work) regularly? If so, that would be impairment. Early in life, at the toddler stage, when the child may be just at home with a parent or babysitter, there are not too many role requirements, so it is especially hard to tell then. However, because daycare is used for younger and younger children, parents receive more complaints now than ever before that their child is not fitting in. Impairment is a difficult criterion to apply at these early life stages, when the child ought not to be expected to do very much. Sleeping, growing, and learning (from exposure to parents and the world) are the key objectives. Any further role demands, like fitting in with many others in a daycare setting, can be a bit unrealistic.

That said, if the child has to be regularly isolated in daycare or is repeatedly kicked out of preschool, this would qualify as impairment. Before the age of four or five, I would not seek any treatment unless there is something more stark (see below). After that, impairment as a criterion becomes more useful. Also, in some cases the behavior might well go away on its own, but the parents can't afford to wait that long. For instance, we have seen two-year-olds at my clinic who have been kicked out of multiple daycare centers for hitting. The hitting may well be a passing phase, but that doesn't matter to parents or daycare workers who have to deal with it. So hitting constitutes a sign of impairment here, even if it's not necessarily a sign of a serious long-lasting problem.

Even if we raise the bar for impairment in the early stages of life, it may become clear to a parent as she or he interacts with a young child that something potentially troubling is happening. The child will not eat, for instance, or does not respond physically (an infant who pushes away, for example), make eye contact, or turn around to look when you say his name. The normal range can be wide at this age, so don't panic, but you should probably visit a pediatrician just to bring up these concerns and get questions answered.

Change in behavior. A behavior may take on significance and become a problem because it represents a break from the usual pattern. Two different children might mope, tend to stay in their room, and not want to be with friends. For one child, this may be pretty much how she acts and has always acted, which is also, by the way, kind of like how her dad acts. For the other child, who is usually actively involved in things and pretty cheerful (when not giving the usual attitude, of course), moping and standoffishness mark a notable change. In the case of the latter child, a parent should be more alert to the possibility of depression. The change marks the behavior as clearly not a matter of temperament or enduring personality style, but something else.

Signs of distress. Is the child showing signs of stress that coincide with exposure to an event or stressor? Here I'm talking about, for instance, exposure to a disaster (anything from the grand scale, like a hurricane, down to something in the household, like a fire), domestic violence, death of a relative, peer bullying, sexual abuse, or even exposure to violent TV, be it *CSI* or news footage. The child may show lack of sleep, nightmares, anxiety, clinginess, or impairment as noted above. Many of the effects are transient, depending on the child and the nature of the event. If they do not go away or lessen after a few weeks (depending on the child and severity of the exposure to the event), consider seeking help.

Danger and risk of danger. Is the child's behavior dangerous to himself or to others? This may involve aggressive behavior that could hurt others or self-injury that is not accidental, which runs a range from poking pins into his own arm to setting fires to attempting suicide. One of my cases is a nine-year-old boy who slaps his new infant brother across the face in exactly the way a woman rebuffing a romantic advance would slap a man in an old movie. Another one of my cases, an eleven-year-old boy, placed a pillow over his six-month-old infant sister, which could have resulted in suffocation. In case you think that's not scary enough, he looked up at his mother, who had caught him in the act, and said, "Do you think she's dead yet?" He was brought to the emergency room and then to the inpatient unit I was directing at the time. These are, of course, clear cases of danger to others requiring immediate attention, whatever the child's intentions might be. If the baby is smothered, it doesn't really matter whether it was the result of malice or unwise play.

A child talking about killing himself or others must be taken seriously. The statements alone serve as a basis for seeking help or intervention. Sometimes, the decision is easy to make. A twelve-year-old boy was brought to my clinic because he kept telling a teacher he was going to kill her. This was not an isolated event or just a statement made in a moment of rage. He was calm, methodical in his presentation, and noted that his father had guns he would bring to school one day. An eight-year-old girl said she did not want to live and just wanted to kill herself. Again, she said this repeatedly and not just when prompted by a moment of strong emotion (for example, *I'm so embarrassed, I could just kill myself*).

Sometimes, the decision to seek help is harder to make. I'm not saying that you have to haul your four-year-old to the emergency room because he mimics a cartoon character saying, *I could just die.* Context matters. A young child may make an isolated statement or two, but the child seems fine at home, at school, and when playing with friends, and the statements disappear after a couple of days. That's one kind of context, and it would argue for just keeping an ear out for further statements. Another kind of reassuring context can be found in the minuscule suicide rate among the very young. But suicide attempts and suicide run in families, so that's part of the context, too, and it argues for alertness. And if a twelve-year-old girl says the same thing, that's different. Rates of suicide attempts and depression increase sharply with the onset of adolescence, especially for girls. Other context variables — not being involved with peers at school, the presence of a gun in the home, a "contagious" event in the media (a celebrity's recent suicide, for instance) that might inspire imitation — make the statement gain in seriousness until it's clear that you need to seek help for her.

Danger to oneself or others is a special case in which you should err on the side of obtaining an evaluation. When in doubt, get a professional opinion.

Behavior in relation to age. One complexity in judging the behavior of children is that they're changing so fast, presenting a moving target for your judgments about the relative seriousness of their problems. The behavior itself may not always be at issue; sometimes, it's the behavior in relation to the child's age. For instance, not being toilet trained by age three, four, or five is not a psychological calamity or even a problem, except that parents are sick and tired of changing diapers and don't want to deal with it anymore. More specifically, for children of five and under, bedwetting is not very significant in relation to current or future adjustment, but after the age of ten it becomes a risk factor that may presage serious psychological problems later in life. It's the same behavior, but the different age changes its meaning. Not being toilet trained by age ten or twelve predicts later aggression. The same is true of fears — of darkness, monsters, separation from a parent — all of which are a "normal" part of development for most children, even when those fears really do bother them. But the fears usually go away on their own. If they don't, the same problem with fear in middle or later childhood (ages ten to twelve) could reflect a more serious anxiety disorder.

Unusual behaviors and extreme symptoms. Here we arrive at a far and often disturbing end of the area defined as problem behavior. Is the child reporting hearing voices that tell him to do dangerous or harmful things, or engaging in endless repetitive behaviors (for example, with toys or objects) for hours on end? We have had cases in which voices tell the child to hurt others or to set fires. Seeing things that aren't there, believing that some spirit is controlling one's mind — these can be significant signs pointing to a serious disorder. Moreover, and it's worth repeating, it's a serious disorder whether or not the child acts on what the voices tell him to do.

Again, a parent should look for departure from the everyday. Much of early childhood and normal development includes imaginary play, imaginary friends, dialogues between stuffed animals, and just plain talking to yourself, sometimes in different voices. That is all part of play, a critical aspect of context. A five-year-old muttering to himself in two or three different voices while playing with toy soldiers on the floor is quite normal. A twelve-year-old sitting by himself, muttering in different voices, bears closer attention, especially if it happens more than once.

When in Doubt

Pediatricians, psychologists, and child psychiatrists are the first line of inquiry about how a child is doing. Pediatricians do not specialize in social, emotional, or behavioral problems and psychiatric disorders; their primary training is in medicine and physical health. But a large percentage of children (up to 40 percent) who are brought to them have psychological problems. Thus, pediatricians very often serve as parents' first contact with specialists who can treat such problems or make referrals to mental health professionals. Psychologists and child psychiatrists are trained to provide systematic evaluation, meaning that they use various standard psychological measures to see how the child is doing in many areas of social, emotional, cognitive, and behavioral functioning. And they're trained to look at different contexts — how the child is doing at home, in school, in peer relations — and assess any signs of trouble requiring follow-up. Sometimes this kind of evaluation is vitally important.

For example, a ten-year-old girl was referred to me because she was very disruptive at home and her parents could not manage her. Also, she couldn't sleep at night and seemed perturbed. The parents brought her to our clinic, and we did an evaluation, which included separate meetings with the parents and child. The evaluation revealed that she had many tantrums as part of home routines (such as eating and going to bed) and high levels of anxiety, as the parents had indicated. However, unbeknownst to the parents, she was clinically depressed and had very extensive suicidal thoughts — not just passing fancies but frequent thoughts, and a plan to kill herself with pills from her mom's medicine cabinet. She had, in fact, attempted suicide with a high dose of her mother's pills in the previous week, which had made her very sick. The parents just thought she was ill and let her stay home from school. We alerted the parents to this in the middle of the evaluation, suggested inpatient hospitalization for an evaluation, and then arranged at that moment for the girl to be admitted.

Another case involved a twelve-year-old boy who was doing very poorly at school because he got into many fights and wouldn't do any assigned work, be it in class or homework. Full evaluation revealed that he also met criteria for ADHD. The dominant symptoms were hyperactivity and inattentiveness. We began treatment at our clinic to address many of the behavioral problems, but we also encouraged his parents to work with a child psychiatrist with whom we consulted to consider a regimen of stimulant medication. Within ten days, the child was on medication and doing much better at school and at home.

Getting Help: Leads and Contacts

This section will necessarily be partial and open-ended, but there are some guidelines to bear in mind as you research the best way to get help for your child.

The first step is to find out what you can about the problem your child might have. Don't just Google the problem and click on whatever links you might find there. The Internet is filled with misinformation about clinical problems and effective treatment. You must go to a source where the information has been provided or screened by professionals. The Web pages listed below are reliable sources that meet these criteria. Currently, there's no Good Housekeeping Seal of Approval for websites' accuracy, but the federal government and other organizations mentioned below go to special lengths to present the latest and most accurate facts and findings.

The many professionals and others who offer services to treat particular problems are not all alike. Different psychologists, psychiatrists, social workers, family therapists, pastoral counselors, and others may all take different approaches to the same problem. Yes, you will want to start by making sure that the person you choose is a professional who is credentialed and licensed in the state in which he or she practices. But that's not enough, so it's your responsibility to ask questions and get second opinions. High on your list of questions to any professional should be

- What is the treatment you provide for my child's problems?
- How long have you been providing this treatment?
- Has this particular treatment been studied and does it have scientific evidence in its favor?
- What are treatment options other than the one you provide?

There's a delicate point to navigate here. Many of the treatments offered in clinical practices are not based on evidence of their effectiveness. It's likely that if you're seeking treatment for your child, you will encounter a warm, persuasive, reasonable, well-intentioned professional who has the requisite credentials, seems like a good person, and otherwise meets your expectations. The waiting room will look right. The office will look right. There will be framed certificates from suitably impressive and accredited institutions of higher learning and professional organizations. But none of this — *none* of it — guarantees that you will get worthwhile treatment. You need to be a critical consumer of mental health services, as critical as you would be when buying a car or a house. You have to find out if there's any evidence that the therapy provided by this professional actually works, and if the therapy is recognized as the treatment of choice. Ask. If you don't like the answer, ask somebody else. Even if you do like the answer, ask somebody else. It's a rare professional who will say, "I do this kind of therapy, but there are other therapies, which I don't use, that are even more effective and that have scientific research behind them." You will have to find such things out for yourself.

I won't list the various organizations' Web addresses, because they tend to change, but the information below is intended to at least get you started. (And you can start with a look at my website — http://www.childconductclinic .yale.edu/ — which has links to others.) For information about children's mental health and treatment services, go to the websites of the National Institutes of Health, the American Psychological Association, and the American Academy for Child and Adolescent Psychiatry. If you're trying to find therapists for children or families, you can try the websites of the National Register of Health Services Providers in Psychology or the Association for Behavioral and Cognitive Therapies, or you can ask the psychological association in your state (for example, the California Psychological Association, New York Psychological Association, or Illinois Psychological Association). Type the state followed by "Psychological Association" in your favorite search engine and the site will come up. It's also your responsibility to find out if there's good evidence for a particular treatment's effectiveness. The Cochrane Library, which can be found online, provides rigorous reviews of evidence related to medical and psychological treatments.

Conclusion
Positive Parenting

The mental health professions have tended to focus on deviance, violence, and illness — all important, to be sure, but not a full picture of human experience. They have put less emphasis on improving everyday life. But a few years ago, one of the leaders in my field, Martin Seligman, started an approach called "positive psychology." I admit that I skeptically rolled my eyes when I first heard the term, thinking that here was yet another approach that strayed from science into wishful vagueness. But I was wrong. Positive psychology turned out to be an effective approach that uses good science to help people make better lives. It is now an area of serious research, with a body of supporting studies — evidence that it works — that trumps many longer-established techniques in the field.

My method, which is in sympathy with positive psychology's intent to "build resilience, promote adaptive coping skills, and teach effective problem-solving" (as Seligman and his colleagues put it), does not focus narrowly on behavior to the exclusion of the rest of what makes a person a person. Nor do I think of my job as getting rid of the bad or repairing what's broken. Using science to help people build more positive lives for themselves and their families means that I often need to go beyond behavior and work on the larger relationship between parent and child.

With that in mind, let's reconsider the focus of the previous chapter, which was on the negative: impairment, danger, and problems that resist solution. If chapter 11 were all you read of this book, you might well spend the next few days, months, and years following your child around the house, hyper-alert for drastic changes or other potential warning signs of serious trouble. But to close the book in a way consistent with its emphasis on positive opposites, I want to turn the discussion around to consider your relationship with your child as a set of opportunities for what I'll call "positive parenting."

Whether or not you're actively engaged in a program to change your child's behavior, there is so much you can do to help your child, so much you can do to prevent or minimize social, emotional, behavioral, and adjustment problems. It's important, I think, to mention some of these things you can do, even if they're not all exactly techniques for changing behavior, and even if you've heard some of them before.

But even if we're just concentrating on my method and on making the program work better, bear in mind that the effectiveness of the principles and techniques I discuss in this book can be helped or hindered by the context in which they are applied, and that's where general parenting practices can really affect a program's success. I already devoted a chapter to parenting stress and household chaos, and in that discussion I went beyond behavior to consider what you can do to reduce the general level of stress and chaos for your family. There is much more to say about parenting and family life on this more general level, going beyond specific techniques for addressing specific behaviors. This discussion does not substitute for the methods we have discussed. General improvements in the tone of family life will not teach specific behaviors or eliminate those that cause problems around the home, but they can greatly influence a child and enhance the effects of the programs we have suggested.

Think of child-rearing in relation to that most mundane of health-care issues, the care of your teeth and gums. Your dentist tells you that you can do certain specific things to care for your teeth: brush, floss — you know the drill. You also know the stakes. Plaque causes gum disease, which can not only wreck your smile but is also associated with heart and lung diseases. Specific practices like brushing and flossing are roughly analogous to the specific methods I've presented to you in this book to address specific conditions such as tantrums, acting up in the supermarket, or not doing homework. But in both child-rearing and dental care there are also more general steps one can take, things *not* specifically addressed to any particular problem (plaque, tantrums), that have broad positive effects *and* a very significant effect on the specific problem. Engaging in regular exercise, getting good nutrition, and maintaining a normal weight, for instance, are three general conditions that reduce the likelihood of gum disease.

And there are analogous parenting practices, not specifically aimed at tantrums or resisting homework or any other particular behavior problem, that can greatly influence children's behavior. These practices will also have broader good effects on the child and the home — in much the same way that exercise, nutrition, and weight control do more for you than simply fighting gum disease. The nature of life and work these days seems to lead us away from many of these basics of child-rearing, and we have to resist that pull.

So I'm going to tell you about some things you can do to improve my method's chances of success — and improve your family life, too. I fully realize that I'm running a risk that you'll see the headings (instruct calmly, listen to your child, solve problems together, and so on) and say to yourself, *Oh, of course I know I'm supposed to do* that. *It's common sense, and every parenting expert out there talks about this stuff.* I can understand why you might respond that way, at least initially. But give me a chance to show you what's fresh and useful in even the most familiar-sounding advice.

First, and most important, there's plenty of research showing that general parenting strategies can be crucial to the success of any program for changing specific behaviors. I don't want to withhold important guidance from you just because some other parenting books have given similar pieces of advice, perhaps in useful ways, perhaps in less-than-useful ways that had no connection to the research. So I'll run the risk of telling you some things you probably know already in order to give you the best chance at success, the best-equipped toolbox that science can offer. I know you don't need me to tell you that it's good to hug your kid, but I want you to understand that hugging your kid will lead him to value your praise more and heed your instructions better, which will in turn make it more likely that a point program will succeed in changing his behavior.

Second, all parents, no matter who they are, can use an occasional refresher course in general technique. As I read over the twelve points that follow, I blush to think how many times I, as a father of two daughters (now grown), did the exact opposite of what I'm advising now. ("*Instruct calmly? Instruct calmly?!* I AM INSTRUCTING CALMLY! NOW GET BACK IN HERE AND CLEAN UP THIS MESS!") I've tried to put it all together in a brief guide of the sort I myself would have done well to refer to from time to time when my kids were younger.

When you're done reading this conclusion, stop and ask yourself if you're really already doing everything I advise you to do here. If you are, congratulations — you're a parental superhero. If you're not, you're human. You love your kids, you want the best for them, and you want to be the best possible parent to them. Give me your attention for a few more pages, and I'll take one last opportunity to help you do that.

1. *Instruct calmly.* Although it's normal to be upset occasionally, try to teach your child the critical lesson when you're both calm. The best training does not occur on the battlefield — that is, in the middle of a tantrum or when the eyes of other children or parents are on you. The best training happens when you're not on the battlefield, perhaps when you're sitting together on the couch or taking a walk or talking in the car. Simply modeling calmness when you talk about provocative issues will have the important effect of teaching your child how to handle difficult situations. And you can have a much better effect as a teacher of lessons without the hard feelings, entrenched positions, and test of wills that usually occur in the heat of battle.

You're always teaching your child, even when you're not trying to. Recent research has begun to identify the neurological processes by which a child's brain observes and responds to a parent's reactions. The child's brain learns and mimics most actively when the parent responds to something — an event, an object, other people — with strong negative emotion, like disgust. You may not know that you're teaching, and your child may not know that she's learning, but her brain is busily organizing its activity around the example you set. So by remaining calm you teach a very valuable lesson, and, even more important, you also *don't* teach the more powerful *negative* lesson that you would teach if you lost your temper.

More generally, when you model reasonableness, measured discussion, and not panicking, you make it more likely that your child will consider you a resource and not someone to be escaped and avoided. If you are unreasonable, hot-tempered, and panicky about any particular issue — clothes, hair, drugs, sex, smoking, school, and so on — your child will tend to escape and avoid you whenever that issue comes up. Because parents tend to get most excited about the things that matter most to them, they often succeed in ensuring that their child won't regard them as a resource when it comes to these very things. And if there are too many areas of life like that, you will make escape and avoidance your child's default setting, across the board, in dealing with you.

2. *Listen to your child.* It is good to listen to your child and her opinions, not only because it's good for her mental health and self-esteem but also because of the exchange it represents. You listen because you want your child to share her views with you, and you expect the same from her. The key to negotiation is you listening and then your child listening. Your modeling of this early in life will make later interactions with your child much easier.

In my field we use the term "askable" to describe parents whose children feel comfortable coming to them to talk, especially about touchier subjects. Being askable is especially important, the research tells us, because children and adolescents prefer to get their information about subjects like sex and drugs from their parents. You may be surprised to know that they'd rather talk to parents about these touchy subjects than learn about them from friends, siblings, or the media. And each of these difficult subjects opens up a broader range of important discussion topics that goes well beyond addressing a child's misconduct. When your child wants to talk to you about sex, for instance, you and she will also be talking about love, attachment, intimacy, relationships, sexual orientation, reproduction, and all the related emotions — about life, in other words.

It pays to be askable. It will affect your long-term effectiveness with your child and your short-term effectiveness in changing behavior.

One practical piece of advice: after you have heard what your child has to say, do not begin by refuting it. Point out anything good in what your child said, even if you then propose a different way of thinking about it. And never use "dumb," "stupid," or other belittling words. *Of course,* you're thinking. *What kind of idiot would do that?* Well, lots of parents, even good and loving parents, do something like it. When your child talks, does he get the feeling that you're just waiting for him to finish so that you can state your opinion at length and in detail? Is your child confident that you're really listening or are you just waiting for a chance to lecture?

3. Solve problems together. Think of the kind of behavior you want to teach. One way to do that is to consider what happens in the heat of the battle and what causes those battles — tantrums, shouting, not listening, all those things you find frustrating in your child — and then identify the positive opposites you want to teach. Make a list of the unwanted behaviors and their positive opposites. The list is important because parents are often too vague about their goals for their child's behavior. The more specific your goals, the more likely it will be that you can work effectively with your child toward reaching them. Even when the objective is general — greater kindness or honesty, for instance — the best way to get there is to develop specific behaviors that exemplify it.

One good way to work together on behavior is to take advantage of occasions when you and your child see others doing what you want to talk about. This is easy when it comes to relatively trivial things such as using good manners at a restaurant. Point out the behavior to your child as something that could be and ought to be done differently. Identify exactly what behaviors you think ought to be different, say what exactly should be done, and suggest to your child that she should do the same when she's in a similar situation. Or, conversely, when you see parents or children doing something right — disagreeing without becoming angry, for instance, or showing good manners — point that out as a good model. Be specific: *See how that little girl is looking at her book so nicely and calmly? When we go out to eat at Friendly's, or even at Grandma's for Thanksgiving, and you're starting to get antsy at the table, tell me that you feel that way and I'll make sure to have a book or a toy or something you can quietly play with. And if you absolutely need to run around, just let me know by whispering that to me. It's not a big thing, but it would be great if you would tell me, so I can help you not fidget, like that girl.* The final sentence takes the edge off the instruction, reducing it from *You Must Obey* to something more like *Here's a tool for your toolbox,* which actually increases the chances that the child will use it.

This is problem solving in the sense that you identify a problem (some situation you want to handle differently) and a solution (because you identify different ways of responding). Think of such opportunities as vicarious simulations, another way to engage in reinforced practice. And yes, you can do it even when you are watching TV with your kids.

To make this process less dictatorial, when you point out the problem you see, specify what the other person is doing and ask your child an open-ended question: *So, what do you think would be better to do?* Or give hints: *Do you think it would be better to . . . or to . . . ?* Praise your child's response if it is correct; point out and praise the part that is good if it is partially correct. If it's incorrect, don't dwell on your child's error; just state the correct answer and emphasize the lesson you want to teach. And you can add, *It's good to talk with you about these things* at the end of this exchange, praising reasonable discussion and building your relationship so that the dialogue can continue even when you and your child disagree.

4. Be generous with warm fuzzies. I have spent a great deal of effort in this book encouraging you to praise your child as a reward for the right behavior. And I have stressed the value of physical contact — a hug, kiss, or pat — in making that praise more effective. But I wouldn't want you to come away with the impression that warmth and positive contact should be restricted only to those instances in which you're pursuing a specific program for changing behavior. They're not just reinforcers.

There is a more general role in our approach for warm fuzzies — smiling, hugging, warmth, being together, all those calm, affectionate relationship-building moments that you tend to forget when your parental wrath has been raised. Physical contact is crucial for your child's development, responsiveness to stress, learning, and more. It's probably important throughout life, since positive physical contacts increase both physical and psychological comfort. So hug your child for no good reason, behaviorally speaking, and do it frequently.

These warm-fuzzy moments are not usually the most effective times to directly address or change behavior. Because they're not moments when the unwanted behavior might occur, they don't offer good opportunities for reducing or eliminating it and replacing it with a positive opposite. But warm-fuzzy moments have two very important behavior-related benefits: they provide a buffer of support against stressors and normal anxieties that arise in the world, and they make a parent more effective as a behavior-change agent. The better the parent-child relationship, the more effect the parent's interventions are likely to have, whether they are praise or (mild) punishment.

A solid positive relationship establishes a great basis for effective parenting, which offers yet another reason to emphasize positive reinforcement rather than punishment. You should be a consistent resource and influence for your child in all areas of life, an objective that will be undermined if the child escapes, avoids, and resists the influence of a parent too heavily associated with punishment.

5. *Build competencies* — more than one of them — at different points in childhood. This is *not* a call for more scheduled lessons. I do not want to add to what for many families is already a hectic weekly extracurricular round of soccer, flute, gymnastics, karate, swimming, and so on that produces pressure and anxiety, fostering negative interactions at home. Think of all the times that such an overscheduled week requires you and your child to be ready, have all necessary equipment at hand, and leave and arrive on time. It's a blueprint for parenting stress and household chaos. Think, instead, of what your

child seems to like, and pick perhaps two areas (for a child between one and ten years of age) and help him or her continue in these areas.

Of course, there may be interests you're not willing to support. When one of my daughters was two years old, she wanted a drum set. Knowing how focused she was, we could easily envision her drumming endlessly through the night, inspiring our neighbors to form an angry mob and attack our house. So we said little about a drum set, and soon the request shifted to a different instrument. We enthusiastically praised that new choice and signed her up for lessons right away. (This was a case in which the parents were not just thinking of the development of the child. There was nothing wrong with my daughter's desire for a drum set and nothing better about the instrument she did end up playing. We could have bought ear plugs and said yes to the request for drums. But sometimes you have to let your own well-being influence your decision-making about a child's interests. Be as flexible and open-minded as you can, but recognize that you may end up drawing the line on a competency because you do not wish to live with it, even though there's nothing inherently wrong with it.)

You can help your child pursue an interest or two in a low-key, consistent, but casual way, at least until competence builds and the years of habitual practice add up to the point where a more formal engagement makes sense and is rewarding for the child. Such competencies can be very constructive for your child's development, helping to build friendships, peers, confidence, and some skill likely to influence what the child does and likes later in life. Competencies can also help your child pass a little more smoothly through the adolescent years, a time often associated with a temporary increase in problem behaviors, especially risk-taking: vandalism, experimenting with drugs or sex, driving drunk. The research tells us that a child's connection to one or more ongoing activities in some area of competence can ease all of that by reducing the likelihood of risky behavior. For example, recent findings show that young girls involved in sports during their preadolescent and adolescent years are less likely to be involved in drugs. It's not certain that involvement in sports was the reason they were less involved in drugs, but, until that's totally worked out by further studies, it's a good bet to encourage sports and other competencies.

6. *Encourage social interaction, often under your supervision.* In early childhood, your supervision is required mostly to head off conflict and other such problems, but, as much as you can, be available but resist the urge to referee when your child plays with other kids. In many ways, social interaction is a competency that deserves its own time, not just something that might be allowed to happen in dribs and drabs between school and scheduled activities. Developing friendships and learning how to interact, both under your guidance and beyond it, can have lifelong effects on your child's adjustment and functioning in normal as well as stressful times. By the time your child is fourteen years old, play time is a distant memory and he may well be hanging out in his room with a friend, eating pizza and blasting his tunes. Yes, he may seem cut off from you at that moment, but you're still encouraging social interaction by allowing your son and his friend to do this in your home and perhaps even treating them to the pizza. And he's socializing without entirely breaking his ties to you. Plus you know exactly where your child is, which brings me to the next item . . .

7. *Always know where your child is.* In early childhood, that's a given. And you should model the principle for your child by letting her know where you are, even if it's just in the form of a note left for the babysitter. Keeping in touch, knowing everyone's whereabouts, should be natural and automatic for a family, not just because it's good parenting but also because monitoring should not be something you suddenly spring on an adolescent when the likelihood of risky behavior increases. If monitoring strikes the older child as a brand-new restraint, she'll be more likely to resist it. So start early. As she enters the six-to-twelve age range and begins to have afterschool activities, and especially as peers take on much greater importance for preteens and teens, you need to be more active in order to know where she is. If you cannot be around as much as you want to be, have her call in, or you can call the place where she is supposed to be.

Why is it so important to know where your child is? The research confirms that not knowing where your child is places him at greater risk for all sorts of behaviors, including experimenting with drugs, alcohol, smoking, and sexual behavior (which is occurring at younger and younger ages). Children who are unmonitored are more likely to bond with, connect to, and be encouraged by peers who are themselves not monitored well. As they have more unsupervised time, they talk more about deviant behavior and engage in more of it. Merely keeping better tabs on your child can decrease the risk of his engaging in such behavior. You do not have to be there in person, but knowing your child's whereabouts is absolutely essential. (And, now that children spend so much time online, the monitoring must extend not only outside the house but also into cyberspace.) How long do you have to keep this up? Until your child is not a child anymore.

8. *Plan down time.* Carve out some special time to relax tight restrictions around the house. Chances are that you want homework done, the child out of the house on time, dinner at a certain time and bath at another, and so on. In many homes, the child has the equivalent of a full-time job, with you as a loving but demanding boss. You are under the gun, and like a movie director, you must make sure everyone is in place for the scene, the props are there (clothing, toothbrush, swimsuit), the lighting and camera are ready to go (pay the electric bill, buy a camera, figure out how it works), and that it all comes together in a timely fashion. On a good day, as you drop off to sleep, exhausted, you can call out, *That's a take! Print it!* The scene worked. But, unlike a director, your movie is never done, and you can't just throw away the scenes that didn't work. No matter how well or how poorly it went the day before, you have the next day, and the next.

So, for your own sake as well as your children's, make sure your child has time to chill out. In your mind, at least, program some down time in which you ask for nothing, expect nothing, and will not need to press your child to find out what was accomplished. For younger children, some quiet play time by themselves is valuable. The research shows that children who are allowed to play quietly by themselves are much less likely to be aggressive when they interact with other children. We don't fully understand the reason for this yet, but idle play in child development isn't idle at all.

9. *Put value on quantity time.* Be around, be together, and maintain family routines linked to regular household business, like meals and errands. This kind of mundane quantity time is much more significant than that one memorable quality-time outing to a ball game at which you bought a T-shirt, program, and two hotdogs, and, including parking, spent a couple of hundred dollars. Quality time is nice, but it's never a substitute for quantity time. Imagining that it might be was the rationale of a busy generation. A very special forty minutes of parent-and-child time per weekend is a good thing — and it's lovely that you don't spend that time arguing — but you need plenty of quantity time as well to help get the child to the place you might like him to be in life. Think about quantity versus quality in reading to your child. It's better to read pretty good children's stories to her every day for twenty minutes than to go all week without reading to her and then on Sunday read the greatest children's book ever to her for an hour. She's going to get a lot more out of a daily dose of reading, and it's far more likely to positively affect her reading skills and academic performance. One appealing thing about quantity time is that you don't have to do anything special or have a scheduled activity: just arrange to be around together, to be available to each other and interact normally.

10. *Develop rituals and routines with your child.* Every Friday we go shopping, on Saturdays we have a pancake breakfast, every time we drive home from grandma's house we stop at a certain park, and so on. Rituals and routines can be extremely modest. For instance, a regular drive to a lesson — on Saturdays, you take your daughter to ballet — can double as both simple logistics (the kid has to get to ballet somehow) and a week-ordering routine (that's the time we talk about how things are going with friends, school, romance, and so on). Aim for regularity and frequency, but don't be so rigid that the routine becomes an additional source of pressure. You're trying here to build a reservoir of predictable experiences — which, in addition to all the other benefits, will become the basis of good memories. Good experiences founded in routines will build your relationship and make you more effective in everything you do as a parent, whether you are focusing on the ABC's with a younger child or on potentially serious is-

sues as the child gets older. Small regular investments in your relationship are like regular deposits in your savings. They accrue slowly, and the added amount at any given moment may look like nothing, but the compound interest, building on what has been built, is enormous.

11. *Connect the child to other family members,* including those of different generations. There are lots of benefits of such connections, including family routines that stabilize a child's life and opportunities for the child to bond with and learn from adults who aren't his parents. Extended family connections have not been widely studied in relation to children's behavior, but some recent research shows that children with connections to extended family have a reduced risk of disruptive behaviors.

Families tend to spread out, so it's not always easy to keep in touch, but try to build relationships that provide for continuity and roots (with grandparents and even great-grandparents) and also for bonding with any of your child's closer-in-age relatives (cousins, for instance). If they live eight states away, it's worth bringing everyone together during the holidays, even if all parties have to travel four states to meet in the middle. If you are not around extended family, and especially if you are a single parent, perhaps try to arrange occasions (a picnic, or any kind of visit) on which you and your child can spend time with another single parent with a child. Often a church or other community connection is a good way to find such peers. There is an international organization for single parents and their children, Parents without Partners, which has over two hundred chapters throughout the United States and Canada. It provides structured educational, family, and recreational activities for parents and children — outings, picnics, holiday parties, informal meals, and the like.

12. *Take care of yourself.* It's easy to forget to keep yourself in good mental and physical shape for child-rearing. Parenting, running a household, working, sustaining a relationship, and planning for multiple futures (your children's, your own, perhaps your parents') combine to put a lot of stress on you. The multiple challenges keep coming at you — and coming back at you, because you can't ever set-

tle any one of them for good and cross it off your list of things to do. You're in for a long haul, and you're going to need to be in shape for it. It's important that you see to your own needs, and not just your child's, by building in your own down time, your own social interaction, your own special routines with your spouse or friends. This isn't "me generation" propaganda or "I come first" selfishness; it's what the research on parent-child interaction tells us about the best route to effective parenting. If you're flat-out all the time, you're going to break down or at least show the negative effects of that stress in your interactions with your child. Invest a little of your energy in yourself; it will pay off for your family.

· · ·

Twelve different items seem like a lot, but that's deceptive. Remember the food pyramid? We were supposed to eat all those foods in certain proportions, not that anyone could or did do any such thing. If the list of principles I just presented to you was arranged into some kind of psychological health pyramid, it would have the great advantage that every item fits into multiple categories. Relaxing tight restrictions helps generate quantity time; connecting with other family members can be done by instituting extended-family routines and rituals, and so on. It all seems more practicable when you realize that doing a few of these things leads to doing the rest of them. And doing any or all of them will make a behavior-change program that much more likely to succeed.

· · ·

Parenting books and online parenting coaches often focus on making you feel "empowered," and it *is* important to feel effective and in control of critical parts of your life, such as child-rearing. The research on empowerment tells us that feelings of control actually reduce anxiety, increasing your ability to cope. But there's a catch. There's a difference between *feeling* empowered and actually *being* more effective and in control. The research makes clear that the illusion of control over difficult situations also reduces anxiety. Having *any* answer to questions about parenting, even if it's a wrong or irrelevant one provided by an "expert" who ought to know better, can increase your feeling of being in control. It works the same way with placebos in trials of new medications; the patients taking the sugar pill that looks like real medicine often do report feeling better.

I want you to come away from this book with new confidence in your parenting skills, and with the additional confidence that any greater sense of control and efficacy you feel is not an illusion. It's founded on something real and reliable: scientific research that in recent decades has begun to help parents address age-old challenges of child-rearing. I have arrived at my method by refining the results of a great deal of rigorous discovery conducted by committed scientists, who in turn have drawn on a great deal of parental trial and error in raising children. That's what this book is — a systematic refinement into method of all that experience, of what has been proven to work. Let those parents and scientists, and the kids they raised and studied, help you become a more effective and skilled parent.

APPENDIX

*Age-Appropriate Rewards for Children**

Rewards for preschoolers

Going to the park

Playing with friends

Getting to sleep in the "big bed" with parents

Getting to "camp out" in the living room with parents

Listening to a bedtime story

Playing on a swing set

Spending the night with friends or grandparents

Being lifted into the air

Playing games with a parent

Having a coin-operated ride at the grocery store

Having parents take a photo of the child

Talking into a tape recorder

Going out for pizza

Playing with clay or play dough

Going on a special errand or place alone with dad or mom

Helping plan the day's activities

Helping mom or dad on some grown-up task

Riding on a bicycle with dad or mom

Riding a tricycle

Working on a puzzle with a parent

* For additional information, see http://www.chores-help-kids.com/age-appropriate-rewards.html and http://books.apa.org/books.cfm?id=4441005.

Staying up later than usual
Going on a trip to the zoo
Getting a piggyback ride
Having a bubble bath
Riding on dad's shoulders
Going outside at night
Having a family night
Playing in the sandbox
Sitting in the chair with dad or mom
Going to the library
Going for a picnic
Playing outside

Helping with a baby sister or brother
Reading a story
Baking something in the kitchen
Having a special dessert
Finger painting
Drawing with crayons
Playing a game with parent(s)
Playing a video game
Watching a movie
Renting a video game
Renting a movie
Computer time

Rewards for six- to twelve-year-olds

Taking a trip to the park
Playing with friends
Having an extra bedtime story
Playing on the swing set
Spending the night with friends or grandparents
Going to a ball game
Eating out
Going someplace alone with dad or mom
Baking something in the kitchen
Planning a day's activities
Riding a bicycle
Going on a fishing trip with dad or mom
Choosing a TV program
Taking time off from chores
Using the cell phone
Dressing up in parent's clothes
Setting the table
Camping in the backyard

Going to the library
Decorating the home for the holidays
Helping to prepare some food (e.g., cookies)
Staying up later than usual
Going to the movies, especially with a friend
Playing a favorite tape or CD
Coloring
Taping himself or herself and listening to it
Choosing the menu for a meal
Calling a relative (making the call and greeting the person)
Buying something
Planting something in the house or garden
Going on a picnic
Going skating, swimming, or bowling

Making a special craft with mom
  or dad
Ordering a meal to be delivered
Going for a hike
Going canoeing or camping or
  fishing or skiing
Sleeping in a different place than
  usual in the house
Doing a jigsaw puzzle
Decorating own bedroom
Having a special afterschool
  snack
Choosing a special breakfast

Having a special treat in school
  lunch
Playing a game with mom or
  dad, like checkers, marbles,
  or cards
Listening to a Walkman
Computer time
Playing a video game
Renting a video game
Watching a movie
Renting a movie
Skateboarding

Rewards for adolescents and some preadolescents

Participating in activities with
  friends (e.g., going to a mall,
  the movies, or a concert)
Having one or more friends over
  for an afternoon or a
  sleepover
Taking dance or music lessons
Receiving accessories for
  grooming or for sports
Hanging a special poster in
  bedroom
Redecorating own bedroom
Skating or bowling with friends
Talking additional time on the
  telephone
Having dating privileges
Receiving a gift certificate
Making a trip alone
Finding a part-time job
Taking the car to school for a
  day

Getting to stay out late
Having car privileges
Staying up late
Staying overnight with friends
Taking time off from chores
Having a date during the week
Getting a chance to earn money
Getting to use the family camera
  or getting one's own camera
  (e.g., disposable)
Getting a driver's license or steps
  along the way
Driving the car on a family trip
Camping out
Going to summer camp
Getting a special haircut or
  hairstyle
Going to an amusement park
Being allowed to sit alone when
  the family eats out
Inviting a friend to eat out

Receiving cell phone time

Downloading songs onto one's computer

Getting to use an iPod or other MP3 player

Getting to sleep in late on the weekend

Having one's own checking account

Going shopping

Receiving a magazine subscription

Buying a DVD or CD

Having one's own telephone

Selecting something special for dinner

Buying a book of one's choice on an outing with a parent

Going horseback riding

Computer time

Index